SECURITY V. LIBERTY

SECURITY V. LIBERTY

CONFLICTS BETWEEN CIVIL LIBERTIES AND NATIONAL SECURITY IN AMERICAN HISTORY

DANIEL FARBER
EDITOR

RUSSELL SAGE FOUNDATION • NEW YORK

The Russell Sage Foundation

Library of Congress Cataloging-in-Publication Data

Security v. liberty : conflicts between civil liberties and national security in American history / edited by Daniel Farber.
    p. cm.
   Includes bibliographical references and index.
   ISBN 978-0-87154-327-1
   1. War and emergency powers—United States. 2. National security—Law and legislation—United States. 3. Civil rights—United States.
I. Farber, Daniel A., 1950-
   KF5060.S43 2008
   342.73'062—dc22

                          2007044178

Text design by Suzanne Nichols.

RUSSELL SAGE FOUNDATION
112 East 64th Street, New York, New York 10021
10 9 8 7 6 5 4 3 2 1

TABLE OF CONTENTS

ABOUT THE AUTHORS

DANIEL FARBER is Sho Sato Professor of Law at the University of California, Berkeley.

ALAN BRINKLEY is Allan Nevins Professor of History and provost at Columbia University.

STEPHEN HOLMES is Walter E. Meyer Professor of Law at New York University School of Law.

RONALD D. LEE is a partner of Arnold and Porter LLP in Washington, D.C.

JAN ELLEN LEWIS is professor of history and associate dean of the Faculty of Arts and Sciences at Rutgers University, Newark.

L. A. POWE, JR. is the Anne Green Regents Chair in the School of Law and the College of Liberal Arts at the University of Texas.

ELLEN SCHRECKER is professor of history at Yeshiva University.

PAUL M. SCHWARTZ is professor of law at the University of California, Berkeley Law School.

GEOFFREY R. STONE is the Harry Kalven, Jr. Distinguished Service Professor of Law at the University of Chicago.

JOHN YOO is a law professor at the University of California, Berkeley, a visiting scholar at the American Enterprise Institute, and served in the Bush Justice Department from 2001 to 2003.

CHAPTER 1

INTRODUCTION

DANIEL FARBER

Threats to national security generally prompt incursions on civil liberties. The relationship has existed since the presidency of John Adams and has continued through two world wars, the cold war, Vietnam, and today. This historical phenomenon is commonplace, but the implications of that history for our post-9/11 world are less clear.

In the long run, if we are to cope with present and future crises, we must think deeply about how our historical experience bears on a changing world. This book explores the past and present relationship between civil liberties and national crises, with contributions from leading legal scholars and historians. These individuals seek both to draw historical lessons and to explore how the present situation poses unique issues.[1]

Some definitions are a necessary prerequisite to these issues. The terms *national security* and *civil liberties* may not have been in use during some of these periods or may have been used differently. For our purposes, we define national security as involving a perceived violent threat that implicates either the stability of the government (subversion), the general safety of a large numbers of members of society, or the government's ability to engage successfully in armed conflicts. We define civil liberties to include issues relating to freedom of expression, due process, restrictions on government surveillance, and discrimination against minority groups (thus encompassing what are sometimes called *civil rights*).

The more optimistic accounts of American history hold that restrictions on civil liberties based on national security are few and far between—and are quickly corrected when the precipitating crisis passes. Indeed, optimists believe that the backlash against repression can actually strengthen civil liberties in the long run. More pessimistic observers contend that Congress and the president routinely overreact to domestic or foreign threats and that their interventions leave permanent scars on constitutional freedoms. An intermediate view is that there is no real trend, that each crisis is unique, as is its aftermath.

Unfortunately, serious analysis of such historical trends is scarce, though there is no lack of excellent treatments of individual crises. This book attempts to fill the gap. The first part focuses on specific episodes in American history. The goal is to understand how those episodes bear (or perhaps do not) on present dilemmas.

The authors of these historical chapters develop several themes. The first involves the way in which threats are perceived by political actors, presented to the public, labeled (as wars or otherwise), and absorbed by public opinion. Another involves the political dynamic of civil liberties restrictions: their origin among national leaders or grassroots groups, the resistance to them that develops; and their use in advancing existing agendas. Finally, we consider the historical trajectory: do these crises lead to permanent retrenchment of civil liberties, do the effects fade, or is there possibly a learning curve that ultimately results in stronger protections for civil liberties?

The second part of the book looks both backward and forward from the twentieth century episodes discussed in the first part. The back story behind the twentieth-century experience, given by Jan Lewis, covers key episodes from the Alien and Sedition Acts to the late nineteenth century. Lewis's survey reveals several precursors of twentieth century themes.

The remainder of Part II looks to the future. Recent decades have seen dramatic changes in the world. For instance, the potential access to weapons of mass destruction by nonstate actors may fundamentally change how the government responds to threats. At the same time, technology makes it possible to fight wars without the mass mobilizations required in the past. Other important changes are more subtle. Our current demographics and attitudes toward minority groups have evolved, altering the environment that racial and ethnic minorities weather during crises. The Supreme Court has increasing confidence in its institutional powers, as shown by the justices' intervention in the 2000 presidential race. Finally, America is now the world's sole superpower, but faces a more robust international human rights regime. Some of these changes may turn out not to make a fundamental difference, but all of them have the potential to do so.

This book does not attempt to explore all of these changes, but instead focuses on two key issues: the changing role of the courts and the relationship between technology and privacy. The concluding chapter, by Stephen Holmes, argues that some of the authors may have underestimated the seriousness of the risk posed by terrorism, particularly in connection with weapons of mass destruction. Holmes argues, however, that the Bush administration's insistence on unprecedented levels of secrecy and its brusque attitude toward human rights and civil liberties issues have actually been counterproductive in their long run effects.

Most of the heavy lifting is done in the individual chapters, for which this introduction seeks to set the stage, first, by reviewing the current legal situation. Because none of the chapters cover the United States' response to 9/11, a brief overview of this history is in order. Readers may be familiar with many of these events, but it is illuminating to assemble the legal developments into a narrative. Moreover, in even a few years, memories of these developments may fade, so a reprise may be useful for later readers.

It is also helpful to piece together the stories in each chapter to provide a larger view of the historical trajectory. Each episode has its own peculiarities and historical texture, but certain themes are consistent. Some are discussed in the concluding chapter. Others are sketched here to make the individual chapters cohere.

Finally, there is the question of how history reproduces itself in new circumstances, or fails to do so. The 9/11 response has some striking similarities to earlier episodes—not entirely coincidentally, in that some earlier actions (especially in World War II) served as models for the Bush administration. But there are also some equally striking differences, which reflect changes in technology, legal culture, and internationalization. The introduction closes with a few thoughts about the similarities and differences.

CIVIL LIBERTIES AND THE RESPONSE TO 9/11

The government response to 9/11 and the war on terror raised a number of civil liberties concerns. Perhaps the most fundamental centered on the treatment and trials of individuals detained as suspected terrorists. Almost none were United States residents or citizens, so the American public was not directly affected. What makes these issues fundamental, however, is that they go to the applicability of the rule of law in a period of emergency, because the executive branch initially claimed the power to deal with detainees free from judicial or congressional restrictions and any due process requirement. The result was a prolonged confrontation between the judiciary and the president, with Congress attempting to oust the courts and impose restrictions of its own on the president. I will consider the detention issue in depth and then briefly review other civil liberties concerns.[2]

The detention issue arose only a few months after 9/11. Congress passed a resolution authorizing the president to "use all necessary and appropriate force" against "nations, organizations, or persons" that he determines "planned, authorized, committed, or aided" in the attacks.[3] As part of this response, the president ordered an invasion of Afghanistan to attack al Qaeda and the Taliban regime.

On November 13, 2001, President Bush issued a military order regarding the detention of terrorists.[4] Section 1 of the order states that "to protect the United States and its citizens, and for the effective conduct of military operations and prevention of terrorist attacks, it is necessary for individuals subject to this order under section 2 to be detained, and, when tried, to be tried for violations of the laws of war and other applicable laws by military tribunals."

Section 2 defines who is subject to this order, or, more precisely, authorizes the president to do so in the future. The president need merely make a written finding that there is "reason to believe" that a person was a member of al Qaeda, has engaged in acts of international terrorism against the United States, or has harbored such individuals. The president must also find that "it is in the interest of the United States that such individual be subject to this order." Essentially, then, the targets are everyone who has assisted al Qaeda or engaged in terrorism against the United States—or, more precisely, those who are suspected of doing so by the president. Individuals covered by this order do not include American citizens.

Section 3 provides for detention of these individuals, who are to be "treated humanely" and "afforded adequate food, drinking water, shelter, clothing, and medical treatment." Section 4 then provides that "any individual subject to this order shall, when tried, be tried by military commission for any and all offenses triable by military commission that such individual is alleged to have committed and may be punished in accordance with the penalties provided under applicable law, including life imprisonment or death." Subsection (c) sketches the procedures for such trials, which are to provide a "full and fair trial." Finally, section 7 provides that individuals "shall not be privileged to seek any remedy or maintain any proceeding, directly or indirectly, or to have any such remedy or proceeding sought on the individual's behalf, in (i) any court of the United States, or any State thereof, (ii) any court of any foreign nation, or (iii) any international tribunal."

Three months later, the president supplemented this order with a classified directive not fully declassified until June 2004, denying the protections of the Geneva Conventions to supporters of al Qaeda, whether captured during the Afghanistan conflict or elsewhere. The first paragraph concludes that "the war against terrorism ushers in a new paradigm, one in which groups with broad, international reach commit horrific acts against innocent civilians, sometimes with the support of states." "Our Nation recognizes," the memo continues, "that this new paradigm—ushered in not by us, but by terrorists—requires new thinking in the law of war, but thinking that should nevertheless be consistent with the principles of Geneva."

The second paragraph considers applying the Geneva Conventions to al Qaeda and the Taliban. As to al Qaeda, the president concludes: "I accept the legal conclusion of the Department of Justice and determine that none of the provisions of Geneva apply to our conflict with al Qaeda in Afghanistan or elsewhere throughout the world because, among other reasons, al Qaeda is not a High Contracting Party to Geneva."

The president rejected the sweeping argument that because Afghanistan is a failed state, the Geneva Conventions did not apply to the conflict as a whole. He did not, however, provide Taliban supporters with prisoner of war status, notwithstanding contrary arguments by the U.S. State Department (Powell 2002). Nevertheless, "as a matter of policy," the memo directs the armed forces to "continue to treat detainees humanely and, to the extent appropriate and consistent with military necessity, in a manner consistent with the principles of Geneva."

The document was based in part on the advice of White House counsel (and later briefly Attorney General) Alberto Gonzales (Gonzales 2002). Gonzales argued that "the war against terrorism is a new kind of war." He continued:

> The nature of the new war places a premium on other factors, such as the ability to quickly obtain information from captured terrorists and their sponsors in order to avoid further atrocities against American civilians, and the need to try terrorists for war crimes such as wantonly killing civilians. In my judgment, this new paradigm renders obsolete

Geneva's strict limitations on questioning of enemy prisoners and renders quaint some of its provisions requiring that captured enemy be afforded such things as commissary privileges, scrip (i.e., advances of monthly pay), athletic uniforms, and scientific instruments.

Gonzales argued, however, that the United States would continue to be constrained by several factors: "(i) its commitment to treat the detainees humanely and, to the extent appropriate and consistent with military necessity, in a manner consistent with the principles of [Geneva], (ii) its applicable treaty obligations, (iii) minimum standards of treatment universally recognized by the nations of the worlds, and (iv) applicable military regulations regarding the treatment of detainees."

The memo was sharply contested by the legal adviser to the State Department, William H. Taft IV, who argued that the Geneva Convention should apply to Taliban detainees in Afghanistan (2002). But the president ultimately sided with Gonzales, except to the extent that he was willing to classify Taliban members as unlawful combatants under Geneva rather than as being entirely outside the purview of the Geneva Conventions.

Besides eliminating the substantive provisions of Geneva as applied to al Qaeda, the president's decision also effectively eliminated its procedural ones as well (for a detailed critique of the president's position and its legal rationale, see Jinks and Sloss 2004, 97). Under Article 6, "should any doubt arise as to whether persons, having committed a belligerent act and having fallen into the hands of the enemy," constitute POWs, "such persons shall enjoy the protection of the Present Convention until such time as their status has been determined by a competent tribunal." Article 6 might apply to Taliban and perhaps to some of their al Qaeda supporters in Afghanistan. Common Article III imposes other requirements in an "armed conflict not of an international character occurring in the territory of one of the High Contracting Parties." In such conflicts, punishment is not allowed "without previous judgment pronounced by a regularly constituted court, affording all the judicial guarantees which are recognized as indispensable by civilized parties." Thus, where they apply, the Geneva conventions not only provide substantive protection but require significant procedural safeguards beyond those promised in the president's detention order.

Failure to comply with Geneva was potentially be more than an international embarrassment if the conventions apply. Under a federal statute, the War Crimes Act,[5] United States nationals or members of the armed forces who commit war crimes are subject to life imprisonment or the death penalty if the victim dies. War crimes include "any conduct . . . defined as a grave breach" in the Geneva conventions and any violation of common Article 3. Geneva III, article 130, lists "willfully depriving a prisoner of war of the rights of fair and regular trial prescribed in this Convention" as a grave breach. Thus, failure to follow proper procedures before imposing punishment on detainees potentially was a serious federal offense, even a capital one. The president sought to avoid these potential consequences—and with them the need to provide procedural protection—by ruling the Geneva Conventions completely inapplicable to al Qaeda and its supporters, and by classifying Taliban soldiers as unlawful combatants.

The Supreme Court proved resistant to the president's decisions. Perhaps the contemporaneous publicity about abuses at the Abu Ghraib prison impaired the administration's standing with the Court, as L. A. Powe points out. In any event, its initial encounter with the detention issues in June of 2004, the Supreme Court split in its rationale but agreed almost unanimously in the result: eight justices rejected the government's position that it had an nonreviewable right to detain "enemy combatants" without a hearing.[6] The individual detained in that case was a American citizen, which undoubtedly made the government's argument more difficult. Four justices, led by O'Connor, held that the detainee was entitled to some form of due process hearing. Justice O'Connor's opinion acknowledged a power of detention but also began to stake out limits: for example, detention cannot be solely for the purposes of interrogation and cannot extend beyond the armed conflict at question. Justice O'Connor was thus faced with the difficult question of how to determine whether an individual fell within what she called the narrow category of unlawful combatants. She attempted to provide a fair process for determining the facts, allowing the government to begin the process by filing factual affidavits but then allowing the petitioner in the case, Hamdi, the chance to provide evidence in rebuttal. Four other justices, in two different opinions, would have held Hamdi's detention squarely unlawful. Only Justice Thomas voted in favor of the government's position.[7]

In a later case decided in June of 2006, *Hamdan v. Rumsfeld*,[8] the Court again rebuffed the administration's efforts to evade legal restrictions. Hamdan involved the use of military commissions to try enemy belligerents under the presidential order discussed earlier. In an opinion by Justice Stevens, the Court held that the president lacked the power to establish military tribunals under congressional enactments and under the Geneva Convention. Again, the president's effort to operate free from outside legal restrictions was rebuffed.

After Hamdan, Congress stepped into the detainee issue. The Military Commissions Act of 2006 modifies the rules governing detainees while attempting to limit judicial review.[9] It prohibits enemy combatants subject to the act from invoking the Geneva Convention as a source of rights. The statute attempts to provide a fairer hearing by sending appeals to the Court of Military Commission Review rather than the secretary of defense and by protecting the military judges in tribunals from adverse career consequences. The statute guarantees the defendant's right to be present at all points in the proceeding (contrary to the president's order), but allows classified material to be edited before being introduced at trial. It also allows the use of some coerced statements against the defendant. Finally, the statute makes it clear that conspiracy to violate the laws of war is a separate offense. This point was for some time hotly contested.

The most fundamental change, however, is to eliminate the writ of habeas corpus for "any alien detained by the United States who has been determined by the United States to have been properly detained as an enemy combatant or is awaiting such determination." The term *enemy combatant* is broadly defined to include anyone who provides "material support" for hostilities and appears to apply even to permanent residents in the United States. The statute also attempts to oust the courts from independently interpreting the Geneva Conventions. Notably, however, Congress did not contest the Court's determination that the Geneva Conventions do apply to the detainees.

The new statute has already been challenged in court. As L. A. Powe points out in chapter 7, there are two ways to view Hamdan. One is based on separation of powers, a demand that Congress be brought into the process of deciding how to treat detainees. The other is a rule of law demand that procedures be consistent with the due process clause. How the Court handles the habeas issue remains to be seen at this writing.[10] In the meantime, the political balance of power has shifted, with the demise of the Republican majority in both houses of Congress. Given that the Military Commissions Act narrowly passed Congress on a highly partisan vote, the detainee issue may not have reached its final legislative resolution.

Quite apart from its invocation of military authority as a basis for detention, the administration also used the immigration laws as a basis for detention after 9/11. The attorney general used this authority to detain more than 5,000 foreign nationals (Cole 2004, 1753, 1777–8). Many of these individuals were held for extended periods before being released. Others were deported after closed hearings. Section 1226a of the USA PATRIOT Act authorizes the government to detain any alien whom the government has "reasonable grounds" to believe involved in any activity that "endangers the national security of the United States." Because of ambiguous language in the statute, it is unclear if the statute authorizes indefinite detention of such aliens, although it does appear that such a detention decision at least would have to be renewed every six months.

This detention provision was only one aspect of the PATRIOT Act, Public Law 107-56, which was enacted only six weeks after 9/11. Few congressional committee hearings about the legislation were held, and there was little debate within Congress. The final legislation was not crafted by the usual conference committee, but instead reconciled in private negotiations between administration officials and a small group of legislators. It was only several years later, when the PATRIOT Act was renewed in March 2006, that any extensive congressional debate took place. The result was to temper some of the statute's provisions but to reenact the bulk with few changes.

Among its other provisions, the PATRIOT Act broadly authorizes the government to obtain private records in the hands of third parties, such as records of library use. It also expands the use of electronic surveillance. As it turns out, however, the statutory expansion of electronic surveillance was more or less a red herring, given that the government's real surveillance program is extra-statutory and much broader.

In the aftermath of Vietnam and Watergate, Congress had enacted a statute extensively regulating the use of surveillance for intelligence purposes. The Foreign Intelligence Surveillance Act (FISA) gives the United States broad authority to intercept communications between foreign powers, but a special court must give approval if the surveillance is likely to involve communications with an American citizen or resident alien. In an emergency, the attorney general may authorize surveillance for seventy-two hours without a court order.

Not content with the authority provided by FISA, the president authorized a far more sweeping interception program soon after 9/11, eliminating any use of warrants or court orders. The administration claimed that these interceptions were justified under the president's inherent executive authority and also under the statute authorizing the use of military force (AUMF) after 9/11. (Note that this is the same AUMF that the Bush administration used to justify detainee treatment and military trials. The Supreme Court viewed the statute as authorizing some military detentions but not as overriding the Geneva Conventions or existing federal statutes.) The program was in place for several years before it was disclosed through a leak. The president has requested that Congress explicitly authorize the program; so far, he has obtained only temporary authority for a modified version of the program.

Finally, although restrictions on speech have not figured significantly in the response to 9/11, federal law does create a potential chilling effect on freedom of association. Sections 2339A and 2339B of the federal criminal code make it a crime to give "material support" to designated terrorist organizations or to give such support knowing that it will be used for illegal acts. Material support is defined to include "any property, tangible or intangible, or service," including expert advice or assistance. The precise sweep of these provisions is unclear, and not surprisingly, there are allegations that they have chilled charitable contributions to Islamic organizations.

How do these activities compare with past responses to national security crises? By examining the historical chapters in this book, we can begin to answer that question.

RESPONSES TO CRISES IN AMERICAN HISTORY

The primary purpose of this book is to set these recent events in historical context. Part I focuses on the twentieth century experience. Alan Brinkley describes the experience during World War II and the ensuing Red Scare. World War I engendered a violent reaction to dissent—a somewhat ironic turn for a war that, after all, was supposed to make the world forever safe for democracy. But the grand democratic ambition of the war also provided an ironic justification for repression: anyone who opposed the war clearly posed a grave danger to the future of world democracy, making a small current sacrifice in liberty reasonable to secure a more glorious future.

The espionage and sedition acts were reminiscent of the alien and sedition acts more than a century earlier. The Espionage Act of 1917 made it illegal to discourage enlistment in the military and banned seditious materials from the mails. The postmaster general interpreted the term *seditious* to include anything critical of the government's motives. Unhappy that its powers were not even broader, the Wilson administration obtained the passage of the Sedition Act of 1918, which made it a crime to insult the government, the flag, or the military. The Sedition Act also banned any activities that interfered with war production or the prosecution of the war. Beyond these legal measures, the government also encouraged extralegal attacks on dissidents. The greatest burden again fell on immigrants.

After the war, demands for loyalty revived in the great Red Scare. The Justice Department made 6,000 arrests on a single day. Most people were eventually released, though some were deported and others remained in custody for weeks.

These government actions created a backlash. Building on the earlier Free Speech League, Roger Baldwin helped create the National Civil Liberties Bureau in 1917, which was renamed the American Civil Liberties Union three years later. On the Supreme Court, Justices Holmes and Brandeis moved toward a libertarian interpretation of the First Amendment, creating the foundation of modern free speech doctrine.

Brinkley argues that governments have often used crises to seize power in excess of what is really needed, pursuing preexisting agendas in the name of national security. The victims tend to be chosen because of their lack of political influence rather than because of any real danger they pose.

A contrasting view appears in John Yoo's appraisal of civil liberties during World War II. In his view, FDR adopted policies that went well beyond those of the Bush administration today in terms of their effects on civil liberties. As Yoo points out, Bush modeled his order on one FDR issued to establish a military commission for the trial of Nazi saboteurs. FDR intimated that he would execute the prisoners without regard for the Supreme Court, and the Court quickly upheld the convictions. Unlike the post-9/11 regulation created by the Defense Department and then modified by Congress in the Military Commissions Act of 2006, FDR's order did not define commission procedures or delimit the crimes that the tribunals could try.

FDR also engaged in much more sweeping detention than the Bush administration did, beginning with 3,000 Japanese citizens and then confining more than 100,000 Japanese-Americans. Congress soon gave its approval with a statute criminalizing violations of the evacuation order. Even before Pearl Harbor, FDR issued a broad authorization of electronic surveillance of suspected subversives, but requested that such investigations be kept to a minimum and limited as much as possible to aliens.

Yoo asks about the differences between the responses FDR and Bush adopted. Why was Bush's response more limited? The answer, Yoo believes, lies in the nature of the conflicts. The deepest incursions into civil liberties were in the world wars, where the threat to national security was the greatest. This, he suggests, explains the "relative restraint—from a historical perspective—of the Bush administration." Because of the networked nature of modern terrorism, a more focused response was required.

In terms of the differing reactions to the government's actions, Yoo also emphasizes the greatly strengthened role of the Supreme Court in American society. He speculates that "the Bush administration's acceptance of judicial supremacy," all too common in his view among political actors these days, "may have led it to moderate its policies in anticipation of court challenges." In contrast, FDR had much less reason to be concerned about the views of the courts.

After World War II, of course, Russia replaced Germany as America's greatest adversary, and internal security policies shifted accordingly. Ellen Schrecker's chapter probes the history of the early cold war. She reminds us of some of the excesses of the period: the FDA inspector dismissed because he refused to answer questions about his hiking companions; the cook who was considered a security risk in Sacramento because the city is a state capitol; the loyalty oath for anyone seeking a fishing permit in upstate New York. Schrecker examines these incidents not as aberrations, but as reflective of the worst incidents of political repression in American history.

Schrecker views the Communist Party as the most dynamic force on the left during the 1930s, because the party's front groups dominated left wing culture. After the war, when the party represented a legitimate security threat, the Truman administration overreacted to the threat of subversion. Admittedly, Schrecker says, information about Soviet espionage did justify many of the security precautions of the postwar era. But espionage was not really the central concern of the Truman White House's anticommunism effort. The administration was more concerned about threats of sabotage by communist union officials who might use strikes to cripple the defense program. Waterfront unions were a particular target of anticommunist activities. Employers then co-opted anticommunist efforts to eliminate union activists.

Because party membership was secret, members could only be identified by behavioral cues. Unfortunately, many on the left who were not Communist Party members evinced similar behaviors. The security program thus turned into a witch hunt that cost people their jobs or security clearances for sometimes trivial conduct. In statistical terms, the effort to avoid false negatives inevitably led to a large number of false positives. Because the FBI relied on secret informants and sometimes illegal procedures, it was unwilling to divulge the bases for accusations, making defense against the charges impossible.

More fundamentally, Schrecker contends, the security issue was ultimately fueled by partisan politics. Truman made serious revisions in the loyalty program only after the Republicans took control of Congress, but this did not defuse Republican use of the issue. Republicans recognized that the issue provided the most effective way to challenge Truman. For this reason, the Republican leadership encouraged Senator Joseph McCarthy's anticommunist crusade. The Eisenhower administration toughened the security program, eager to distinguish itself from its predecessor. But by 1954, when the issue was losing political appeal, Eisenhower had decided to bring McCarthy down. Eisenhower recognized that the political momentum of the anticommunist crusade was fading.

In Schrecker's view, the kind of repression that occurred during the early cold war—and the Court's initial collaboration with and later rejection of that repression—recurs with such frequency during crises as to cast doubt on optimistic scenarios about long-term progress on civil liberties issues. The author of chapter 5 takes a less pessimistic view.

Geoffrey Stone brings the historical progression to a close with his analysis of the Vietnam War era. He focuses on surveillance issues. Both Johnson and Nixon were appalled by the intensity of the opposition to the war. By the mid-1960s, however, it had become impossible to base prosecutions on mere dissenting speech. Instead, the government prosecuted individuals for conduct, such as burning draft cards; more important, it used domestic surveillance to disrupt the antiwar movement.

As that movement expanded in the mid-1960s, the FBI expanded its domestic surveillance efforts beyond suspected communists. In 1965, it began wiretapping the Students for a Democratic Society (SDS) and the Student Non-Violent Coordinating Committee (SNCC). The anticipated evidence of ties with the Communist Party did not materialize. President Johnson also requested FBI reports on antiwar members of Congress, journalists, and professors. In 1968, the FBI's activities turned from surveillance to disruption. FBI agents infiltrated antiwar groups to destabilize them.

Other government agencies undertook their own investigations. At the urging of President Johnson, the CIA began an effort to infiltrate and monitor antiwar activities, as well as opening international mail of individuals involved in the antiwar movement. Even army intelligence officers got into the act, assigning 1,500 undercover agents and ultimately collecting evidence on more than 100,000 opponents of the war. In 1969, the National Security Administration (NSA) began to intercept phone calls of antiwar advocates.

When President Nixon took office, these activities expanded. For instance, the Central Intelligence Agency provided the FBI with more than 12,000 domestic intelligence reports annually (all quite illegal, given the CIA charter's prohibition of CIA involvement in domestic security). The Nixon administration also used the IRS to identify supporters of antiwar organizations and then target them and their organizations with tax investigations. By 1970, the administration began assembling an enemies list and moved to centralize domestic intelligence in the White House.

These programs remained secret until an antiwar group broke into an FBI office to steal and then release about 1,000 sensitive documents. As more of the government's activities became public, congressional investigations began. A Senate committee found that the FBI alone had more than half a million domestic intelligence files.

During the 1970s, Congress and the president enacted restrictions to halt such activities. The army terminated its program and destroyed its files. President Ford banned the CIA from conducting surveillance on domestic activities and prohibited the NSA from intercepting any communication beginning or ending on American soil. Ford's attorney general imposed stringent limits on FBI investigations. Federal legislation limited electronic surveillance without a warrant from a special court.

One of the lessons of this history is that neither repression nor opposition to repression has an inherent partisan bias. The Democratic Johnson showed no more regard for civil liberties than the Republican Nixon; on the other hand, ameliorating the worst abuses of the Vietnam era was also a bipartisan effort.

As Stone observes, many of these post-Vietnam safeguards have now been dismantled or at least significantly weakened since 9/11. In 2002, Attorney General Ashcroft authorized the FBI to attend, for surveillance purposes, any event open to the public. The USA PATRIOT Act authorizes the government to demand medical records, financial records, and other documents from third parties without probable cause. Most important, the Bush administration began a secret electronic surveillance program that disregarded the statutory restrictions enacted in the 1970s.

This brings us directly to the topic of the next section. How much does the present response to antiterrorism mirror past national security efforts? How has the reaction to current government programs compared with past reactions? In short, what can we learn from this history that is relevant today?

THE MORE THINGS CHANGE?

How much of our recent experience, and of the modern experience described in Part I, was a surprise? Part II addresses the question. First up is Jan Lewis, who provides an overview of national security issues through the turn of the last century.

She begins with the Alien and Sedition Acts passed by Congress in 1798. In the congressional debates over these bills, she sees signs of conflicting conceptions of citizenship and national security. Against the background of the French Revolution, Federalist anxieties about the nation's security were acute and focused on their political opponents and on immigrants. At Federalist urging, the naturalization period was increased to fourteen years to limit citizenship to individuals who had fully assimilated American culture. The Alien Enemies Act and Alien Friends Act, between them, authorized the president to deport any alien who was a native of an enemy country or whom he considered "dangerous to the peace and safety of the United States." Although no one was ever deported, the statutes cut off the flow of immigration to the United States and caused some resident aliens to flee. This was the first of many times that immigrant communities came under special suspicion during a national security crisis.

More notorious than either of these, however, was the Sedition Act, which made it illegal to defame any branch of the federal government. The Federalists considered their Republican opponents to be enemies of the state, not legitimate political adversaries. Fourteen prosecutions were brought under the Sedition Act, and Lewis observes that they were specifically designed to silence the president's critics and ensure his reelection. In the eyes of the Federalists, however, this targeting was not a matter of party politics but of national security, because they considered their opponents to be advocates of an international revolutionary ideal. Lewis believes that, as a result of Federalist attacks, the left wing of the Republican party was effectively silenced.

Lewis then briefly examines a largely forgotten episode, the War of 1812. New Englanders traded with the British enemy, interfered with militia recruitment, and sometimes seemed to welcome a British victory. Mobs attacked opponents of the war, especially in Baltimore, but the Madison administration chose not to renew the Sedition Act. On the other hand, in a remarkable incident, General Andrew Jackson detained judges who had attempted to issue habeas corpus writs or otherwise challenge his military rule of the city of New Orleans.

The remaining civil liberties episodes discussed by Lewis revolve around issues of race. Before the Civil War, the government sharply restricted abolitionist speech. Abolitionist tracts were banned from the mail in the South with the tacit consent of the federal government; a gag rule prevented congressional consideration of abolitionist petitions; and anti-abolition riots were not uncommon. A lesser known incident took place in 1836, when seditious libel charges were brought based on possession of abolitionist publications in Washington, D.C. The prosecutor was Francis Scott Key (notwithstanding the "land of the free" line in the anthem he penned). The jury acquitted, but only after the defendant had languished in jail for eight months.

The civil liberties issues of the Civil War are more familiar fare. Lincoln suspended habeas corpus and authorized widespread military arrests. In terms of the effects on dissenters, Lewis observes, the pattern was to clamp down and then let up on particular dissenters. Efforts to suppress newspapers or Democratic critics were often met with political outcries, at which point the government would retreat.

The story of civil liberties in the South, during and after the war, is less familiar. Travel within the Confederacy required a passport. As in the North, habeas corpus was limited and political dissidents were targeted during the war. Civil liberties fared poorly again in the South as Reconstruction wound down in the 1870s. Southern mobs routinely broke up political meetings and attacked dissidents. Black voters were subject to intimidation and violence. In an 1898 riot in Wilmington, a mob of two thousand burned down a newspaper office and gave the mayor a day to leave town. The number of black victims is still not known.

Lewis finds that national security (at least in the sense of foreign threats) was sometimes but not always the basis for infringing civil liberties during the nineteenth century. But even when the country faced no foreign threat, the targets of government restrictions were always social outsiders such as blacks; indeed, attacks on them were one way of defining nationalism. Lewis also finds that the process of limiting civil liberties was entangled with party politics in each instance, not only in its origins but in its ability to reshape the political landscape.

An observer who is familiar with the early twentieth-century experience would find much that is familiar in this even earlier history: targeting outsider groups such as immigrants and ethnic minorities in World War I, using national security measures against political dissidents and partisan opponents. This is not too surprising: the individuals who were in power in the first third of the twentieth century were very likely to have come of age during the nineteenth. Thus there are clear continuities bridging the turn into the twentieth century.

What about continuities between the current century and its predecessor? Do current clashes between civil liberties and national security reflect the same dynamics as twentieth-century episodes, or should we expect a different dynamic?

Many readers may be startled by John Yoo's assertion that the Bush security program is more restrained than its predecessors. Yet a review of the history shows that the latest response to a national security threat has not included some of the major abuses of previous periods. Unlike the Alien and Sedition Act, the Civil War, World War I, or the cold war, there have been no prosecutions based on dissent from government policies. Compared with the Alien and Sedition Act, World War I, or World War II, ethnic communities or immigrants as a group have not been branded as disloyal, let alone confined to internment camps. Although some actions focused on immigrant communities and some security measures have had a greater impact on Arab-Americans, we have not seen the deliberate targeting of an ethnic group of earlier periods. This is not meant to minimize impacts on Arab-American communities, but instead to address their proper scale relative to the vigilante efforts of World War I or the internment camps of World War II. Also, so far as we know, surveillance has not— unlike in the Vietnam era—targeted domestic dissenters. And unlike the Civil War or World War II, there have been no mass detentions of American citizens.

These changes are due in part to the changed nature of the threat, as John Yoo and others observe. The current situation is different because technological advances give enemies of the state a greater ability to organize, communicate covertly, and unleash mass destruction. Thus, unlike most previous crises, this one does not involve fears of a potential mass movement against government policies, rather, the task of identifying a small network of opponents and neutralizing their efforts. Also, unlike the Civil War or either World War, neither the war on terror domestically nor American military actions in the Middle East has required mass mobilization or placed serious burdens on large sectors of the public. For this reason, there may be less reason for security measures to degenerate into campaigns against political dissidents. On the other hand, surveillance issues loom very large,[11] but, at the same time, few members of the public have any direct tie to the foreign nationals who are the major targets of interrogation, detention, and possible trial.

Another significant change pertains to the role of the courts. Yoo notes that many lower courts have been less willing to defer to the executive than in past crisis periods. In his chapter on the role of the Supreme Court, Powe views the Court as historically uninterested in protecting civil liberties except during the Warren Court period. Even the Warren Court, he observes, was unwilling to act when it faced strong opposition from Congress. Still, Powe admits that he is surprised by the relatively high protection given to civil liberties in the past few years.

In terms of the judicial role, then, the current era may be different. Hamdi seemed to break the historical pattern of judicial passivity, although the ruling can be read as retaining at least some level of deference to the executive. The more recent ruling in Hamdan clearly showed an unwillingness to defer to either the president or Congress, striking down military tribunals despite Congress's apparent effort to derail the litigation. As Powe observes, this is a sharp deviation from prior practice. Moreover, as Yoo speculates, the Court's greater aggressiveness may reflect society's growing acceptance of judicial primacy in interpreting the Constitution. He also observes that Bush did not have the opportunity to reshape the judiciary that FDR had enjoyed by the time of World War II, further weakening Bush's position.

If Powe is right that congressional opposition has a damping effect on the Court, removing such opposition with the 2006 switch in congressional control to the Democrats may further embolden the justices. Of course, some justices may find more reason to leave issues to the other two branches on the theory that divided government will lead to a more vigorous and constructive political debate. The response to the most recent congressional legislation should therefore shed significant light on how the Court responds to shifts in political power.

To some extent, all of this may be seen as confirming the optimistic view of an upward trend in crisis treatment of civil liberties over the course of American history. Political resistance to the executive programs has been outspoken, in contrast to both world wars. Compared with even the Vietnam era, courts have been more aggressive in supporting civil liberties and the executive's incursions on civil liberties have been less blatant.

For instance, even if the administration had tried to target political dissenters, it would have been unlikely to succeed because First Amendment doctrine has greatly solidified, even since the Warren Court era. One of the few points on which both liberal and conservative justices agree is the need for staunch protection of free speech. This is one area where the optimistic story seems correct. Beginning with the Holmes and Brandeis efforts to defend speech after World War I, constitutional doctrine has become progressively more protective of dissent. And given the Court's increased prominence and power—enough to allow it to intervene for the first time in history in a presidential election—there is little reason to think the Court would have backed down on this issue had there been a post-9/11 effort to suppress dissent.

But before applauding our progress over the past, it is also important to consider the changed context in which today's civil liberties concerns arise. Unlike past crises, the current threat arises from an ideological and religious movement that has never had any significant traction on American soil. This, as much as increased respect for civil liberties, may explain why dissenters have not been targeted by the government for prosecution or surveillance. Mass detention of American Arabs was not a plausible option, given that the attackers were all foreigners (rather than American citizens or permanent immigrants) and that the United States has important Arab allies (especially Saudi Arabia). Thus, many of the repressive actions of earlier periods were probably not available to the Administration after 9/11 even if it had wanted to use them. There may also be some tendency for administrations to avoid measures that caused controversy in immediate preceding crises, either reverting to still earlier measures (such as the revival of military trials by the Bush administration) or creating novel measures (FDR's use of wiretapping).

Another important respect in which this crisis differs from its predecessors is the role of international law. From the first, the administration was aware of the potential application of the Geneva Conventions to its activities. Even more so, the administration's legal memoranda showed keen awareness that both the Geneva Convention and antitorture norms had been incorporated into domestic law, thereby raising the threat of criminal penalties for violations. This was not a legal situation that presidents had ever faced. Military lawyers were also outspoken in their concerns about compliance with international law, as well as conformity to what they regarded as the dictates of due process. In Hamdan, the Supreme Court relied in part on the Geneva Conventions to invalidate the administration's unilateral effort to create military tribunals. In response, Congress attempted to oust the Court from reliance on international law, but made its own effort to meet the demands of Geneva and other international requirements.

The increased profile of international law in this crisis period partly reflects fundamental changes in the international system. In no small part because of American efforts in the postwar period, multilateral institutions have become much stronger and international human rights law has emerged. That some of these human rights guarantees have been adopted into domestic law merely reflects the growing acceptance of international norms. Once given the sanction of the United States criminal code, international law provisions had to be dealt with one way or another, not simply ignored.

A recurrent theme in American history has been the formation of national identity. As early as the Alien and Sedition Acts, national security disputes were entangled with divergent views of national identity. At that time, Jeffersonian Democrats resisted incursions of civil liberties, Federalist advocates considered Democrats tainted with internationalist ideals at the expense of distinctly American values. Today, a somewhat similar struggle seems to be taking place over the extent to which America should remain free from the entanglements of international norms.

Both the increased sway of international law and the entrenchment of the Supreme Court's role as constitutional arbiter can be seen as reflections of the same fundamental trend toward a legalist regime, in which government decisions are seen as essentially governed by legal norms rather than discretion. The Bush administration has fought against this regime with strong arguments for unilateral presidential authority. In turn, this effort has encountered sharp resistance, not only from courts but as well from other segments of the legal profession (including the American Bar Association, military lawyers, and State Department counsel). The resistance is probably heightened by the perception that the threat of terrorism has no clear end point, so that the administration is demanding a permanent rather than temporary deviation from the legalist regime.

Future national security efforts will also be shaped by technological changes. Technology creates the possibility of asymmetrical warfare. Small groups can threaten powerful nation states, using electronic communications to operate and potentially gaining access to weapons of mass destruction. In their contribution, Paul Schwartz and Ronald Lee point to an ongoing dialectic between civil liberties and national security. They argue that technological change can both aid and harm national security and civil liberties, leading to a continual evolution of legal regulation. On the one hand, they note, technological changes may create continual policy flux, eliminating the time needed to reach a deliberative balance between civil liberties and national security. On the other hand, the private sector's important role in developing and commercializing technology may lessen the government's ability to preside over the civil liberties and national security dynamic. If one thing is clear, it is that technology will continue to develop in new and sometimes unexpected ways, posing ongoing challenges for the advancement of both national security and civil liberties.

CONCLUDING THOUGHTS

Civil liberties and national security have been in tension since the early days of the republic. Technology, international human rights laws, and judicial independence have all brought important changes. The contributions to this volume illuminate several important continuities.

First, presidents of all political parties and ideological stances have focused almost exclusively on national security in times of crisis, with little or no thought of civil liberties. Liberal Democrats like Woodrow Wilson,

Franklin Roosevelt, and Lyndon Johnson seemed to waste no time worrying, any more than moderate Republicans like Richard Nixon or conservative Republicans like George W. Bush did. The only exception is the cold war, where the impetus for incursions of civil liberties came from Congress, and presidents were less enthusiastic—though generally acquiescent. It may have been significant that cold war subversion charges were often leveled against government officials (including ultimately military officers), impairing the functioning of the bureaucracy the president heads.

Second, responses to crises have always been intertwined with partisan politics. Presidents use national security as a partisan weapon. Support for civil liberties is most likely to come from the president's partisan political opponents if it exists at all within the political mainstream. We see this pattern as early as the Alien and Sedition Acts and as recently as the 2006 elections.

Third, conflicts over civil liberties and national security often are entangled with disputes over national identity. The question is what it means to be a loyal American. Sometimes, as in the case of German Americans in World War I or Japanese Americans in World War II, the issue concerns ties to foreign nations or cultures. Sometimes, the issue is the extent to which American identity is consistent with attachments to international ideas (for which Jeffersonian Democratic Republicans, McCarthy-era "subversives," and Clinton Democrats were equally attacked).

Although the optimistic view of ever-upward progress on civil liberties is too simple, there is some support in recent history for this hypothesis. In particular, the aftermath of the Vietnam era, as exemplified in the Watergate scandal, seems to have permanently changed the degree of deference that courts, the press, and the public are willing to give unilateral presidential action. Moreover, as noted earlier, the result of earlier crisis has been to solidify First Amendment doctrine as a barrier to repression of dissenters.

Trends regarding other issues are less clear. For instance, military tribunals played a major role in the Civil War era, were submerged again until World War II, and then were forgotten until resurrected by the Bush administration. With regard to surveillance, changes in technology seem to play an equal role with changes in legal norms, making prediction difficult.

Obviously, references to history cannot dictate answers to the questions of today. Hopefully, however, the historical perspective this volume provides will help illuminate current issues. We seem to be repeating the past in both obvious ways and more subtle ways. History can provide fresh insights into our current situation because of these enduring themes.

Equally important, the terrorist threat differs in significant ways from previous national security issues. As we have seen, the response to the threat has also been distinctive in important respects, and it has taken place in a changed setting of increased judicial independence. It also bears noting that another major terrorist attack, on the scale of 9/11 or above, would shift American policies and politics in ways that cannot be readily predicted. In this book, we do not attempt to speak to hypothetical future events and their relationship with past episodes.

The chapters that follow this introduction probe the continuities and discontinuities from the John Adams administration through the George W. Bush administration from the perspectives of historians and constitutional lawyers. We do not attempt to present any orthodoxies, if indeed there is any orthodoxy to be found on these issues today. The authors have different perspectives and sometimes speak in different voices. They include at least one architect of Bush administration policy as well as some outspoken critics, and others who take the stance of the detached observer.

Our goal is to foster a discussion among key issues about the ways in which history can (and cannot) illuminate current clashes between national security and civil liberties. Although no book could hope to settle the ongoing debate about the relationship between civil liberties and national security, at least the debate may proceed more intelligently if we take care to understand the implications of past episodes for today's disputes.

NOTES

1. The Russell Sage Foundation also contemplates a separate volume of comparative perspectives on these issues, which is the reason that the current volume focuses exclusively on the United States.
2. For an excellent collection of background materials on these issues, see Abrams 2005.
3. U.S. Congress, Authorization for Use of Military Force (AUMF), 115 Stat. 224 (2001).
4. The order is most readily accessible on the White House website, http://www.whitehouse.gov/news/releases/2001.
5. 18 U.S.C. 2441.
6. *Hamdi v. Rumsfeld*, 542 U.S. 507 (2004).
7. *Hamdi* is notable as evidence that ideology is not everything, even in the hardest constitutional cases. The critical vote for Justice O'Connor's position was Justice Breyer, commonly considered a member of the liberal block. Chief Justice Rehnquist, a strong conservative voice, also allied himself with O'Connor's centrist views. In the meantime, the two most conservative members of the Court (Thomas and Scalia) came to diametrically opposite

conclusions, and Scalia was joined by Justice Stevens, the most liberal member of the Court.

8.   *Hamdan v. Rumsfeld*, 548 U.S. forthcoming (2006).

9.   Pub. L. No. 109-366.

10. For a more detailed history of the detainee issue, see Margulies 2006. Readers should keep in mind his perspective as counsel for certain detainees. See also two leading authorities on federal jurisdiction, Fallon and Meltzer 2007, 2031.

11. For a discussion of the surveillance issues, see the chapter by Schwartz and Lee, as well as Donohue 2006, 1059.

REFERENCES

Abrams, Norman. 2005. *Anti-Terrorism and Criminal Enforcement.*

Cole, David. 2004. "The Priority of Morality: The Emergency Constitution's Blind Spot." *Yale Law Journal* 113(8): 1753–78.

Donohue, Laura K. 2006. "Anglo-American Privacy and Surveillance." *Journal of Criminal Law and Criminology* 96 (3): 1059–108.

Fallon, Richard H., Jr., and Daniel J. Meltzer. 2007. "Habeas Corpus Jurisdiction, Substantive Rights, and the War on Terror." *Harvard Law Review* 120: 2031.

Gonzales, Alberto R. 2002. Memorandum for the President, "Decision re Application of the Geneva Convention on Prisoners of War to the Conflict with al Qaeda and the Taliban." January 25, 2002.

Jinks, Derek, and David Sloss. 2004. "Is the President Bound by the Geneva Conventions?" *Cornell Law Review* 90(1): 97.

Margulies, Joseph. 2006. *Guantanamo and the Abuse of Presidential Power.* New York: Simon & Schuster.

Powell, Colin L. 2002. Memorandum to Counsel to the President, "Draft Decision Memorandum for the President on the Applicability of the Geneva Convention to the Conflict in Afghanistan." January 26, 2002.

Taft, William H., IV. 2002. Memorandum to Counsel to the President, "Comments on Your Paper on the Geneva Convention." February 2, 2002.

PART I

THE MODERN AMERICAN EXPERIENCE

CHAPTER 2

WORLD WAR I AND THE CRISIS OF DEMOCRACY

ALAN BRINKLEY

The American involvement in World War I and its aftermath produced one of the most widespread and virulent assaults on civil liberties in American history. It also created a powerful reaction that helped produce some of the first firm defenses of our modern notion of what civil liberties mean. But unlike other wartime battles over civil liberties, which largely pitted government self-interest against popular expectations, the conflicts of the World War I era pitted one set of fervent democratic passions against another. On one side was President Woodrow Wilson, fired with a mission to redeem the world. On the other was a range of individuals and groups who, whether or not they shared Wilson's international hopes, rejected his belief that they justified a suspension of democratic freedoms at home. The highly ideological character of this struggle—before, during, and after the war—at times pitted democratic ideals against democratic practices.

WILSON'S MISSION

On the surface, nothing could seem more different from the bellicose American unilateralism of today than the shining, idealistic internationalism of Woodrow Wilson. Wilson took America into World War I calling for a "peace without victory," a "world made safe for democracy," and he sought to negotiate a "people's peace" that would establish democratic principles for international governance and national self-determination—principles to be enforced by a robust League of Nations in which the United States would be a responsible partner. For a time, his vision captured the global imagination and made Wilson the individual (and the America he represented) a symbol of selfless idealism to the world. When he arrived in Europe in 1919 to begin negotiations with the other victorious powers on the shape of the peace, he was greeted in London and Paris with such enormous popular adoration and hope that it frightened some European leaders (and even some Americans) with its intensity and fervor.

The failure of Wilsonian internationalism, and the tragic personal fate of Woodrow Wilson during his effort to save it, are part of American folklore. But that failure was not just the result of feckless opposition in Europe and in the U.S. Senate, as most accounts of the Wilson legend suggest. It was also a product of the messianic character of Wilson's approach to the war and its damaging, perhaps fatal, impact both on the peace and on the stability of progressive hopes at home. When Wilson began to explain to himself, and to the world, America's reasons for entering World War I—an intervention highly controversial with the public up to, and indeed after, the declaration of war—he gravitated instinctively to a highly moral justification, one that rested on his vision of America's special obligation to export its democratic ethos to the world. At the same time that he sketched out his plans for a new internationalism, he displayed thinly concealed disdain for the nations with which he was proposing a partnership. Wilson at times seemed to imply that America's wartime allies were as much in need of redemption at the hands of the United States as the "backward nations" Theodore Roosevelt had once eagerly proposed to "civilize."

The new Bolshevik government in Russia was also central to Wilson's thinking as he shaped his war aims. The Fourteen Points he proposed in January 1918 as a basis for peace were in part a response to Lenin's Principles of Diplomacy, issued a few weeks before. Lenin called for no forcible annexation of territory, the restoration of independence to all occupied nations, self-determination for all national groups that had not previously been independent, and no economic coercion of weaker nations by stronger ones. Eighteen days later, Wilson proposed virtually the same things (Mayer 1959, 1967). He also, of course, included other proposals that he had framed before the war (with the League of Nations serving as a global equivalent of the enlightened commissions, regulatory agencies, and reformed legislatures that progressives were creating at home).

When America entered the war, Wilson refused to allow American troops to join forces with the Allied armies that had by then been fighting in the trenches for three years. Instead, he created the American Expeditionary Force, an almost entirely separate army with an entirely separate command to avoid the "pollution" of America's moral army. After the war, in Paris, buoyed by his spectacular popular greeting, Wilson insisted that only his plan adequately reflected the democratic yearnings of the world. "I have uttered as the objects of this great war ideals and nothing but ideals," he said on the eve of the negotiations, "There is a great wind of moral force moving through the world, and every man who opposes that wind will go down in disgrace" (Kennedy 1980, 355–7). By the end of the negotiations, the European leaders had come so to resent Wilson's condescension that they resisted him almost as much because of their dislike of him as because of their opposition to the substance of the proposals.

Clemenceau, looking back at his own handiwork in Paris, conceded, "This treaty will bring us burdens, troubles, miseries, difficulties, and that will continue for long years." The *Nation* magazine argued at about the same time that "in the whole history of diplomacy there is no treaty more properly to be regarded as an international crime than the amazing document which the German representatives are now asked to sign" (Dawley 2003, 256). Wilson, however, defended the agreement as a nearly perfect instrument of peace. "Dare we reject it," he asked, "and break the heart of the world?"

WAR, PEACE, AND THE BATTLE OVER CIVIL LIBERTIES

The highly ideological character of the war, and the debate over the peace, was the context within which the battle over civil liberties emerged. The war for democracy and enlightenment ushered in one of the most repressively reactionary periods in American history. Mobilizing the nation behind a great mission to remake the world inspired, and appeared to many leaders to require, a mighty effort to suppress dissent and division at home—a project that was, in fact, eagerly supported by many important reformers themselves. Even notable progressives responded to critics of American intervention with harsh attacks on their patriotism, damaging the reputations of such notable antiwar reformers as Jane Addams. The young progressive Randolph Bourne decried this "herd mentality" among liberal intellectuals in a famous attack on his one-time idol John Dewey, a whole-hearted supporter of both the war and a harsh critic of its opponents. Dewey's philosophy, Bourne wrote,

> breaks down noisily when it is used to grind out interpretation for the present crisis. . . .
>   A philosopher who senses so little the sinister forces of war, who is so much more concerned over the excesses of the pacifists than over the excesses of military policy, who can feel only amusement at the idea that anyone should try to conscript thought, who assumes that the war-technique can be used without trailing along with it the mob-fanaticisms, the injustices and hatreds, that are organically bound with it, is speaking to another element of the younger intelligentsia than that to which I belong. (1965, 53–54)

The Wilson administration too responded to dissent with an aggressive campaign of intimidation and coercion to silence or marginalize opponents of the war. Even before America entered the war, Wilson made clear his unwillingness to tolerate opposition and urged Americans to accept the belief "once and for all that loyalty to this flag is the first test of tolerance" (Murphy 1979, 54). At the center of the government's effort were two extraordinary pieces of legislation—the first antisedition legislation passed in the United States since the Alien and Sedition Acts of 1798. The Espionage Act of 1917, fiercely debated in Congress, made illegal acts of "disloyalty" such as discouraging enlistment in the military, and it gave the postmaster general authority to ban all "seditious" materials from the mails. The early versions of the bill contained a press censorship provision for statements that might undermine support for the war, but members of Congress— perhaps aware in a way Wilson apparently was not, of the danger of the path on which they were embarked—refused to allow that provision in the bill. Whatever restraint legislators may have thought they had built into the Sedition Act had little impact on the Department of Justice and the other agencies tasked with enforcing the law. Attorney General Thomas Gregory, when asked about opponents of the war, said shortly after the passage of the bill, "May God have mercy on them, for they need expect none from an outraged people and an avenging government" (Murphy 1979, 163–4, 191–2). The postmaster general, with great relish, announced that "seditious" materials included anything that might "impugn the motives of the government and thus encourage insubordination," anything that suggested "that the government is controlled by Wall Street or munitions manufacturers, or any other special interests." All publications of the Socialist party were banned by definition.

Even so, the government remained unhappy with the Espionage Act. Gregory complained shortly after its passage that "most of the teeth which we tried to put in [the bill] were taken out." In 1918, the administration proposed amendments to expand the government's powers to suppress antiwar activities. The amendments eventually became the Sedition Act of 1918, which, made it a criminal offense to use "any disloyal, profane, scurrilous, or abusive language about the form of government of the United States or the Constitution of the United States, or the flag of the United States, or the uniform of the Army or Navy," or any language that might bring those institutions "into contempt, scorn, . . . or disrepute" (Murphy 1979, 79–82). The more important provision of the act, however, was the more prosaic ban on any activities that might curtail production of war goods or otherwise interfere with the government's effort to conduct the war. That provision made possible the arrest and prosecution of many dissenters who opposed the draft or discouraged military recruiting.

This Sedition Act was particularly useful to the government as an instrument for suppressing radicals and labor unionists, but it also made possible increased harassment of homosexuals and labor activists and successful prosecutions of anyone who opposed the war, protested the draft, or defamed the president. This was the first time since 1798 that the government had formally outlawed speech, and it eventually produced the largest number of political prisoners in American history to that point (Dawley 2003, 157). "You shall not criticize anything or anybody in the Government any longer," Senator Hiram Johnson of California caustically remarked, "or you shall go to jail" (Peterson and Fite 1968, 16). As if to prove his point, the Justice Department in the spring of 1918 arrested Eugene V. Debs, the leader of the American Socialist Party and an outspoken critic of American intervention in the war, for speaking out in defense of fellow party members already imprisoned for their beliefs. They were, Debs said, "simply paying the penalty, that all men have paid in all the ages of history for standing erect and for seeking to pave the way to better conditions for mankind." Debs was convicted and sentenced to ten years incarceration— a sentence commuted in 1921 by President Warren G. Harding after Debs had spent more than two years in prison.

Government policies helped encouraged widespread popular intolerance of dissent and difference. The American Protective League was founded in 1917 by a group of mostly wealthy private citizens to assist the government in the task of maintaining loyalty and was endorsed and partially funded by the attorney general. Its 250,000 members spied on their neighbors, eavesdropped on suspicious conversations in bars and restaurants, intercepted the mail and telegrams of suspected dissidents, and reported to the authorities any evidence of disenchantment with the war effort. They made extralegal arrests. Attorney General Gregory encouraged APL members in late summer 1918 to organize "slacker raids" against perceived draft resisters—an incident that horrified even many otherwise loyal members of the Wilson administration. One member of the Justice Department later described the raids as one of the "chief embarrassments . . . of the war mania" (Kennedy 1980, 291–2), but he—and almost everyone else—remained silent at the time.

The American Protective League was only the largest of a number of such organizations. There was also the National Security League, the Knights of Liberty, the American Defense Society, even one modeled on the Boy Scouts—the Boy Spies of America. Established institutions also took up the cause of loyalty. Industrial espionage helped employers fire thousands of workers suspected of radicalism (which often meant unionization). Schools, colleges, and even prominent universities such as Columbia dismissed faculty who criticized the war.

The greatest impact of this frenzied crusade for loyalty fell on immigrants. The primary target, although not the only one, was German Americans. State education boards banned the teaching of German in the public schools. Libraries removed German books from their shelves. Merchants and others dropped German words from the language. Sauerkraut became liberty cabbage; frankfurters became liberty sausage. (Could the creative members of Congress who coined the term freedom fries in a spasm of anti-French sentiment in 2002 have known of this earlier linguistic inventiveness?) German faculty members were fired from universities. German musicians were fired from orchestras. There were widespread rumors of plots by German Americans to put ground glass in bandages sent to the front, and so people with German names were barred from the Red Cross. In Minnesota, a minister was tarred and feathered because he was overheard praying with a dying woman in German. In southern Illinois, a man was lynched in 1918, for no apparent reason except that he happened to be of German descent.

This overwrought nativism—generated, even if sometimes inadvertently, by government policy and rhetoric—extended to other ethnic groups as well: to the Irish (because of their hostility to the English), to the Jews (because many were hostile to an American alliance with the anti-Semitic Russian government), and to others simply because their ethnic distinctiveness came to seem a threat to the idea of *one-hundred percent Americanism*, a phrase widely used at the time to describe national unity. Immigrant ghettoes in major cities were strictly policed and became frequent targets of vigilante groups. Even many settlement house workers came to feel it their duty to impose a new and more coercive conformity on the immigrants they served. A settlement worker in Chicago said in 1918 that the war had made her realize that "we were a nation only in a very imperfect sense. We were stirred to a new sense of responsibility for a more coherent loyalty, a vital Americanism" (Higham 1955, 242–3).

Hardly had the war ended before the same frenzied demand for loyalty revived in the form of the first great Red Scare. It was in part a response to the Bolshevik revolution in Russia, and the tremendous fear that event had created throughout the capitalist world. It was also a product of the great instability of postwar America, which many middle class people feared was being orchestrated by revolutionaries. There was widespread labor unrest, racial conflicts in cities, economic turbulence, and a small but, to many people, frightening wave of violence and terrorist acts by radicals. But the Red Scare was above all a result of the deliberate strategies of ambitious politicians, who saw a campaign against Bolshevism in America as a useful spur to their careers.

The Justice Department, now under Attorney General A. Mitchell Palmer (who had presidential hopes for 1920), was the leading actor in inflaming the Red Scare. An attempted bombing of his house helped legitimize the major campaign against radicals that he was already planning and that he launched in 1920. On New Year's Day, he ordered simultaneous federal raids (orchestrated by a young and ambitious Justice Department employee, J. Edgar Hoover) on suspected radical centers all over the country. There were 6,000 arrests, amid enormous publicity. They have become known as the Palmer Raids, and they were arguably the greatest single violation of civil liberties in American history (Dawley 2003, 269).

Most of the people arrested were not radicals at all, and even the relatively few genuine radicals rounded up could not be shown to have violated any laws. Most were eventually released, though many remained in custody for weeks and even months without facing formal charges, without access to attorneys or even their own families. Several hundred foreign radicals and presumed radicals were deported to Russia, where they arrived, many of them speaking no Russian and knowing nothing of the country, in the middle of a civil war. Palmer himself looked back on this sorry episode a year later without repentance. "Like a prairie fire," he said,

> the blaze of revolution was sweeping over every American institution of law and order a year ago. It was eating its way into the homes of the American workman, its sharp tongues of revolutionary heat were

licking the altars of the churches, leaping into the belfry of the school bell, crawling into the sacred corners of American homes, seeking to replace marriage vows with libertine laws, burning up the foundations of society (Higham 1955, 229–30).

War Department officials, in the meantime, were creating top-secret plans (labeled War Plans White) to defeat what they feared was an impending revolution in the United States. Breathtaking in their scope, these plans were nothing less than preparations for the military to go to war against American dissenters—not just political dissidents and radicals, but much larger groups, including ethnic communities that had resisted the pressure to Americanize. The likely targets, the War Department report claimed, were people "susceptible to hostile leadership against Anglo-Saxon institutions" (Dawley 2003, 274–5).

Woodrow Wilson reputedly predicted in early 1917, "Once lead this people into war, and they'll forget there ever was such a thing as tolerance. To fight, you must be brutal and ruthless, and the spirit of ruthless brutality will enter into the very fibre of our national life, infecting Congress, the courts, the policeman on the beat, the man on the street" (Dos Passos 1962, 175). That this statement is so widely considered apocryphal is perhaps in part because it appears to be such an uncannily accurate and self-fulfilling prophecy. The behavior Wilson supposedly predicted, and certainly helped to create, was a product not just of the war and not just of social instability, but of the self-righteous moralism and messianic sense of mission that blanketed American actions both at home and abroad in this age of war and revolution.

PROGRESSIVISM REBORN

To some progressives, both at the time and later, there was a bright light amid the darkness of these troubled times. Progressivism was largely purged from American national politics by the harsh impact of the war, but it was in some ways strengthened in grass-roots movements and in new forms of dissent. Examples include the international peace movement of the 1920s, in which many prominent American progressives (among them Jane Addams, the first president of the Women's International League for Peace and Freedom, who eventually won a Nobel Peace Prize for her efforts) were active; a spirited movement of opposition to imperialism (both the formal imperialism of Britain and France and the American occupations and interventions in Latin America and the Caribbean); the slow rebuilding of the labor movement and its expansion to embrace workers abroad (through, for example, the International Federation of Working Women); and the continuing commitment of a small but influential group of progressive intellectuals.

But the most significant progressive awakening of the postwar years was the birth of a vigorous defense of civil liberties that eventually, though not wholly until the 1960s and 1970s, gave the Bill of Rights an expansive meaning in American life for the first time. Before World War I, support for civil liberties had been largely theoretical. There was no significant jurisprudence capable of giving real meaning to the Bill of Rights; and though people of wealth and standing took freedoms for granted, most others could have no reasonable expectation that the law would protect their right to free speech and other liberties. One scholar, for example, later wrote of the first century and a half under the Bill of Rights as "140 years of silence" (Murphy 1979, 22). As Zechariah Chafee, a great champion of free speech in the 1920s and 1930s, later wrote of the World War I era: "The First Amendment had no hold on people's minds, because no live facts or concrete images were then attached to it. Consequently, like an empty box with beautiful words on it, the Amendment collapsed under the impact of Prussian battalions, and terror of Bolshevik mobs" (1952, 4).

The heavy-handed actions of the federal government after the war created a powerful backlash, which destroyed the political career of A. Mitchell Palmer, almost nipped in the bud the bureaucratic ascent of J. Edgar Hoover, damaged the Democratic party, and helped create some of the first significant institutional and judicial defenses of civil liberties (see Murphy 1979). Among the first formal organizations to defend the First Amendment was the Free Speech League, which early in the century had defended citizens against the antianarchist laws that followed the assassination of President McKinley. A small but courageous organization centered in New York City, it continued to fight government suppression of speech through World War I. Partly in response to the work of the League, Roger Baldwin—a former settlement house worker—became incensed by the violations of rights he witnessed in the war years and became, for the first time, a civil-liberties activist. (He believed, with some reason, that he was responsible for introducing the term *civil liberties* into popular discourse.) In 1917, he helped create the National Civil Liberties Bureau, which in early 1920, in response to the Palmer Raids, was reorganized and renamed the American Civil Liberties Union. Baldwin insisted that the best way to establish the principle of robust civil liberties would be to defend the most unpopular people and causes. He was especially outspoken on behalf of the radical anarchists of the Industrial Workers of the World, particular targets of government harassment, arguing that by standing up for the Wobblies he was casting light not just on the role of government but also on the role of industrial capital in repressing the rights of individuals.

The third great contribution to the creation of the modern regime of civil liberties was the slow but growing support for the idea within the judiciary. Not until the Warren Court decisions of the 1950s and 1960s did protecting civil liberties become a major item on the Supreme Court's agenda, and even then the courts at lower levels were slow to embrace the cause. The gradual shift of judicial thinking on the issue, though, became visible within months after the end of the war, less in the actual decisions of the courts than in several notable dissents that created the intellectual foundation for an expanded legal notion of free speech.

The most important figure in this process—although not the first—was Oliver Wendell Holmes. During and immediately after the war, Holmes showed little more inclination than any other members of the Supreme Court to challenge the government's aggressive use of the Espionage and Sedition Acts to silence opposition. Early in 1919, the Court accepted an appeal on behalf of Charles Schenck, a socialist who had been convicted of violating the Espionage Act for passing out leaflets denouncing the war and encouraging young men to resist the draft. Holmes wrote the majority opinion, which affirmed both Schenck's conviction and the constitutionality of the law. "The question in every case," he wrote in a highly controversial decision, "is whether the words used are used in such circumstances and are of such a nature as to create a clear and present danger that they will bring about the substantive evils that Congress has a right to prevent" (Murphy 1979, 266–7). Schenck's words, he insisted, were designed to undermine the draft and were therefore unprotected speech. "When a nation is at war," he added, "many things that might be said in time of peace are such a hindrance to its effort that their utterance will not be endured so long as men fight, and that no Court could regard them as protected by any constitutional right."

Holmes's decision in the Schenck case (and to some degree his almost perfunctory decision in 1919 to reject the appeal of Debs's conviction earlier that year) evoked a storm of protest, not just from civil liberties activists but also from legal scholars and fellow jurists whose opinion he valued. Among his critics was the distinguished jurist, Learned Hand, then a New York district court judge with an admiration for Holmes that his biographer described as "extreme" and close to "idolatry" (Gunther 1994, 162). But he differed sharply, if cordially, with Holmes on the Schenck case. While Holmes gave only glancing attention to the First Amendment in his decision, arguing that free speech was always weighed against and often less important than other values, Hand considered free speech a fundamental right, "a hard-bought acquisition in the fight for freedom" (Stone 2004, 201). Shortly after the passage of the 1917 Espionage Act, Hand considered an appeal by the radical periodical *The Masses*, which the attorney general had banned from the mails because of a cartoon critical of the draft and a poem honoring Emma Goldman and Alexander Berkman, who were serving prison terms for their opposition to the war. Hand—fully aware that he was jeopardizing his likely promotion to the court of appeals by doing so—ruled on behalf of the *Masses*, arguing that the material in question could not be shown to be a danger to the prosecution of the war. To decide otherwise, he argued, would open the way to "the suppression of all hostile criticism, and of all opinion except what encouraged and supported the existing policies" (Murphy 1979, 196–7). Although his opinion was later overturned by the court of appeals, and although his opinion did very likely cost him a promotion to the higher court for a time, Hand's commitment to opposing the suppression of speech only intensified in coming years and led him to join in the criticism of Holmes's Schenck decision, a painful stance to Holmes. Ernst Freund, the great legal scholar, published a highly critical article of Holmes's wartime decisions in the spring of 1919, calling Holmes's opinions "unsafe doctrine" and offering the withering argument that "the peril resulting to the national cause from toleration of adverse opinion is largely imaginary" (Stone 2004, 201).

Although it is impossible to prove that the criticism of his Schenck and other wartime decisions actually caused Holmes to reconsider his position on free speech (something Holmes himself always staunchly denied), it is clear that the small avalanche of criticism he was receiving from respected colleagues coincided with a significant shift in Holmes's own position beginning in 1919. The most important evidence of this change was the case of *Abrams v. U.S.*, which reached the court in 1919 and was decided in 1920. The case asked the court to overturn the conviction under the Sedition Act of a Russian immigrant who had passed out leaflets critical of the American military intervention in Russia after the Bolshevik revolution. Holmes dissented from a decision upholding the conviction in language that sharply differed from his earlier opinions and helped shape eventual judicial support for a robust defense of free speech. No one should be confident, he said, that the passions of the moment would withstand the scrutiny of history. For

> when men have realized that time has upset many fighting faiths, they may come to believe even more than they believe the very foundations of their own conduct that the ultimate good desired is better reached by free trade in ideas—that the best test of truth is the power of the thought to get itself accepted in the competition of the market, and that truth is the only ground upon which their wishes safely can be carried out. That, at any rate, is the theory of our Constitution. It is an experiment, as all life is an experiment. Every year, if not every day, we have to wager our salvation upon some prophecy based upon imperfect knowledge. While that experiment is part of our system, I think that we should be eternally vigilant against attempts to check the expression of opinions that we loathe and believe to be fraught with death. . . . I had conceived that the United States, through many years, had shown its repentance for the Sedition Act of 1798.[1]

Given Holmes's own halting and sometimes grudging movement toward a robust defense of the First Amendment, it is hard to see his argument in *Abrams*—coming well after the fiercest wartime passions had abated—in the same courageous light that one might look at Hand's decision in the *Masses* case. Even in 1920, the year of a Wall Street bombing that killed more than thirty people and wounded hundreds more, strong sentiment remained for taking virtually any imaginable steps to curb anarchists and radicals, and Holmes's opinion was not without powerful critics, both from within the Wilson administration, defensively upholding its increasingly unpopular policies in its waning months, and among significant legal scholars and jurists, who were as shocked by Holmes's apparent change of position as others had been shocked by his weak defense of the First Amendment in Schenck.

A year later, Louis Brandeis, who, like Holmes, had been relatively slow to resist the march toward censorship during the war, made another significant contribution to the case for expanding the definition of free speech. In a dissent against the court's ruling in *Gilbert v. Minnesota*, in which the Court upheld a Minnesota law under which Joseph Gilbert had been convicted of speaking against the draft, Brandeis wrote:

> I have difficulty in believing that the liberty guaranteed by the Constitution . . . does not include liberty to teach, either in the privacy of the home or publicly, the doctrine of pacifism. . . . I cannot believe

that the liberty guaranteed by the Fourteenth Amendment [in other words, the Fourteenth Amendment's extension of First Amendment and other protections to all citizens] includes only liberty to acquire and to enjoy property.

In 1927, still dealing with the fallout from wartime repression, Brandeis wrote yet another influential opinion in *Whitney v. California*. He concurred on technical grounds with the 1919 conviction of Anita Whitney for joining a communist party in California and advocating the overthrow of the United States government, but dissented sharply from the Court's expansive view of the state's power to suppress dangerous speech:

> Those who won our independence by revolution were not cowards. They did not fear political change. They did not exalt order at the cost of liberty. To courageous, self-reliant men, with confidence in the power of free and fearless reasoning applied through the processes of popular government, no danger flowing from speech can be deemed clear and present [a not very subtle slap at Holmes's *Schenck* decision], unless the incidence of the evil apprehended is so imminent that it may befall before there is opportunity for full discussion. If there be time to expose through discussion the falsehood and fallacies, to avert the evil by the processes of education, the remedy to be applied is more speech, not enforced silence. . . . It is therefore always open to Americans to challenge a law abridging free speech and assembly by showing that there was no emergency justifying it. . . . The fact that speech is likely to result in some violence or in destruction of property is not enough to justify its suppression. There must be the probability of serious injury to the State. Among free men, the deterrents ordinarily to be applied to prevent crime are education and punishment for violations of the law, not abridgment of the rights of free speech and assembly (*Whitney v. California*, 268 U.S. 375 (1925)).

In these and other dissents, Holmes, Brandeis, and a slowly expanding group of other judges and justices began laying out much of what became the legal and moral basis for our modern conception of civil liberties.

A HISTORY OF STRUGGLE

The history of civil liberties in America during World War I, as through much of American history, is a story of struggle. Even in peacetime, Americans have engaged in an ever-changing negotiation between the demands of liberty and the demands of order and security. But in times of national emergency, the conflict between these two demands has becomes particularly intense—and the relative claims of order and security naturally become stronger. Every major crisis in our history has led to abridgments of personal liberty, some of them inevitable and justified. But in World War I, and in most other times of crisis, governments have also used the seriousness of its mission to seize powers far in excess of what the emergency required. They pursue existing agendas in the name of national security. They target unpopular or vulnerable groups in the population less because there has been clear evidence of danger than because they have been able to do so at little political cost. During World War I, the victims of government repression were labor leaders, anarchists, and socialists, none of whom posed any danger to the war effort but all of whom were widely disliked. In World War II, the victims were Japanese Americans, who were stripped of all the rights of citizenship not because there was any evidence that they were disloyal but because they were feared on largely racial grounds. In our own time, the victims are mostly Arab Americans and foreign nationals, who have been subject to mass arrests and considerable harassment on the basis of little or no evidence of danger or disloyalty.

That makes it particularly important that vigilant citizens, such as those who created the ACLU, have usually been willing to make the case that the defense of our liberties is not an indulgence, but an essential part of democratic life. Civil liberties, in short, are not a gift from the state that can be withdrawn when they become inconvenient. They are the product of continuous effort, which has extended over two centuries and must continue into a third—in dangerous times as well as in tranquil ones—if personal freedom is to remain a vital part of our national life.

NOTE

1.   *Abrams v. United States*, 250 U.S. 616 (1919).

REFERENCES

Bourne, Randolph. 1965. "Twilight of the Idols." In *War and the Intellectuals: Essays by Randolph Bourne 1915–1919*. New York: Harper & Row.
Chafee, Zechariah. 1952. *Thirty-Five Years with Freedom of Speech*. New York: Roger N. Baldwin Civil Liberties Foundation.
Dawley, Alan. 2003. *Changing the World: American Progressives in War and Revolution*. Princeton, N.J.: Princeton University Press.
Dos Passos, John. 1962. *Mr. Wilson's War*. Garden City, N.Y.: Doubleday.

Gunther, Gerald. 1994. *Learned Hand: The Man and the Judge.* New York: Alfred A. Knopf.

Higham, John. 1955. *Strangers in the Land: Patterns of American Nativism, 1860–1925.* New Brunswick, N.J.: Rutgers University Press.

Kennedy, David M. 1980. *Over Here: The First World War and American Society.* New York: Oxford University Press.

Mayer, Arno. 1959. *Wilson v. Lenin: Political Origins of the New Diplomacy.* New Haven, Conn.: Yale University Press.

———. 1967. *Politics and Diplomacy of Peacemaking: Containment and Counterrevolution at Versailles, 1918–1919.* New York: Alfred A. Knopf.

Murphy, Paul L. 1979. *World War I and the Origin of Civil Liberties in the United States.* New York: W. W. Norton.

Peterson, H. C., and Gilbert Fite. 1968. *Opponents of War, 1917–1918.* Seattle, Wash.: University of Washington Press.

Stone, Geoffrey R. 2004. *Perilous Times: Free Speech in Wartime from the Sedition Acts of 1798 to the War on Terrorism.* New York: W. W. Norton.

CHAPTER 3

FDR, CIVIL LIBERTIES, AND THE WAR ON TERRORISM

JOHN YOO

It is commonplace to hear today that the war on terrorism has reduced civil liberties in America. Much of the focus has been on the PATRIOT Act, which expanded the authority of the federal government to seek records and to intercept communications of suspected terrorists within the United States.[1] As staff writer Rick Weiss explained in a *Washington Post* article in late 2003, Al Gore called for the act to be repealed, accused the Bush administration of suspending civil liberties, and claimed that the government was using "fear as a political tool to consolidate its power and to escape any accountability for its use" ("Gore Criticizes Bush Approach to Security," November 10, 2003, A2). During the 2004 presidential campaign, then candidate and now chairman of the Democratic Party Howard Dean called the act "morally wrong," "shameful," and "unconstitutional" (David Tell, "The Patriot Act's Surprising Defenders," *Weekly Standard*, vol. 9, issue 8, November 3, 2003).

Similar criticism from the media, the academy, and civil liberties groups has greeted other elements of the Bush administration's terrorism policies. Bush's decision to detain al Qaeda suspects as enemy combatants and to try them using military commissions has sparked years of litigation that has reached the Supreme Court. The Justice Department's effort immediately after 9/11 to investigate, detain, and deport aliens, mostly from the Middle East, illegally in the United States, has been called ethnic profiling on a grand scale. Most recently, as Hope Yen wrote in the *Washington Post*, revelations that the Bush administration has ordered the National Security Agency to intercept suspected al Qaeda communications into or out of the United States without a warrant has led to claims of violations of privacy ("Probe Sought on NSA Surveillance," December 19, 2005, A5).

We can gain a useful perspective on the civil liberties question in the current war by comparing the Bush administration's terrorism policies to the wartime measures of President Franklin Roosevelt. FDR was faced with a devastating surprise attack on the United States at Pearl Harbor on December 7, 1941. He responded with domestic wartime policies that went well beyond those of today in their effect on civil liberties. It is difficult to judge how the World War II experience should bear on current controversies. One could argue that the Bush administration's approach is legal because it falls well within the markers set out by FDR's World War II policies, which went unchallenged by the courts. But the nature of the threat posed by the al Qaeda terrorist network is different enough that past legal models may not prove to be a helpful analogy. If it is difficult, however, for policy makers to develop optimal strategies for defeating terrorism, it will be doubly difficult for courts to review them with any competence. This may be the final, and most important, legal lesson to be learned from FDR—in World War II, the courts deferred to the political branches until the war ended, whereas the Supreme Court shows every indication today of joining the fray, despite the difficulties posed by the new type of war that began on 9/11.

MILITARY COMMISSIONS

One of the first Bush administration initiatives to receive strong criticism was the president's order in November 2001, creating military commissions.[2] On September 11, 2001, members of the al Qaeda terrorist organization crashed two civilian airliners into the World Trade Center in New York City, a third into the Pentagon in Arlington, Virginia, and headed a fourth toward Washington, D.C., crashing in Pennsylvania because the passengers resisted. Approximately 3,000 civilians were killed, billions of dollars in property were destroyed, and the nation's transportation and financial systems were temporarily closed. In part, the United States responded by sending forces to Afghanistan, where the ruling Taliban militia had harbored al Qaeda for several years.

Another aspect of the war on terrorism focused on the detention and trial of captured al Qaeda members. Military commissions are a form of military tribunal used to try captured members of the enemy for violations of the laws of war. American generals have used military commissions from the Revolutionary War through World War II (for a critical review of the history, see Fisher 2005). They are not created nor regulated by the Uniform Code of Military Justice, which governs courts-martial,[3] but instead have been established by presidents as commanders in chief and by military commanders in the field. Bush's military commissions apply to any individual for whom there is "reason to believe" is or was "a member of al Qaeda" and has engaged in or planned to commit terrorist attacks against the United States.[4] Al Qaeda had carried out attacks on the United States and thereby "created a state of armed conflict."[5]

Critics lambasted the idea. According to an article by Thomas Friedman in the *New York Times*, "in the place of fair trials and due process," President Bush "has substituted a crude and unaccountable system that any dictator would admire" ("A Travesty of Justice," November 16, 2001, A24–25). Some members of Congress reacted harshly; according to a *Washington Post* article, Senator Patrick Leahy claimed that the commissions "cut out Congress in determining the appropriate tribunal and procedures to try terrorists" (George Lardner Jr., "Democrats Blast Order on Tribunals," November 29, 2001, A22). More than 700 law professors and lawyers signed a letter claiming that the commissions "undermined the separation of powers."[6] Litigation has followed, with one federal district judge in Washington, D.C., enjoining the military commissions from operating, but the U.S. Court of Appeals for the D.C. Circuit overruling the decision.[7] As of this writing, the Supreme Court had granted certiorari to hear the case, but Congress then enacted a law declaring that habeas corpus jurisdiction does not extend to the base at Guantanamo Bay, Cuba, where the commissions would take place.[8]

Yet President Bush's military order was not unprecedented. In fact, Bush administration lawyers modeled it closely on an executive order by President Roosevelt in 1942 establishing a military commission for the trial of Nazi saboteurs.[9] World War II witnessed the widespread use of military commissions. While the most famous of them were the Nuremberg trials, military commissions heard charges of war crimes against former leaders of the German and Japanese regimes at the end of the war. But the first was the case of the German saboteurs. In June 1942, eight Nazi agents covertly landed in Long Island, New York, and Florida. Their plans included attacking factories, transportation facilities, and utility plants.

All had lived in the United States before the war, and two were American citizens (Danelski 1996, 61–63). One of them decided to turn informer. After initially dismissing his story, the FBI soon decided to arrest the plotters and their capture was revealed by the end of June (64–65). Members of Congress and the media demanded the death penalty, even though no statutory provision established capital punishment for non-American citizens.

Upon the arrest of the saboteurs, Attorney General Francis Biddle informed Roosevelt, who responded by seeking a trial outside the civilian judicial system. On June 30, he wrote to Biddle supporting the idea of using military courts because "the death penalty is called for by usage and by the extreme gravity of the war aim and the very existence of our American government" (Danelski 1996, 65). Roosevelt already thought they were guilty, and the punishment was not in doubt: "Surely they are just as guilty as it is possible to be . . . and it seems to me that the death penalty is almost obligatory" (65). Two days earlier, Biddle and Secretary of War Henry Stimson had worried that the plot was not far enough along to win a conviction with a significant sentence—perhaps two years at most. Stimson was surprised that Biddle was "quite ready to turn them over to a military court," and found, over a dinner with Felix Frankfurter, that Frankfurter also believed a military court preferable (66).

On June 30, Biddle wrote to Roosevelt summarizing the advantages of a military commission. It would have the advantage of speed, violations of the laws of war would be easier to prove, and the death penalty would be available (Danelski 1996, 66). Biddle also believed that using a military commission would prevent the defendants from seeking a writ of habeas corpus. "All the prisoners can thus be denied access to our courts" (66). Biddle did not commit to writing another important consideration: secrecy. According to Stimson, Biddle favored a military commission because the evidence would not become public, particularly the fact that the saboteurs had been captured because of an informant and the ease with which the Nazis had infiltrated American lines. Biddle recommended that FDR issue executive orders establishing the commission, defining the crimes, appointing its members, and excluding federal judicial review (66–67).

Following Biddle's advice, President Roosevelt issued two executive orders on July 2. The first created the commission and defined its jurisdiction. It stated:

> All persons who are subjects, citizens, or residents of any nation at war with the United States or who give obedience to or act under the direction of any such nation, and who during time of war enter or

attempt to enter the United States or any territory or possession thereof, through coastal or boundary defenses, and are charged with committing or attempting or preparing to commit sabotage, espionage, hostile or warlike acts, or violations of the law or war, shall be subject to the law of war and to the jurisdiction of military tribunals; and that such persons shall not be privileged to seek any remedy or maintain any proceeding directly or indirectly, or to have any such remedy or proceeding sought on their behalf, in the courts of the United States, or of its States, territories, and possessions, except under such regulations as the Attorney General, with the approval of the Secretary of War, may from time to time prescribe.[10]

The second order established the procedures for the military commissions.

The Commission shall have power to and shall, as occasion requires, make such rules for the conduct of the proceeding, consistent with the powers of military commissions under the Articles of War, as it shall deem necessary for a full and fair trial of the matters before it. Such evidence shall be admitted as would, in the opinion of the President of the Commission, have probative value to a reasonable man. The concurrence of at least two-thirds of the Members of the Commission present shall be necessary for a conviction or sentence. The record of the trial including any judgment or sentence, shall be transmitted directly to me for my action thereon.[11]

By the end of World War II, several military commission cases would reach the Supreme Court and would be affirmed.[12] FDR's 1942 order was the first, however, and represented far more of an intrusion on civil liberties than Bush's. It was also, at the time, of more questionable constitutionality. At the time that FDR issued his order, the governing case on the books was the Civil War precedent, Ex Parte *Milligan*, in which the Supreme Court had reversed the conviction by military commission of a Union civilian who sympathized with the Confederate cause and had planned acts of sabotage behind the lines. The Court held that the government had to use the federal courts because the defendant was not a member of the enemy armed forces and the civilian courts were "open to hear criminal accusations and redress grievances."[13] Nonetheless, FDR created commissions to avoid Milligan, to charge the defendants with violations of the laws of war, and to oust any form of judicial review. Military counsel for the Nazi saboteurs challenged FDR's commissions on this ground; they claimed that the military commission could not exercise jurisdiction because courts were open, the defendants were not in a war zone, that violations of the laws of war were not subject to prosecution under federal law, and that a military commission violated the Articles of War enacted by Congress (Danelski 1996, 68–69).

FDR's desire to secure a conviction and death penalty was not deterred by the news that the Supreme Court had agreed to hear the defendants' claim that the military commissions were illegal. As the Supreme Court Justices gathered in conference before oral argument, for example, Justice Roberts reported that Biddle had communicated his concern that FDR would order the execution of the saboteurs without regard to the Court. Chief Justice Stone, whose son was working on the defense team, said "that would be a dreadful thing" (Danelski 1996, 69). Although Stone did not recuse himself, Justice Murphy—who was at the conference in uniform as a member of the army reserve—did so, but Justice Byrnes, who had been serving as an informal advisor to the administration, did not (69). Biddle himself argued the case and urged the Court to overrule Milligan. After two days of oral argument, the justices decided to uphold trial of the prisoners by military commission. The great pressure on the Court is reflected in the Court's decision to deliver a per curiam opinion on July 31, the day after oral argument, but to announce that it would not issue an opinion until later (71).

The military commission began the trial the next day and three days later convicted and sentenced the defendants to death. Five days later, FDR approved the verdict but commuted the sentences of two (Danelski 1996, 72). An important point of contrast between FDR's commission and that of the Bush administration is the rules of the proceedings themselves. Roosevelt's two executive orders remained the only ones that provided guidance for the commissions with regard to the rules of procedures and the definition of the substantive crimes. There was no definition, for example, of the elements of any of the violations of the laws of war, nor were there any procedures given aside from the votes required for conviction and the admission of evidence. President Bush's initial order contained a similar, bare-boned set of rules that consciously paralleled FDR's order. Unlike World War II, however, the Defense Department exercised its delegated authority under the presidential order to issue two lengthy codes, one defining the elements of the crimes triable by commission, the other setting out the procedures. The Defense Department's regulations, for example, set the standard for conviction at proof beyond a reasonable doubt and provided defense counsel with access to exculpatory evidence in the hands of the prosecution. They also recognize the right against self-incrimination and the right of cross-examination, and require a unanimous vote of the commission members for the death penalty.[14] These procedures have been criticized because they do not reach the same standards of due process applicable in domestic criminal trials. Some features of the FDR and Bush commissions remain similar, such as the standard for the admissibility of evidence (evidence that is probative to a reasonable person) and review ultimately to the president rather than to federal courts. Nonetheless, it seems clear that the Bush commission rules are far closer to the standards governing courts-martial than the rules set out by FDR, and in fact recognize more procedural rights than those of FDR.

Similarly, the Bush Defense Department's articulation of the crimes subject to trial by military commission go well beyond FDR's short, undefined "sabotage, espionage, hostile or warlike acts, or violations of the law or war." Take, for example, the Bush Defense Department's effort to define spying:

(6) Spying
  (i) Elements.
    (A) The accused collected or attempted to collect certain information;
    (B) The accused intended to convey such information to the enemy;
    (C) The accused, in collecting or attempting to collect the information, was lurking or acting clandestinely, while acting under false pretenses; and
    (D) The conduct took place in the context of and was associated with armed conflict.
  (ii) Comments.
    (A) Members of a military organization not wearing a disguise and others who carry out their missions openly are not spies, if, though they may have resorted to concealment, they have not acted under false pretenses.
    (B) Related to the requirement that conduct be wrongful or without justification or excuse in this case is the fact that, consistent with the law of war, a lawful combatant who, after rejoining the armed force to which that combatant belongs, is subsequently captured, can not be punished for previous acts of espionage. His successful rejoining of his armed force constitutes a defense.[15]

Again, some may criticize the Bush military commission's efforts to be more precise in its definition of the crimes and elements punishable by military commission. One could also argue that the definition of these crimes will make little difference if the procedures do not give the defendants the chance to profit from them. Nevertheless, it seems beyond doubt that the Bush administration's effort has gone further than FDR's orders on the scale toward protection of civil liberties.

When the Court issued its opinion in the Nazi saboteurs case months later, it worked hard to distinguish Milligan and so uphold FDR's decision. Milligan, according to Chief Justice Stone's opinion, was subject to trial in civilian court because he had never associated himself with the enemy armed forces; the saboteurs, however, clearly had joined the Nazi armed forces (Danelski 1996, 74). The Bill of Rights was no obstacle, nor was the separation of powers. According to Stone, congressional creation of the courts-martial system and the absence of any criminal provisions to punish violations of the laws of war did not preclude FDR's use of military commissions. Stone read the Article of War recognizing the concurrent jurisdiction of military commissions as a congressional intent to incorporate by implication the laws of war as federal law punishable by commissions. The justices decided not to address the issue that had divided them behind the scenes—whether Congress could require the President to give the saboteurs a trial at all—because they did not read the Articles of War as precluding military commissions anyway (76–78).

DETENTION

Perhaps the sharpest contrast between the Bush and FDR war policies lies in the area of detention. In the wake of the September 11 attacks, the Bush administration set two policies in motion. The first was the FBI's massive investigation into the attacks themselves, known as PENTTBOM (see Office of the Inspector General 2003). Attorney General Ashcroft ordered the FBI to use "every available law enforcement tool" to arrest anyone linked to the terrorist attacks (1). A primary tool became the power to detain aliens who remained in the United States in violation of the immigration laws, usually because they lacked a valid visa or had entered the country illegally (1). According to figures assembled by the inspector general of the Department of Justice, the Department of Justice initially arrested and questioned 1,200 citizens and aliens nationwide, with many of them subsequently released. But 762 aliens, of whom twenty-four were already in the custody of the Immigration and Naturalization Service (INS) at the time of the 9/11 attacks, were detained and were investigated for ties to the 9/11 attacks or terrorism (2). They were eventually brought before immigration judges, with counsel but in closed hearings, and almost 500 aliens were eventually removed from the country (105). Detained aliens, their families, and advocacy groups filed lawsuits claiming that the detentions were illegal, that the closed hearings violated the INS statute, and that some detainees were abused in INS detention facilities.

A second policy authorized the detention without criminal charge of members of al Qaeda as enemy combatants, whether they were citizens or not (Ho and Yoo 2003). In the wake of the September 11 attacks, the United States invaded Afghanistan, toppled the ruling Taliban militia, and installed a friendly government. In the course of hostilities, it captured several hundred Taliban and al Qaeda fighters, whom the United States armed forces sent to a detention camp at the naval station in Guantanamo Bay, Cuba (Ho and Yoo 2003). In February 2002, President Bush announced that the detainees would be designated as enemy combatants, but that they would not be entitled to prisoner of war status under the Geneva Conventions because al Qaeda was not a signor nation and the Taliban had failed to obey the rules of warfare (Office of the Press Secretary 2002). The Bush administration claimed that the laws of war allowed the detention of enemy combatants without criminal charge or access to the courts until the end of hostilities. Only one American, John Walker Lindh, was initially captured in the operations in Afghanistan. He was transferred to the custody of the Justice Department and tried in federal district court in Alexandria.

The policy was applied to two American citizens, however. The first, Yaser Hamdi, who grew up in Saudi Arabia but was born in Louisiana, was captured in the fighting in Afghanistan. The second, José Padilla, was captured attempting to enter the United States at Chicago O'Hare airport as part of an al Qaeda plot, according to the Bush administration, to explode a radioactive device in a major American city. President Bush justified both detentions on his power as commander in chief and under Congress's authorization to use military force passed on September 18, 2001. After Hamdi's father sought a writ of habeas corpus, the Supreme Court in 2004 upheld his detention under Congress's September 18 authorization, even though it did not specifically mention detention, instead providing the president with the power to use "all necessary and appropriate force" against those connected to the September 11 terrorist attacks.[16] After the Court's decision, the Bush administration released Hamdi to the custody of the Saudi Arabian government. It moved Padilla, who argued that he was not covered by the authorization because he was captured outside any recognized battlefield, to the civilian criminal justice system. A federal jury in

Miami convicted Padilla of the crime of providing material support to terrorists in August 2007 ("Jury Convicts Jose Padilla of Terror Charges," *Washington Post*, August 17, 2007, A01). As of this date, no American citizens remain detained as enemy combatants.

In the wake of the December 7, 1941, attacks, President Roosevelt engaged in a far more sweeping detention. After the attacks and the German and Italian declarations of war, President Roosevelt authorized the Departments of War and Justice to intern German, Japanese, and Italian citizens in the United States. In February 1942, roughly 3,000 Japanese aliens had been detained (Irons 1983, 19). Detention of the citizens of an enemy nation had long been a conventional feature of the rules of war, and was authorized by the Alien Enemy Act.[17] That same month, however, FDR went even further and authorized the detention of American citizens on more questionable grounds. On February 19, 1942, FDR signed Executive Order 9066 allowing the secretary of war to designate parts of the country as military zones "from which any or all persons may be excluded."[18] By the end of 1942, the government had moved 110,000 Japanese American citizens to ten internment camps because they might provide aid to the Japanese Empire (73). Recent historical work suggests that Roosevelt took a far more active role in the detention decision than has been commonly understood (see Robinson 2003).

The story of the internments is well known (see, for example, Irons 1983; Robinson 2003; Yamamoto 2001). General John DeWitt, commander of the Fourth Army on the West Coast, initially opposed the mass evacuations, as did officials in the Justice Department and several prominent Roosevelt advisors. But by late January, 1942, thinking had changed. A popular movement on the West Coast demanded removal of the Japanese Americans to the nation's interior, a movement that gathered momentum as Japan won a string of military victories in the Pacific (Robinson 2003, 89–90). It appears that the precipitating factor was the release of the Roberts commission report into the Pearl Harbor attacks (95). Although the commission only briefly mentioned that Japanese in the Hawaiian islands, along with Japanese consular officials, had sent intelligence on military installations before the attacks, it "attracted national attention and transformed public opinion on Japanese Americans" (95). Newspapers, California political leaders, and military officials began demanding that the Roosevelt administration intern Japanese Americans out of a fear of further Japanese sabotage and espionage (95–97). Some in the War Department, however, discounted the effect espionage on the West Coast would have on the course of the war, and FBI Director J. Edgar Hoover dismissed the Army's claims of espionage and sabotage by Japanese Americans (100–1).

FDR's cabinet members raised the issue twice with the president before the final executive order. First, Biddle met FDR for lunch in early February, at which the attorney general conveyed his doubts about the need for evacuations. Though he did not make a decision at that time, he concluded the lunch by saying he was "fully aware of the dreadful risk of Fifth Column retaliation in case of a raid" (Robinson 2003, 104). A few days later, Secretary of War Stimson called President Roosevelt after learning that General DeWitt would recommend that military necessity required evacuation of the Japanese Americans. News that Singapore had fallen to the Japanese had arrived the day before Stimson's call, making it unlikely that FDR would be open to second-guessing claims of military necessity. Nonetheless, Stimson—who had his own doubts about the need for evacuations and their legality—proposed three options: massive evacuation, evacuation from major cities, or evacuation from areas surrounding military facilities (104–5). Roosevelt responded that Stimson should do what he thought best, and that FDR would sign an executive order giving the War Department the authority to carry out the evacuations. DeWitt soon found the evacuations militarily necessary, and Stimson and Biddle agreed on a draft of the executive order, which was based on Roosevelt's constitutional authorities as chief executive and as commander-in-chief (107–8). FDR signed Executive Order 9066 on February 19, 1942.[19] It does not appear that FDR expressed any concern for the civil liberties of the Japanese Americans when he made his decision but instead based his decision on the military's claim of wartime necessity.

Others have observed that Roosevelt was not especially vigilant in protecting civil liberties (Irons 1983, 57). In this case, according to one biographer, the decision was easy. FDR believed that the military "had primary direct responsibility for the achievement of war victory, the achievement of war victory had top priority, and 'victory' had for him a single simple meaning" of defeating Germany and Japan. Victory, for Roosevelt, "was prerequisite to all else" (Davis 2000, 424). To make matters easier, there was no great outcry from liberal leaders, there was no cabinet meeting or forum for debate within the administration, and the attorney general came to agree with the War Department that the measure was legal. Recent historical work argues that the internment decision did not arise solely because of misinformation about the Japanese Americans or the pressure of events in the early months of the war, but also because FDR's racial views about Japanese Americans led him to believe the worst about their potential for disloyalty to the government (Robinson 2003, 118).

Both Congress and the Court approved FDR's order. In March 1942, Congress enacted a law establishing criminal penalties for those who refused to obey the evacuation orders.[20] Support for the law was so broad that it was approved in both the House and Senate by voice vote with only one speech made in opposition, by Republican Senator Robert Taft of Ohio (Irons 1983, 68). The Supreme Court would not directly address the constitutionality of the detentions until the war's end. In *Korematsu v. United States*, the Supreme Court upheld the detention of the Japanese Americans. According to the Court, the mass evacuation triggered strict scrutiny under the Equal Protection Clause because it discriminated on its face on the basis of race.[21] Nonetheless, the order survived because the Court agreed with the executive branch that such security measures in wartime could present a compelling government interest, and the Court deferred to military judgment concerning whether the measures were needed. According to Justice Black's 6-3 majority opinion, "we are unable to conclude that it was beyond the war power of Congress and the Executive to exclude those of Japanese ancestry from the West Coast war area at the time they did."[22] Recognizing the deprivation of individual liberty involved, the majority observed that "the military authorities, charged with the primary responsibility of defending our shores, concluded that curfew provided inadequate protection and ordered exclusion."[23] As with an earlier case upholding a nighttime curfew on Japanese Americans in the western military region, the Court concluded, "we cannot reject as unfounded the judgment of the military authorities and of Congress that there were disloyal members of that population, whose number and strength could not be precisely and quickly ascertained."[24]

Historical work since has revealed that some government officials in fact doubted whether the evacuation order responded to any real security threat. Nonetheless, the Justice Department chose in its case before the Supreme Court to assert that military authorities believed the evacuations necessary because of an alleged threat against the West Coast (see brief for the United States, Korematsu (No. 22), United States, Kurland, and Casper 1975, 197; Robinson 2003, 210). A companion case, Ex Parte *Endo*, however, found that the government could not detain a Japanese American citizen whom the government had conceded was "loyal and law abiding."[25]

To this day, the debate over the necessity of the measures continues. But regardless of which side one falls on that debate, it seems clear that the internment of the Japanese Americans in Korematsu represents a far more serious infringement of civil liberties than the current enemy combatant detention policy pursued by the Bush administration. The first and most obvious difference is one of magnitude. FDR interned without trial about 110,000 Japanese Americans on suspicion of disloyalty to the United States in wartime. The Bush administration detained two citizens—José Padilla and Yaser Hamdi—without criminal charge in connection with the war on terrorism, and tried a third, John Walker Lindh, in federal district court. The second difference is one of justification. FDR ordered the detention of the Japanese Americans not because any had been found to be enemy combatants, but because of their assumed loyalty, based on their ethnic ancestry, to a nation at war with the United States. FDR could have pursued a narrower policy that detained individuals based on their ties to a nation with which the United States was at war. In wartime, the citizens of Japan, Germany, and Italy could be interned as a matter of course, and anyone fighting or working for the enemy, regardless of citizenship, could be detained. FDR's internment policy did neither—instead, it tried to sweep in people presumed disloyal based solely on their ethnicity. The Bush administration detained Padilla and Hamdi not on the grounds that they might be disloyal, but because they are in fact enemy combatants who had allied themselves with al Qaeda. It placed Padilla and Hamdi not in the same category as the Japanese Americans, but as the Nazi saboteurs in Ex Parte *Quirin*. Detention was not based on potential disloyalty, but on actions that demonstrated allegiance to a foreign enemy. As a result, race has not served as a proxy for loyalty in the wartime detentions in the war on terrorism, as it did in World War II.

ELECTRONIC SURVEILLANCE

As of this writing, many civil libertarians see the greatest threat from the war on terrorism in the area of electronic surveillance. In December 2005, the *New York Times* reported that the Bush administration had ordered the National Security Agency to monitor international communications either ending or originating within the United States that involve a suspected member of al Qaeda. Some media reports allege that the NSA has also intercepted calls linked to terrorism that took place wholly within the United States. For many years, the NSA had monitored the communications of non-American citizens outside the United States, which are not understood to be protected by the Fourth Amendment.[26] Nor is the monitoring of potential foreign threats prohibited by statute; if anything, it is the primary reason for the NSA's existence.

Interception of calls that begin or end inside the United States, however, even if they involve foreign threats to the national security, are subject to much heavier regulation. Under the Foreign Intelligence Surveillance Act, the government must seek a warrant from the Foreign Intelligence Surveillance Court in order to monitor the communications of potential threats to the national security.[27] To receive such a warrant, the government must show that there is "probable cause" to believe that the target is the agent of a foreign power. Although this probable cause requirement is not the same as that in the Fourth Amendment, FISA requires that when the target is an American citizen that the showing be close, if not identical, to the Fourth Amendment standard.[28] FISA also contains a provision that prohibits any electronic surveillance that is not undertaken under the normal criminal justice methods on its own terms, or unless authorized by another statute.[29]

Civil libertarians have raised two objections to the policy. First, they claim that the NSA monitoring program violates FISA, which purports to be the only legal method for surveillance of national security threats. Second, some argue that warrantless surveillance, even in wartime, might violate the Fourth Amendment, though this argument has been muted. In response, the Bush administration argues that the president has the constitutional authority to gather signals intelligence involving the activities of an enemy at wartime.[30] It supplements this argument with the claim that Congress expressed its support when it authorized the president to use all necessary and appropriate force against those responsible for the September 11 attacks, or those that aid or harbor them.[31]

It is not the purpose of this chapter to re-hash the legal arguments made by both sides in the debate over the NSA wiretapping program. Rather, the NSA program provides another useful point of contrast between the war on terrorism and the policies of President Roosevelt during World War II. President Roosevelt has been described by one historian as the president most interested and involved with covert intelligence after President George Washington, who personally managed spies and directed the interception of British communications (Andrew 1995, 6–9, 76). During World War I, Roosevelt had served as assistant secretary of the Navy, with responsibility for naval intelligence. During World War II, his interest in covert operations led to the establishment of the well-known Office of Strategic Services under Colonel William Donovan.

Less well known are Roosevelt's actions with regard to the interception of electronic communications. According to one historical study, FDR's administration initially had not engaged in any wiretapping for national security purposes. Believing that such electronic surveillance violated the Federal Communications Act of 1934,[32] Attorney General Robert Jackson had issued an order prohibiting the Federal Bureau of Investigation from intercepting electronic communications without a warrant. As Europe plunged into war, however, J. Edgar Hoover grew increasingly concerned about the possibility of individuals inside the United States cooperating with Germany, Italy, or Japan to undermine American national security. But, knowing of Jackson's order, Hoover instead went to Treasury Secretary Henry Morgenthau and asked him to speak to Roosevelt to authorize the interception of the communications of potential foreign agents who might sympathize with Germany.

Roosevelt had long been concerned with the potential threat of a so-called fifth column inside the United States. Apparently the spectacular 1916 sabotage of an American munitions plant that was supplying the allies in World War I remained vivid in his memory (Andrew 1995, 94). As early as 1936, Roosevelt authorized the general investigation by the FBI of "subversive activities in this country, including communism and fascism" (88). When World War II broke out in Europe, Roosevelt further authorized the FBI to "take charge of investigative work in matters relating to espionage, sabotage, and violations of neutrality regulations," and ordered all state and local law enforcement officers to "promptly turn over" to the FBI any information "relating to espionage, counterespionage, sabotage, subversive activities and violations of the neutrality laws" (91). FDR did not define what subversive activities meant.

The quick collapse of France in May of 1940 seemed inexplicable at the time as a military matter, so the idea grew that Germany's victory must have resulted from collaborators and spies behind the lines. As war with the Axis powers drew near, Roosevelt gave an increasing place in his speeches to his concern that the United States, too, might suffer from Axis sympathizers or even covert agents intent on undermining America's efforts to prepare for war.

Even before Hoover came to make his request, through Morgenthau, FDR had already supported amateurish efforts to engage in electronic surveillance. His friend, publisher and real estate developer Vincent Astor, had set up a private group he had called the Room, which included leading figures in New York City (Andrew 1995, 83). As a director of the Western Union Telegraph Company, Astor ordered the covert interception of telegrams, and he and his friends also arranged for the monitoring of radio transmissions in New York City (92). Using its connections, the group also gathered private banking records of companies connected to foreign nations to determine whether they were supporting espionage within the United States. There is no direct record of a presidential order authorizing this surveillance, but historical evidence suggests that the group was acting in response to a request by Roosevelt (92).

Given his suspicions, Roosevelt quickly agreed with Morgenthau and Hoover that wiretapping of suspected agents or collaborators of the Axis powers was necessary to protect national security. The next day, he issued a memorandum to Attorney General Jackson to allow the FBI to wiretap individuals who posed a potential threat to the national security.

THE WHITE HOUSE WASHINGTON
CONFIDENTIAL
May 21, 1940
MEMORANDUM FOR
THE ATTORNEY GENERAL

I have agreed with the broad purpose of the Supreme Court decision relating to wire-tapping in investigations. The Court is undoubtedly sound both in regard to the use of evidence secured over tapped wires in the prosecution of citizens in criminal cases; and is also right in its opinion that under ordinary and normal circumstances wire-tapping by Government agents should not be carried on for the excellent reason that it is almost bound to lead to abuse of civil rights.

However, I am convinced that the Supreme Court never intended any dictum in the particular case which it decided to apply to grave matters involving the defense of the nation.

It is, of course, well known that certain other nations have been engaged in the organization of propaganda of so-called "fifth columns" in other countries and in preparation for sabotage, as well as in actual sabotage.

It is too late to do anything about it after sabotage, assassinations and "fifth column" activities are completed.

You are, therefore, authorized and directed in such cases as you may approve, after investigation of the need in each case, to authorize the necessary investigation agents that they are at liberty to secure information by listening devices direct to the conversation or other communications of persons suspected of subversive activities against the Government of the United States, including suspected spies. You are requested furthermore to limit these investigations so conducted to a minimum and to limit them insofar as possible to aliens.

(s) F.D.R.[33]

Once the Pearl Harbor attacks occurred, FDR authorized the interception of all international communications (Eric Lichtblau, "Gonzales Invokes Actions of Other Presidents in Defense of U.S. Spying," *New York Times*, January 25, 2006, A19). Even though some members of the Supreme Court had criticized wiretapping, the Court had held in *Olmstead v. United States* that electronic communications were not protected by the Fourth Amendment from interception without a warrant.[34] It would not be until 1967, in *Katz v. United States*, when the Supreme Court would hold that electronic communications were entitled to Fourth Amendment privacy protections.[35] It is important to observe, however, that under the Federal Communications Act of 1934, Congress appears to have prohibited the interception of electronic communications, much as the Foreign Intelligence Surveillance Act allegedly does today.

Further points of contrast between FDR's orders and today's controversy over the NSA's interception of communications exist over their potential scope and magnitude. FDR's use of electronic surveillance was formally broader than that of today. According to the Bush administration, the NSA has intercepted only calls where one end of the communication is inside the United States and the other is outside, and where one of the individuals is suspected of being a member of al Qaeda. FDR's pre-war interception order went well beyond this in three respects. First, it applied to anyone "suspected of subversive activities" against the United States government, which included individuals who might be sympathetic to, or even working for, Germany and Japan.[36] But the United States at that time was not yet at war with either Germany or Japan. Second, whereas FDR wanted the FBI to limit the interceptions to the calls of aliens, his order did not exclude citizens. Third, and most important, it was not limited to international calls or telegrams, but included communications that took place wholly within the United States.[37]

Bush's program, however, could prove broader in scope than FDR's order. There is no doubt that electronic communications of all kinds, both domestic and international, have increased by several orders of magnitude since 1940. Email, of course, did not exist in the 1940s, and today accounts for billions of messages every day. International telephone traffic has also grown enormously, and the cost of long distance telephone calls has fallen dramatically in that time. In the 1940s, the FBI might not have had to intercept that many communications to implement FDR's order, because there simply was a smaller population and they were making less telephone calls per person. Today, a narrower order that targets a smaller class of individuals still might involve the interception of a larger number of communications because of the higher amount of phone calls and emails per person.

WHY THE DIFFERENCE?

Two questions arise when comparing the FDR and Bush war policies with respect to civil liberties. First, why the difference in the scope of the policies? Even if they were similar in kind, FDR's policies swept more broadly than those of the Bush administration. Military commissions were used against Nazi saboteurs first, but then they dispensed justice throughout the postwar German occupations zone and American-occupied Japan. Bush has sought to use military commissions to try captured members of al Qaeda, though because of bureaucratic delay and judicial review none has begun. Bush's designation of three American citizens as enemy combatants, even the investigation of illegal aliens from Middle Eastern countries, pales in comparison to FDR's decision to intern 110,000 Japanese Americans. Bush ordered the NSA to intercept international communications involving suspected members of al Qaeda. FDR authorized the FBI to eavesdrop on communications that could be wholly domestic or involve only suspected subversives.

Some have suggested that differences in legal culture might explain these differences. Jack Goldsmith and Cass Sunstein have argued that the difference lies in changes in American legal culture (Goldsmith and Sunstein 2002, 261). They claim that the great expansion in individual rights during the postwar period has both made the government more sensitive to civil liberties and caused the legal culture to react more skeptically to claims of expanded government power in wartime. Geoffrey Stone (2004) and Oren Gross (2003) believe that national security crises have caused the government to panic, but that with the benefit of hindsight we later realize that we have overreacted. In each succeeding crisis, we have moderated our response because hindsight has taught us that the government's security measures went too far the last time. It is doubtful whether this is true as an empirical matter. Perhaps the greatest deprivation of civil liberties in wartime occurred during World War II with the internment of the Japanese Americans; it did not represent an amelioration of even harsher wartime policies that had prevailed in World War I. While there is no doubt that the Alien and Sedition Acts during the Quasi-War with France in 1798 infringed civil liberties, it does not seem to rise to the level of military government during the Civil War. During other conflicts, such as the Mexican American or Spanish American wars, it appears that no significant deprivation of civil liberties occurred at all. The protection of civil liberties in wartime does not appear to have consistently risen throughout history, but rather appears to have fluctuated from war to war.

I believe that the better explanation lies in the nature of the conflicts at hand, rather than in some inexorable historical evolution in legal or political culture. During wartime, the government may adopt policies that restrict civil liberties because it believes that those policies will better allow the nation to defeat its external foe. It seems that the greater the threat posed to the national security, as it appears to decision makers beforehand, the more willing the government may be to allow deprivations of civil liberties necessary to mount an effective response. That threat will depend on the expected harm to the United States the enemy poses, which we can think of as the magnitude of the harm that might come about factored by the probability (as estimated by decision makers based on the evidence they have before the decision) that it will occur. We should expect greater civil liberties deprivations to be proposed and tolerated in situations where the expected harm to the national security is greater. It should come as no surprise, then, that the government decided to engage in the deepest restrictions on civil liberties in the two wars where its safety was under greatest attack: the Civil War, which threatened the dissolution of the Union and which incurred the greatest casualties in American history (as a function of the percentage of the population), and World War II, in which the American Pacific fleet was crippled in a surprise attack and the United States faced a Japan and Germany that had conquered large swaths of territory with only a weakened Britain and Soviet Union on its side. We see comparatively less serious infringements on civil liberties in World War I or the Quasi-War, and almost none in the Spanish American, Mexican American, and numerous smaller conflicts.

Other chapters in this book, and other scholars, have argued that wartime governments have restricted civil liberties by mistake. Governments and presidents can suffer from unfounded fears or panic and enact laws that lean too far in favor of security over liberty. The Alien and Sedition Acts during the Quasi-War with France, which was fought by naval vessels in the Atlantic, and the restrictions on speech in World War I, in which no serious threat to the American homeland emerged from the Central Powers, are examples of this dynamic at work. But it is also the case that governments can err in the other direction—they can underestimate national security threats and fail to take cost-effective measures to ward them off. Japan's Pearl Harbor attack and the 9/11 attacks serve as examples of inadequate attention to security. Rather than panic or surprise, we can think of this as an illustration of estimating the probabilities of future harm to the nation.

This may help explain not just the severity of the Roosevelt response to the gathering storm of war and its impact, but also the relative restraint—from a historical perspective—of the Bush administration. Unlike World War I but akin to the Civil War and World War II, the September 11 attacks involved a direct attack on the United States. The attacks began and were carried out by foreign agents on American soil, who prepared covertly and launched by surprise. Expanded powers for domestic investigation and prevention of attacks seem only inevitable due to the domestic dimension of the September 11 attacks. At the same time, the Bush administration has not approached the magnitude of the policies that the Lincoln and Roosevelt administrations developed. In part, I believe, this is attributable to the difference in the enemy currently faced by the United States. That difference does not arise from the fact that al Qaeda proved it was capable of hitting the United States directly; a direct attack occurred on the United States in the War of 1812, the Civil War, and World War II, and the Soviet Union easily could have launched an attack on the United States from at least the mid-1960s on.

Rather, the difference lies in the nature of the opponent. For the first time, the United States faces a non-nation state, a network of similarly minded Islamic fundamentalists. The members of that network operate by disguising themselves as civilians to launch surprise attacks on civilian targets, and so to spread terror among the population. Success requires gaining information on al Qaeda to prevent future attacks and maintaining the cooperation of communities at home and abroad that could have information on the activity and whereabouts of al Qaeda operatives. This may mean, at times, that counterterrorism policy may be more effective by reducing deprivations of civil liberties to maintain that support and cooperation. Also, because al Qaeda is a small network of operatives, the wholesale, blunt policies of FDR's time would probably prove wasteful as well as counterproductive. To succeed, the United States needs to apply more focused policies to gather intelligence from a relatively small set of individuals and to aim its use of force at a small range of targets.

A second question is why the courts have reacted differently in this war. In previous conflicts, such as World War II, the Supreme Court sided with the president's claims of war power. It upheld military commissions in Quirin and the Japanese exclusion policy in Hirabayashi and Korematsu. Today, however, popular perceptions are that the courts have dealt the Bush administration several setbacks, such as ordering the executive to develop hearing procedures for enemy combatants and enjoining the operation of military commissions. In the past, the courts would defer to the executive during wartime and wait until the war was safely won before exercising a more direct review. I have argued elsewhere that judicial deference in wartime makes sense because courts have little competence in measuring the nature of national security threats, the expected value of potential harms, and balancing them against any costs to civil liberties (Yoo 2003, 2006). In this war, by contrast, at least some lower courts have displayed very little deference to the decisions of the political branches in the war on terrorism. What is important to note, however, is that resistance to deference has come primarily from some lower courts (and by no means all or even most of them), and has yet to characterize the Supreme Court's approach to the war on terrorism. Although the Court's most important terrorism decision thus far, *Hamdi v. Rumsfeld*, agreed that the government should provide some type of hearing for detained enemy combatants, it also displayed a great deal of deference to the executive branch in the formulation of the procedures.[38]

We can conclude by speculating on why the courts today may display less deference to the executive branch in wartime than they did in FDR's day. It is possible that other wartime presidents had less difficulty with the courts because they had the chance to appoint more of their members. By the time of America's entry into World War II, for example, the Supreme Court was filled with members appointed by President Roosevelt. Perhaps the most important factor, again, is the unprecedented and unconventional nature of the enemy. Because al Qaeda is a network rather than a nation-state, it seems more like a criminal organization. Indeed, until the September 11 attacks, our political system consistently treated terrorism as a problem to be handled through the criminal justice system. Because of its structure as a network, al Qaeda seems susceptible to the tools of law enforcement, and this may still raise doubts in the minds of some judges and actors in the political system whether the September 11 attacks really initiated a war—despite presidential and congressional findings.[39] Legal uncertainty about when a conflict against a non-state terrorist organization might end—there is unlikely to be a peace treaty formalizing a termination of hostilities—may also lead some to believe that terrorism is more analogous to crime and hence justifies normal levels of judicial oversight of the executive. The length of the war against al Qaeda—it has already gone longer than World Wars I and II—lead some to doubt that war is the best legal framework for terrorism, though conflicts with terrorists in other countries have come to an end, and there have been wars in international and United States history that gone on longer (such as the Thirty Years' War or Vietnam). Still, deference may become more difficult for courts when they confront unprecedented circumstances outside the normal ken of the judiciary. But new circumstances may also be the time when deference is particularly called for. Confusion about the nature of the terrorist threat may also have combined with the Court's louder assertions of its own supremacy and growing self-confidence in its ability to resolve almost any national problem, a trend much criticized by scholars in areas outside of terrorism.

That may be one last important difference that may help explain the difference Roosevelt and Bush's policies in the war on terrorism. Even as FDR pursued aggressive policies in the areas of military commissions, detention, and surveillance, he did not seem particularly concerned about the role of the courts. Indeed, he appears to have been ready to ignore a judicial decision that would have attempted to curtail his war policies (see Danelski 1966, 69, citing Biddle's apparent concern that FDR would order the execution of the saboteurs without regard to the Court). Judicial supremacy not only was not assured at this time, but FDR himself had engineered an attack on the Court designed to defeat its ability to exercise judicial review over domestic economic policy. Today, the position of the Court in the political system is far stronger, and it is difficult to imagine a decision by the Bush administration to refuse to obey a decision of the Supreme Court in the war on terrorism. Rather than making policy first and worrying about the courts later, the Bush administration's war on terrorism has kept the courts at the center of the action, sometimes intentionally, sometimes not. To be sure, the administration has argued that the courts should follow the political question doctrine and raised justiciability arguments in litigation designed to minimize judicial review. Nevertheless, it does not appear that the Bush administration has ever considered, as FDR and Lincoln had, drastic responses to the courts—such as only enforcing a court's judgment between the parties or refusing to obey a judicial decision. That the administration has gone to Congress on two occasions to overturn the Court's decisions in the enemy combatant cases is in itself is a sign of its respect for the Court's authority if not its agreement with its legal reasoning. The Bush administration's acceptance of judicial supremacy, all too common among political actors these days, may have led it to moderate its policies in anticipation of court challenges. Just as it is difficult to imagine the political system today moving swiftly against the current regime of judicial supremacy, so too it is difficult to imagine FDR developing war policy with great concern for the opinion of the courts.

NOTES

1. USA PATRIOT Act of 2001, Pub. L. No. 107-56, 115 Stat. 272.
2. Military Order of November 13, 2001, Detention, Treatment, and Trial of Certain Non-Citizens in the War Against Terrorism, 66 Fed. Reg. 57,833 (November 16, 2001).
3. See 10 U.S.C. § 821 (2004) ("The provisions of this chapter conferring jurisdiction upon courts-martial do not deprive military commissions, provost courts, or other military tribunals of concurrent jurisdiction with respect to offenders or offenses that by statute or by the law of war may be tried by military commissions, provost courts, or other military tribunals.").
4. Military Order of November 13, 2001, Detention, Treatment, and Trial of Certain Non-Citizens in the War Against Terrorism § 2(a)(1)(i–ii), 66 Fed. Reg. 57,833, 57,833 (November 16, 2001). The order also applies to those who knowingly harbor al Qaeda members who plan to commit terrorist attacks against the United States. 10 U.S.C. § 821 (2004) at § 2(a)(1)(iii).
5. 10 U.S.C. § 821 (2004) at § 1(a).
6. See http://www.law.yale.edu/news/3305.htm.
7. See *Hamdan v. Rumsfeld*, 415 F.3d 33 (D.C. Cir. 2005).
8. Detainee Treatment Act of 2005, Pub. L. No. 109-148, 119 Stat. 2739.
9. Proclamation 2561, "Denying Certain Enemies Access to the Courts of the United States" (July 2, 1942), 7 Fed. Reg. 5101 (1942) (cited in Fisher 2005, 98).
10. 7 Fed. Reg. 5101 (1942); see also Fisher 2005, 98–99.
11. 7 Fed. Reg. 5103 (1942); see Fisher 2005, 99–100.
12. See, for example, In re *Yamashita*, 327 U.S. 1 (1946); *Johnson v. Eisentrager*, 339 U.S. 763 (1950); *Madsen v. Kinsella*, 343 U.S. 341 (1952).
13. 71 U.S. 2, 121–22 (1866).
14. See U.S. Department of Defense, Military Commission Order No. 1, Procedures for Trials by Military Commissions of Certain Non-United States Citizens in the War Against Terrorism para. 5 ("Procedures Accorded the Accused") and para. 6 ("Conduct of the Trial") (March 21, 2002), accessed at http://www.defenselink.mil/news/Mar2002/d20020321ord.pdf; Crimes and Elements for Trials by Military Commissions, 32 C.F.R. 11.3.
15. 68 C.F.R. 11.3.
16. See Authorization for Use of Military Force, Pub. L. No. 107-40, 115 Stat. 224 (September 18, 2001).
17. An Act Respecting Alien Enemies (July 6, 1798), 1 Stat. 577, codified at 50 U.S.C. § 21.
18. 7 Fed. Reg. 1407.
19. Executive Order 9066, 7 Fed. Reg. 1407 (February 19, 1942).
20. Act of March 21, 1942, ch. 191, Pub. L. No. 77-503, 56 Stat. 173.
21. *Korematsu v. United States*, 323 U.S. 214 (1944).
22. Ibid.

23. Ibid.
24. *Hirabayashi v. United States*, 320 U.S. 81 (1943).
25. Ex parte *Endo*, 323 U.S. 283 (1944).
26. See, for example, *United States v. Verdugo-Urquidez*, 494 U.S. 259 (1990).
27. 50 U.S.C. 1801–1862.
28. See In re *Sealed Case*, 310 F.3d 717 (United States Foreign Intelligence Surveillance Court of Review, 2002).
29. 50 U.S.C. 1809(a).
30. U.S. Department of Justice, Legal Authorities Supporting the Activities of the National Security Agency Described by the President (January 19, 2006). On file with author.
31. Authorization for Use of Military Force, Pub. L. No. 107-40, 115 Stat. 224 (September 18, 2001).
32. See, for example, 47 U.S.C. § 605, originally Section 705 of the Federal Communications Act of 1934.
33. Reprinted in Appendix A, *United States v. United States District Court*, 444 F.2d 651, 669–70 (6th Cir. 1971) [Roosevelt 1940 Memorandum].
34. *Olmstead v. United States*, 277 U.S. 438 (1928). FDR is probably referring in his order to Justice Brandeis' dissent in *Olmstead*, at 471, when he mentions Supreme Court criticism of wiretapping.
35. 389 U.S. 347 (1967).
36. See Roosevelt 1940 Memorandum.
37. See Roosevelt 1940 Memorandum.
38. See *Hamdi v. Rumsfeld*, 542 U.S. 507, 527–32 (2004).
39. See Military Order of November 13, 2001, Detention, Treatment, and Trial of Certain Non-Citizens in the War Against Terrorism, 66 Fed. Reg. 57,833 (November 16, 2001); Authorization for Use of Military Force, Pub. L. No. 107-40, 115 Stat. 224 (September 18, 2001).

REFERENCES

Andrew, Christopher. 1995. *For the President's Eyes Only*. New York: Harper Perennial.

Danelski, David. 1996. "The Saboteurs' Case." *Journal of Supreme Court History* 61(1): 61–78.

Davis, Kenneth. 2000. *FDR: The War President, 1940–1943*. New York: Random House.

Fisher, Louis. 2005. *Military Tribunals & Presidential Power: American Revolution to the War on Terrorism*. Lawrence, Kan.: University Press of Kansas.

Goldsmith, Jack, and Cass R. Sunstein. 2002. "Military Tribunals and Legal Culture: What a Difference Sixty Years Makes." *Constitutional Commentary* 19(1): 261–89.

Gross, Oren. 2003. "Chaos and Rules: Should Responses to Violent Crises Always Be Constitutional?" *The Yale Law Journal* 112(8): 1011–134.

Ho, James, and John C. Yoo. 2003. "'The Status of Terrorists." *Virginia Journal of International Law* 44(1): 207–28.

Irons, Peter H. 1983. *Justice at War.* New York: Oxford University Press.

Office of the Inspector General. 2003. *The September 11 Detainees: A Review of the Treatment of Aliens Held on Immigration Charges in Connection with the Investigation of the September 11 Attacks.* Washington: U.S. Department of Justice. Accessed at http://www.usdoj.gov/oig/special/0306/full.pdf.

Office of the Press Secretary. 2002. "Statement by the Press Secretary on the Geneva Convention." Press Release, February 7, 2002. Washington: The White House. Accessed at http://www.state.gov/s/l/38727.htm.

Robinson, Greg. 2003. *By Order of the President: FDR and the Internment of the Japanese Americans,* 2nd ed. Cambridge, Mass.: Harvard University Press.

Stone, Geoffrey R. 2004. *Perilous Times: Free Speech in Wartime.* New York: W. W. Norton.

United States, Philip B. Kurland, and Gerhard Casper. 1975. *Landmark Briefs and Arguments of the Supreme Court of the United States: Constitutional Law,* vol. 42. Washington: University Publications of America.

Yamamoto, Eric K. 2001. R*ace, Rights, and Reparation: Law and the Japanese American Internment.* Aspen Elective Series. Gaithersburg, Md.: Aspen Law and Business.

Yoo, John. 2003. "Judicial Review and the War on Terrorism." *George Washington University Law Review* 72(1–2): 427–51.

———. 2006. "Courts at War." *Cornell Law Review* 91(2): 573–602.

CHAPTER 4

"MERE SHADOWS": THE EARLY COLD WAR

ELLEN SCHRECKER

History shows in one example after another how excessive have been the fears of earlier generations, who shuddered at menaces that, with the benefit of hindsight, we now know were mere shadows. This, in itself, should induce the modern generation to view with prudent skepticism the recurrent alarms about the fatal potentialities of dissent.

William O. Douglas, 1961[1]

In summary, this is my thinking on this matter. Our internal security laws must be adequate. To the extent that they are not adequate now, they should be strengthened. Excessive security, however, can be as dangerous as inadequate security. Excessive security brings normal administrative operations to a standstill, prevents the interchange of ideas necessary to scientific progress, and—most important of all— encroaches on the individual rights and freedoms which distinguish a democracy from a totalitarian country.

Harry Truman, 1950[2]

Kendrick Cole was not a security risk. A New York-based inspector with the Food and Drug Administration, he had been dropped from his position at the end of 1953 under the Eisenhower administration's security program because of his refusal to answer questions about his hiking companions in a supposedly subversive group called the Nature Friends of America. In 1956, however, the Supreme Court decided that, whatever damage Cole's fellow hikers might inflict on the nation's security, there was no way that Cole, whose main duties involved tracking down harmful chemicals, insects, and mouse droppings, could endanger the United States. "It is difficult," John Marshall Harlan explained in the majority opinion, "to justify summary suspensions and unreviewable dismissals on loyalty grounds of employees who are not in 'sensitive' positions and who are thus not situated where they could bring about any discernible adverse effects on the Nation's security."[3] Justice Tom Clark, however, disagreed. In his dissenting opinion, the former attorney general explained that

> the Court's order has stricken down the most effective weapon against subversive activity available to the Government. It is not realistic to say that the Government can be protected merely by applying the Act to sensitive jobs. One never knows just which job is sensitive. The janitor might prove to be in as important a spot security-wise as the top employee in the building.[4]

Clark's position, though in the minority by 1956, had dominated the Court only a few years before when national security not only justified a wide-ranging purge of federal employees, but was also invoked to cover many other manifestations of that repressive outburst we now call McCarthyism. At that time, as it had done so often before, the nation's judiciary condoned the violations of civil liberties that were claimed to be essential for America's defense. It soon recanted, and, again as happened so often in the past, became more protective of individual rights. Because that pattern of repression and repentance occurs during almost every major crisis in our nation's history, it cannot be viewed as a temporary aberration, but rather as a normal part of American political life. That was certainly the case during the late 1940s and 1950s.

This is not to say that all invocations of national security during the early years of the cold war were illegitimate. After all, some American communists had spied for the Soviet Union during World War II; and it was clear that some kind of security precautions were necessary. Nonetheless, most of the dismissals, blacklists, and other sanctions imposed on communists, homosexuals, and other political undesirables during the McCarthy era bore little relation to national security. In fact, when we examine what happened during that period it becomes clear that the definition of what constituted a security threat was elastic in the extreme—often invoked to justify actions against harmless, but politically unacceptable, individuals.

In retrospect, some of these justifications seem rather far-fetched, to say the least. Kendrick Cole's was one of those cases, Another concerned a former seaman who had been barred from sailing under the federal government's Port Security Program and later got a job as a cook in Sacramento. When his previous troubles were revealed, he was fired again. Sacramento was the state capitol and "important people" might show up at his restaurant.[5] A similar concern for the safety of New York City's water supply lay behind the requirement that everyone who applied for a permit to fish in the city's upstate reservoirs had to take a loyalty oath. In 1957 the state's commissioner of water supply, gas and electricity actually refused to grant fishing permits to two Communist Party (CP) leaders (Emerson, Haber, and Dorsen 1967, 269). Sabotage was an equally worrisome prospect in the case of Doris Brin Walker, a clerk-typist in the purchasing department of a pharmaceutical company, fired in 1949 because she was a communist who might adulterate the Cutter Laboratories' "peculiarly sensitive" products.[6]

Nor was the danger only physical. When the *New York Times* fired a copywriter for taking the Fifth Amendment, it did so on the grounds of national security. The man worked on the foreign desk; had he been assigned to the sports pages, the publisher explained, he could have kept his job (Stein 1963, 105). Similarly, the former FBI agents who compiled the entertainment industry's unofficial blacklist, *Red Channels*, claimed that the 151 show business people their volume exposed might use the airwaves to "transmit pro-Sovietism to the American public" (American Business Consultants 1950, 5). Teachers, too, could endanger the United States. For the ever-vigilant J. Edgar Hoover, the menace occurred because their "daily contact" with their students "enables the teachers to effectively control the thinking of the pupils and thus insidiously instill into the minds of children the Communist Party line" (quoted in O'Reilly 1989). Even bad teachers could be dangerous, an Illinois legislator explained. "For an example, when the boys entered the Army it was found that most of them had a deplorable lack of training in mathematics." This might be intentional, he speculated. "Inadequate and improper teaching of any subject could be considered as subversive" (quoted in Harsha 1952, 83–84).

As the preceding examples reveal (and I could have cited dozens more), it is easy to compile a list of the McCarthy era's silliest moments, the ridiculous lengths to which overcautious officials, nervous employers, or publicity-hungry politicians went to guard the nation from the supposed threat of domestic communism. Nonetheless, to treat such excesses as aberrations resulting from some kind of collective hysteria trivializes what was one of the most serious outbreaks of political repression in American history. The congressional inquisitions, political prosecutions, and private blacklists that constituted what we now call McCarthyism could not have gained such traction within the nation's political culture had they not contained considerable plausibility and corresponded at least in some ways with what American policy makers perceived as a real threat to the nation's security. What produced the excesses was the grafting of the anxiety about internal security that developed during the early years of the cold war onto an ongoing campaign against the American Communist Party. Moreover, because of the Supreme Court's long-standing deference to the congressional and executive branches' invocation of national security, there were few, if any, legal obstacles to the violations of civil liberties that occurred.

In the pages that follow, I am going to look at the way in which the activities and ideas of the Communist Party gave plausibility to both the notion that it endangered the United States and the way in which groups and individuals that had long wanted to eliminate radical challenges to the American status quo were able to take advantage of the concern about internal security during the cold war to bring their agenda into the political mainstream. The revelations about the KGB's World War II espionage that emerged in the mid-1990s after the collapse of the Soviet Union, though they established the bona fides of some previously contested testimony about that espionage, do not significantly alter the finding that in many instances national security turned out to be a convenient fig leaf for an essentially political drive to eliminate left wing dissent and curtail liberal reforms. I am not arguing that there were not also legitimate security issues at stake or that a carefully constructed loyalty-security program for federal employees was unnecessary. I am saying merely that for a period of about ten years before such developments as the Cole decision signaled a transformation in the political climate, ideology, partisan politics, and bureaucratic considerations usually determined the way in which security issues were treated. In the name of eradicating the danger of communism, political freedom and the rights of individuals were seriously curtailed.

COMMUNISTS AND ANTICOMMUNISTS

Of course, communism had always been unpopular in the United States. Ever since its founders embraced the Bolshevik revolution and split from the Socialist Party in 1919, the American Communist Party had been viewed with suspicion from many sides. Not only was its revolutionary rhetoric jarringly at odds with the nation's moderate and individualistic ethos, but its conspiratorial tactics and undemocratic practices were equally alien to most law-abiding American citizens. Admittedly, many of those tactics and practices evolved to counter the repression that the party faced in its early days. Hounded by immigration authorities and Justice Department officials and prosecuted under a variety of state-level sedition laws that the Supreme Court did nothing to reverse, the fledgling party turned inward and then went underground.[7] When it emerged as a legal entity in the mid-1920s, it still retained the conspiratorial aura of its origins. It maintained a skeletal clandestine organization and made its members keep their affiliation secret, thus reinforcing its image as a dangerously subversive cabal (Lewy 1990, 39). And, of course, its subservient relationship to the Soviet Union only increased its estrangement from the American mainstream.

Nonetheless, despite its authoritarianism and devotion to Stalin, by the 1930s the CP had become the most dynamic and successful group on the American left, its energy and early opposition to fascism attracting rebels and idealists eager to do something about the Great Depression and the rise of Hitler. At its peak, the party probably had about 75,000 to 100,000 members, with thousands more willing to join the so-called front groups it established or to support the causes that it championed (Klehr 1984; Ottanelli 1991). It was particularly effective within the labor movement, where many of its most dedicated activists worked to organize the industrial unions that constituted the newly formed Congress of Industrial Organizations (CIO). Though never successful in winning their fellow workers to the revolutionary cause, communists did hold a disproportionate share of leadership positions within some of those unions—especially in the electronics, maritime, agricultural, and hard-rock mining industries (Levenstein 1981; Rosswurm 1992). They also established themselves within a few white collar unions, especially those catering to professionals like screenwriters or college teachers who were attracted by the party's intellectual atmosphere and its antifascism (for background on the screenwriters' and teachers' unions, see Ceplair and Englund 1980; Iversen 1959).

The CP's influence extended beyond its members, however, for, during the 1930s and then again during and immediately after World War II, the party was at the center of a vibrant left wing culture that revolved around the myriad activities of its front groups. Schools, civil rights organizations, fraternal societies, literary magazines, student groups, peace groups, summer camps, choral societies, professional organizations, as well as ad hoc groups that sprang up to defend individual victims of political repression or racial injustice—there seemed to be a party-led organization catering to just about every personal interest or left wing cause. Yet, for all its vitality within the left, communism was always marginal to American life. Communists never came to dominate the labor movement or gain control over any significant sector of the economy. Nonetheless, when the cold war turned the party from a minor political sect into a threat to national security, the places from which its allegedly dangerous members had to be purged just happened to be those areas of American society in which the communist movement had been most active.

The party's enemies were legion. As Richard Gid Powers shows, they ranged from genuine crazies to sophisticated socialists and former communists. Most, however, were on the right. Most also viewed American communists through an ideological prism. Like J. Edgar Hoover they regarded the party's adherence to the doctrines of Marxism-Leninism as a threat to the American way of life, treating "resistance to communism," in Powers' words, "as a moral duty" (1995, x). Because of its protean nature, anticommunism could serve many agendas. Antiunion businessmen, for example, had long found Red-baiting useful in combating organizing drives among their workers, and many socialists and liberals embraced it during turf wars within the labor movement and other left wing groups. Conservatives from both political parties discovered the publicity value of charging the New Deal administration with harboring communists. The Catholic Church also opposed the party, alienated by its atheism as well as by its support for the anticlerical loyalists in the Spanish Civil War and, later, by the Soviets' persecution of the church in Eastern Europe. Whatever their motives, by the late 1930s the most dedicated opponents of American communism had coalesced into a self-conscious network of activists who, because of their accumulated experience in the field, were to provide leadership for the anticommunist crusade after World War II (for a more extensive discussion of the anticommunist network, see Schrecker 1998, 42–85).

That crusade was largely—though not entirely—a top-down phenomenon, one that began in Washington, D.C., and spread to the rest of the country. Although grassroots right wingers eagerly embraced the movement, they would have remained a largely insignificant factor had they not received the imprimatur of the federal government, with its emphasis on national security. The cold war was the critical catalyst. The nation's main policy makers in the Roosevelt and Truman administrations, though certainly unsympathetic if not hostile to the CP, had tried to keep their distance from the anticommunist crusade, which they viewed in part as a veiled attack on their own accomplishments. When, however, the tension-filled wartime relationship with the Soviet Union turned increasingly bitter, the nation's leaders could no longer resist the pressure to eliminate communism from American life (for the clearest presentation of this essentially oversimplified argument, see Freeland 1971). Although it had been possible to overlook or at least downplay the party's activities as long as it was viewed only as a radical political organization, once the cold war broke out, the party's longstanding connection to Moscow made it a matter of national security. It was not unreasonable to assume that communists might well be working in the interests of the nation's new foreign enemy—as, in fact, some were. Unfortunately, however, because of partisan pressures and bureaucratic politics, as well as the Truman administration's own hostility toward and lack of knowledge about the Communist Party, what might have been a reasonable set of security regulations turned into a much broader witch hunt that legitimized the political purges of the McCarthy era.

Communism was a mystery to most Americans in the early years of the cold war; few, after all, had ever come into contact with the small, secret, and marginalized party. They knew they were "agin" it, but, as contemporary research showed, they had little idea of what it actually was. A Texas banker in a 1953 survey, when asked why he suspected an acquaintance of communism, explained "just his slant on community life and church work. He was not like us." Another respondent noted that the party wanted to "wipe out everybody who has any money." Most, however, focused on its atheism and on the possibility that its members could convert unsuspecting individuals to their way of life (Stouffer 1955, 156–85). Not surprisingly, stereotypes abounded. Though highly exaggerated, many of the stereotypes did bear some relationship to reality. Thus, for example, the party's rigid discipline and its ties to the Soviet Union made it easy to portray all communists as puppets under Kremlin control. So, too, the CP's secrecy allowed for the depiction of its members as devious and immoral, and its cadres' activism could be interpreted as attempts to take over and subvert every organization the cadres joined.

In short, everything communists did could be considered part of a dangerous Moscow-led conspiracy against the United States. This was not an accident. FBI Director J. Edgar Hoover and his anticommunist allies worked hard to disseminate this image by supplying evidence of the party's past offenses and warning about future ones. They made the most of many venues to spread the word—from criminal trials and congressional hearings to the mass media and friendly politicians. Former Communist Party members were particularly valuable here. The sometimes lurid stories they told about their experiences in the party reinforced the negative stereotypes that dominated the way most Americans thought about communism by the late 1940s. As we shall see, these stereotypes shaped the anticommunist crusade by making it possible to portray American communists as a threat to the nation's security.

THE THREAT OF SUBVERSION

That threat was specific: subversion, espionage, and sabotage.

Subversion was the traditional danger that all revolutionary organizations presented. It was also the most unlikely. There was, to put it mildly, not a scintilla of evidence that a communist uprising was in the offing. Even so, the specter of revolution dominated much of the public discourse about American communism. In a rare 1947 congressional appearance, J. Edgar Hoover offered the scary statistic that "in 1917 when the Communists overthrew the Russian Government there was one Communist for every 2,277 persons in Russia. In the United States today there is one Communist for every 1,814 persons in the country" (U.S. House 1947b). Hoover was hyping the danger of revolution in large part because of his desire to use the criminal justice system against the Communist Party. He and his aides hoped that a successful prosecution would "result in a judicial precedent being set that the Communist [P]arty as an organization is illegal," and thus open the way for future charges against its "individual members and close adherents or sympathizers."[8] Because such a prosecution would probably rely on charging the party with violating a criminal syndicalism law like the 1940 Smith Act that made it illegal "to knowingly or willfully advocate, abet, advise, or teach the duty, necessity, desirability, or propriety of overthrowing or destroying any government in the United States by force or violence," it made sense to emphasize the CP's revolutionary goals.[9] And when the Supreme Court upheld the Smith Act conviction of the party's leaders, in its 1951 Dennis decision, Chief Justice Fred Vinson's majority opinion bought into the FBI's characterization, noting the deepening cold war and invoking the danger to the nation's security posed by "the development of an apparatus designed and dedicated to the overthrow of the Government, in the context of world crisis after crisis."[10]

An equally unlikely scenario, but one that surfaced in the Smith Act trial as well as in many other anticommunist proceedings of the era, was the notion that the CP might subvert the nation's military effort if the United States went to war against Russia. According to this thesis, communists would embrace the "revolutionary defeatism" that Lenin had called for in the middle of World War I when he urged Russian soldiers to turn their guns on their officers and join the revolution (United States 1977, Herbert Philbrick, testimony, April 8, 1949 and Louis Budenz, testimony, March 29–30, 1949). Though extrapolating from the beaten Russian armies of 1917 to the mid-century United States required a considerable suspension of disbelief, Paul Robeson's 1949 remark urging African Americans not to fight for their segregated country seemingly updated the danger (Duberman 1988, 336–62; Dudziak 2000, 62). As a result, it became common for congressional committees, loyalty-security boards, and even faculty investigations to question suspected communists about their willingness to defend the United States against the Soviet Union (Schrecker 1986, 225).

Actually, most of concern about subversion that manifested itself during the early cold war revolved around the essentially partisan allegations of people like Senator Joseph McCarthy that communists in positions of influence in or near the government had sabotaged United States foreign policy in the interests of their Soviet masters. Alger Hiss was an iconic figure here. Hadn't he been at Yalta where, so it was claimed, Stalin had bamboozled FDR and Churchill into handing Eastern Europe over to the Red Army and giving him a free hand in China (Theoharis 1970)? Although Hiss may well have been spying for the Russians, it is unlikely that he subverted American policy. He dealt with administrative details, not substantive issues (for a complete picture of Hiss and his activities, see Weinstein 1997). Harry Dexter White, a Harvard-trained economist who served as assistant secretary of the Treasury, was a more likely candidate. He was the most highly placed American official linked to the Soviet apparatus by the testimony of the key ex-communist witnesses Elizabeth Bentley and Whittaker Chambers. Given that White seems to have been involved in what his biographer calls "a species of espionage," the allegations that he used his position to aid the Kremlin in other ways do have some plausibility. It is possible, in fact, that he may have tried to help the Soviets obtain better terms in a postwar loan. But, because the transaction was aborted, whatever White did had no effect (for the most recent, balanced, and comprehensive treatment of White's activities and the case against him, see Craig 2004).

The charges of subversion that gained the most attention during the 1950s involved the so-called loss of China, the notion that, as one Midwestern senator put it, communist traitors within the State Department and their allies had influenced policy, "which has helped bring about the entire subjugation of China by Communist forces directed from Moscow" (Karl Mundt, quoted in Donovan 1982, 135). Embraced by Republican politicians eager to embarrass the Truman administration, this scenario formed the core of Joe McCarthy's original charges against the government. Given that China was hardly America's to lose, those charges had no basis in reality. Nonetheless, because they contained enough circumstantial evidence to create a plausible scenario, they gained considerable traction. Legitimized by a series of congressional investigations and loyalty-security hearings, that scenario became especially potent after the outbreak of the Korean War. It involved the Institute of Pacific Relations (IPR), an independent think tank that offered expertise on East Asia in the period before the nation's research universities entered the field. State Department officials as well as businessmen and academics, everybody, in fact, who dealt with that part of the world, had some connection with the IPR. Unfortunately, some of its staff members, in particular its American general secretary, were in or near the Communist Party. Given the assumptions about communism that were then ascendant, such a conjuncture made it possible for right wing politicians like McCarthy, as well as the denizens of the so-called China Lobby, to make the claim, albeit with some probably perjured testimony, that the Communists in the IPR had conspired with the State Department's leading China hands to undermine Chiang K'ai-shek.[11]

A similar charge of subversion surfaced in the nation's most high-profile loyalty-security case, that of J. Robert Oppenheimer. Again, there was some plausibility to the charges. Though the Atomic Energy Commission panel that deprived him of his security clearance gave short shrift to the charge that his opposition to developing the hydrogen bomb had been designed to promote Soviet interests, Oppenheimer's admitted ties to the communist movement in the 1930s as well as his injudicious behavior in lying about a friend's transmission of a Soviet request for information did make it possible to raise questions. Even so, it was obvious that political considerations—the desire of his opponents within the military and the scientific community to silence his dissenting views about nuclear strategy— drove Oppenheimer from power (see, especially, Bird and Sherwin 2005). Nonetheless, the fact that such an accusation had even been considered with regard to the nation's most famous scientist reveals how seriously such charges of subversion were being taken.

SOVIET ESPIONAGE

In the letter to J. Edgar Hoover that triggered Oppenheimer's loyalty-security case, William L. Borden, the former chief of staff for the Joint Congressional Committee on Atomic Energy, also accused the Manhattan

Project leader of spying for the Russians (for a text of Borden's letter, see Polenberg 2002, 304–7). That accusation was entirely gratuitous. Nonetheless, whereas subversion was an imaginary threat, espionage was not. Before and, especially, during World War II, some American communists had spied for the Soviet Union.[12] As a result of the recent declassification of some World War II KBG telegrams that the American intelligence agencies deciphered during the early cold war, we now know that at least 100 (and perhaps many more) Americans had given unauthorized information to the Russians. These telegrams, the so-called Venona decrypts, not only revealed the identities of at least three spies within the Manhattan Project, as well as dozens of other Soviet agents elsewhere within the federal government and private industry, but also indicated that the Communist Party helped recruit many of them (Benson and Warner 1996; Haynes and Klehr 1999). Although the Venona code-breaking project was so highly classified that it was even concealed from President Truman, enough information about Soviet espionage surfaced during the late 1940s and early 1950s to justify many of the era's security precautions, both within the federal government and elsewhere (Moynihan 1998, 71–72).

During World War II, however, few high officials worried about Russian spying. The United States and the Soviet Union were allies; and, though both the FBI and military intelligence kept Soviet diplomats in the United States under surveillance, they failed to catch the Kremlin's spies. As a result, it was not until the bulk of the espionage had already taken place that American policy makers began to take it seriously. The most important early indication that Soviet agents had been active in Washington came from Canada, where the September 1945 defection of Igor Gouzenko, a code clerk in the Soviet embassy, revealed the existence of an espionage ring of Canadian communists and sympathizers. Gouzenko, who had taken a sheaf of documents with him to buttress his allegations, claimed that the Soviet military intelligence apparatus was running similar agents within the American government including an unnamed "assistant secretary of the Secretary of State's Department." Because the Canadian government was still trying to maintain cordial relations with the Kremlin, it did not publicize Gouzenko's charges until they were leaked to the Washington columnist Drew Pearson the following February (Whitaker and Marcuse 1994).

By then, the FBI had dozens of names. They had been provided by Elizabeth Bentley, a former courier for the KGB, who turned herself in to the bureau's New York office in November 1945. Most of Bentley's agents were left wing New Dealers, working in the Treasury Department or such wartime outfits as the Office of Strategic Services (on Bentley, see

Olmsted 2002). Some, including Hiss, had been previously identified by the penitential former communist Whittaker Chambers in 1939 when he told a State Department official about his clandestine network of federal employees. At that time, Chambers did not claim that his contacts had been involved with espionage, only that they were secret Communist Party members (see Tanenhaus 1997). In any event, though the FBI made a few stabs at following up on Chambers' revelations, the communists-in-government issue drew little attention. Thus, even when the head of the House Un-American Activities Committee, Texas Congressman Martin Dies, forced the administration to let the FBI investigate a list of some 1,121 suspect civil servants in 1942, the attorney general quashed the bureau's findings. Most of Elizabeth Bentley's agents were on that list (Schrecker 1998, 110–2). But, like Nathan Gregory Silvermaster, one of the key Washington spies, whose position in the wartime government was saved with the help of Harry Dexter White and Lauchlin Currie, FDR's top economic advisor, they were able to keep their jobs (Craig 2004, 108). Until the cold war got under way, security screenings of alleged communists in the government rarely led to dismissals.

The administration's tolerant attitude toward domestic communism during World War II did not guarantee immunity to every individual identified as a communist. Julius Rosenberg, who was managing an industrial espionage ring of his former City College classmates, was fired by the signals laboratory at Fort Monmouth because of his Communist Party ties. He was a trained engineer, however, and so soon found another defense-related position within private industry (Radosh and Milton 1983, 56, 70). Security officials on the West Coast forced Ross Lomanitz and Martin Kamen from their Manhattan Project jobs in Berkeley's Radiation Laboratory. Unlike Rosenberg, neither man was a spy and Kamen was not even a communist. Lomanitz's attempt to organize his colleagues into a left wing union caused his ouster, and it was Kamen's discussion of basic science with a group of Soviet officials at a San Francisco restaurant that brought him down (for an up-to-date discussion of these stories, see Herken 2002, 106–10, 122–3).

Despite their precautions, however, the Manhattan Project's security officials had overlooked the two main atomic spies, Klaus Fuchs and Theodore Hall, as well as Rosenberg's brother-in-law David Greenglass, who had been serendipitously posted to the Los Alamos machine shop after being drafted. It wasn't until the Venona cryptographers began producing results in 1948 that the FBI realized that the KGB had penetrated the bomb project. By then, Hall had gone on to graduate school, Greenglass was out of the army, Rosenberg's network was no longer functioning, and only Fuchs, by then scientific head of the British nuclear weapons project, was still sending information to the Russians (on the atomic spies, see Radosh and Milton 1983; Williams 1987; Albright and Kunstel 1997). It is hard to tell what kind of security measures would have prevented the espionage at Los Alamos. All three spies were or had been in the communist movement; and it is possible that a more rigorous screening process might have weeded them out. But it might have also eliminated several of the project's most valuable scientists including its director, J. Robert Oppenheimer. In any event, by the time the Soviet Union detonated its first nuclear weapon in 1949, the anticommunist security measures then in place would certainly have kept them from such a sensitive project.

The other espionage agents we know about, mainly Bentley's contacts within the wartime New Deal, were providing political and military information of various types—some sensitive, some routine. However valuable that data was to its Soviet recipients, Bentley's defection cut off the flow. The KGB immediately severed all ties with its American agents and called its Russian operatives home. True, Kim Philby and his circle of British spies did continue to send information to the Kremlin, but by the time the KGB tried to restart its American operation, most of its former contacts were out of the government, a more stringent security program was in place, and the Communist Party was much too beleaguered to recruit any new agents. As a result, from the 1950s on, Soviet spies were nonideological individuals who worked for money. In other words, by the time it became a major political issue, communist espionage, though a reality during World War II, had essentially disappeared—and J. Edgar Hoover knew it (Weinstein and Vassiliev 1999, 286–300; West and Tsarev 1998, 174).

SABOTAGE

Actually, Truman and his advisors had never believed that communist spies were a serious threat to the government.[13] The danger to national security that did concern the administration—and that most policy makers as well as professional anticommunists paid attention to—was that of sabotage, the possibility that Soviet sympathizers might cripple the nation's physical infrastructure or otherwise undermine its ability to defend itself. All sorts of scenarios circulated among officials and within the media. Significantly, most of them took off from the Communist Party's activities within the labor movement. Here the danger was not so much that Soviet agents could destroy power plants or blow up bridges as it was that communists in positions of power within the nation's unions might, as Truman's secretary of labor explained, call "strikes which, while ostensibly for good trade union objectives, are designed to disrupt the defense program and, thereby to advance the foreign policy of Soviet Russia" (U.S. Senate 1952, 122, Maurice Tobin testimony).

There was little evidence that any such walkouts had ever occurred or had even been planned. True, during the Nazi-Soviet Pact period before the United States entered World War II, communist-led unions had shut down two California aircraft factories and the Allis-Chalmers machine tool plant outside Milwaukee. Although these were ordinary labor disputes, similar to those that many noncommunist unions were mounting at the time, these strikes came to figure prominently in the early cold war rhetoric about the threat of communist sabotage, cited repeatedly by antiunion employers, politicians, and rivals within the labor movement (on the so-called defense strikes of 1940 and 1941, see Lichtenstein 1982; Meyer 1992). The 1941 Allis-Chalmers walkout drew particular attention when the same UAW local struck again after the war and the company mounted a massive Red-baiting campaign that included planting more than fifty articles in the local press and bringing a special congressional committee to Milwaukee. The pièce de résistance of that campaign was the almost certainly perjured testimony of the professional witness Louis Budenz that he had been at a meeting where the party's general secretary ordered the local to go out on strike to shut down the defense effort.[14] So pervasive was this story about the Allis-Chalmers strike that it even surfaced in the Supreme Court's 1950 decision to uphold the Taft-Hartley Act's imposition of a noncommunist affidavit on union officials.[15] Though the affidavit clearly impinged upon constitutionally protected matters of belief, the invocation of the (far-fetched) dangers of a political strike induced the Court's majority to go along with what was to become a bruising assault on the left wing of the labor movement.

A similar rationale lay behind the federal government's Port Security Program, which took advantage of the crisis caused by the Korean War to impose an anticommunist political test on all the nation's maritime workers. The waterfront unions on the West Coast, the International Longshoremen's and Warehousemen's Union (ILWU) in particular, were traditional bastions of radicalism whose communist leaders retained the loyalty of their members despite repeated attempts by employers, politicians, and rival unions to dislodge them (on the maritime unions, see Kimeldorf 1988; Nelson 1988). Shortly after the Korean War broke out, a group of shipping company executives, anticommunist union leaders, and federal officials met in Washington and recommended that the government adopt a program that would, in the words of the measure's official sponsor, Washington Senator Warren Magnuson, "clean out whatever subversive influences may exist around the waterfronts." Magnuson was explicit about the targets of his legislation. "Some of the last strongholds of the Communist [sic] in this country exist in some of the waterfront unions, despite the efforts of patriotic maritime labor leaders to clean out some of these unions" (cited in Brown and Fassett 1953, 1187). Eliminating communists from the maritime unions would, it was claimed, protect the nation from the danger of "Trojan horse ships bringing in atomic bombs or facilities for bacterial warfare" as well as from "acts of sabotage such as sinking vessels in harbors or channels or at sea, causing fires, explosions or other damage to structures, implements, machinery and supplies, inducing unrest, strikes and work slow-downs."[16]

That the waterfront unions were the intended targets became clear as the program went into effect. Many of the nearly 4,000 dock workers and seamen that the Coast Guard screened off the waterfront were union activists. Security was not an issue here; some of the sailors were able to book passage on the ships from which they were barred, and one man, a petty officer in the naval reserve, had, his lawyer explained, "full and complete access to the very bases from which, as a longshoreman, he was screened."[17] Left-led unions in other industries encountered similar problems. The Atomic Energy Commission refused to let two of those unions represent the workers in its nuclear weapons laboratories and installations. One was the United Electrical, Radio, and Machine Workers of America (UE), the largest industrial union under communist control. The other, the United Public Workers (UPW) represented 80,000 government employees (O'Brien 1968, 191). Industrial security programs, congressional hearings, and the creation of a rival CIO union soon crippled the once powerful UE, while the federal Loyalty-Security program undermined the UPW by singling out its leading activists. At least 50 percent of the questions that the Loyalty Review Board asked Dorothy Bailey, the Labor Department examiner whose dismissal became the main test case of the government's loyalty program, involved her union work.[18] It was not even necessary for the Justice Department to place the UPW on the attorney general's list, as it once seriously considered doing. By 1952, the union was down to 2,500 members (O'Brien 1968, 191).

That so many of the men and women who clashed with the various public and private loyalty-security programs of the McCarthy era were union activists like Bailey raises the possibility that those programs might have been motivated as much by an antilabor animus on the part of the employers as by a concern for security. It was obvious, for example, that Doris Brin Walker's leadership within her local of the left wing United Office and Professional Workers of America (UOPWA), not the danger she posed to the nation's public health, had caused her dismissal from a California pharmaceutical company (on Walker's experiences, see Schrecker 1998, 299–301). Other antiunion employers, also eager to crack down on organized labor, found the government's security regulations a godsend, because they made it possible to fire militant workers otherwise protected by union contracts and labor laws. In 1949, for example, the business representatives who were advising the military on its industrial security program clamored to extend that program to all their operations, not just the ones working on classified projects or government contracts. So eager, in fact, were these corporate officials to use security procedures to purge their work force that, as early as 1948, the United States Army (not normally, it must be noted, a partisan of organized labor) complained about being "put on the spot and charged with the removal of individuals whose only offense has been labor activity and who are therefore troublesome to management" (Fordham 1998, 137–8).

Significantly, in all these cases, the nation's judiciary went along with the assault on civil liberties. The Supreme Court either invoked national security, as it did in the Dennis case and in its 1950 Taft-Hartley decision, *American Communications Association v. Douds,* or else it simply avoided dealing with the First Amendment issues such cases presented. Thus, for example, it ruled that the firing of Doris Walker by the Cutter Laboratories because of her party membership did not violate the Constitution because the federal government was not involved—and, even if it were, security dictated her dismissal since she might engage in "acts of sabotage . . . at any time such acts may be directed by the party leaders."[19]

SECURITY AND THE IDENTIFICATION PROBLEM

Scarcely less crude than the attempts of antiunion employers to eliminate union activists from their payrolls were the ways in which people were able to inject their personal biases into the national security apparatus. An unrelated sex panic, for example, made it possible to eject homosexuals from the federal government on security grounds by claiming that their sexual orientation exposed them to blackmail, though, as a recent study reveals, the most serious consequence they needed protection from was their dismissal from government service (Johnson 2004). What had seemed most shocking to liberals at the time about the case of the union activist Dorothy Bailey was the grilling she endured about her support for racial equality, in particular, about a letter she had written to the wartime Red Cross opposing its policy of segregating the blood of African Americans. Other UPW members faced the same question.[20] Nor were they alone. As the loyalty security program got under way, it became clear that civil rights activists were as vulnerable to dismissal as labor militants. The Post Office Department, which had long served as a route to the middle class for upwardly mobile African Americans, fired so many black postal workers that the normally accommodating NAACP felt moved to protest.[21]

Although the Post Office defended those dismissals on the grounds that it was necessary to protect the important information that went through the mails from being stolen or compromised if an envelope broke open in the presence of a subversive postal worker, the racial biases that crept into its loyalty program not only revealed the prejudices of the bureaucrats who administered it, but also reflected their assumptions about communists and their allies.[22] Because the CP was the only significant American organization not specifically devoted to civil rights that fought for racial equality, it was not necessarily irrational (though it was unfortunate) for loyalty-security officials to assume that individuals who defied racial segregation might have a communist connection. Because many segregationists saw little difference between red activists and black ones, such assumptions became toxic when translated into the political tests that undergirded the economic sanctions of the McCarthy era.

Even so, when we look at the problem from the perspective of the Post Office's security officials, we can understand why they may have asked white suspects if they had black friends and blacks if they had white ones. Their mission, after all, was to eliminate communists from their department's work force. However, because party members kept their affiliation secret, identifying them was no simple matter. Here, we encounter the other reason why the invocation of national security during the McCarthy period produced so much injustice. Besides relying on plausible, but exaggerated and unrealistic, assessments of the dangers of domestic communism, the men and women who operated the nation's loyalty-security machinery in the Post Office and elsewhere also sought to identify alleged subversives in accordance with a definition of communism that was so vague it encompassed most forms of left wing dissent.

J. Edgar Hoover was the most powerful figure to embrace that definition. As far as the FBI director was concerned,

> the open avowed Communist who carries a card and pays dues is no different from a security standpoint than the person who does the party's work but pays no dues, carries no card, and is not on the party rolls. In fact, the latter is a great menace because of his opportunity to work in stealth. (U.S. House 1947b)

It was necessary, therefore, to develop adequate criteria for identifying party members and their "innocent, gullible, or willful allies." Most of those criteria were ideological, designed to smoke out those who, in Hoover's words, "consistently follow the ever-changing, twisting party line" (U.S. House 1947b). What that meant in practice was the assumption that someone belonged to the CP if he or she supported the causes the Communist Party espoused or joined the groups it sponsored.

Such suppositions were not irrational. It was, in fact, quite likely that someone who subscribed to the *Daily Worker*, helped organize a left wing union, bought insurance from the International Workers Order (IWO), and urged the United States to keep out of war in 1940 was or had been in or near the Communist party. After all, the party did demand obedience from its members, expect them to become active in their unions, and provide them with dozens of social and cultural activities. Thus, although someone's party membership was secret, his or her participation in a front group or attendance at a CP-sponsored rally was not. One could, therefore, identify communists by applying the so-called duck test. If someone looked like a duck, quacked like a duck, and waddled like a duck. . . . That method of wildlife identification, however, led to what came to be known as guilt by association. Enshrined in Truman's Executive Order 9835 of March 1947, creating the federal government's loyalty-security program, it made "membership in, affiliation with, or sympathetic association with" one of the supposedly subversive organizations listed by the attorney general grounds for dismissal (for the best discussion of the program and its criteria for dismissal, see Bontecou 1953).

In operation, however, the loyalty-security program turned into a Kafkaesque nightmare that soon spread throughout the rest of society, as employers in both the public and the private sector also sought to purge communists from their payrolls. Thousands of people lost their jobs or security clearances, sometimes for something as trivial as having gone to college with Julius Rosenberg or citing publications from the Institute of

Pacific Relations in their dissertations.[23] The FBI, which largely created and administered the program, was responsible for much of the injustice that ensued. Because it relied on illegal procedures and secret informers, the bureau refused to let the people charged with disloyalty know who made the accusations against them. Nor did it give more information to the panels that reviewed the cases of these men and women (Yarmolinsky 1955, 164–8). National security, it claimed, would be endangered if the identities of its undercover agents were revealed (Theoharis and Cox 1988, 256). As a result, vagueness, hearsay, and anonymous accusations marred proceedings under the loyalty-security program, making it difficult for people to clear themselves even when they were genuinely innocent of communism.

As L. A. Powe shows in his contribution to this volume, it was not until the mid-1950s that the Supreme Court imposed any meaningful constraints on the government's employment security program—and even then, it waffled. Thus, although several justices were horrified by the prospect that the charges of unknown accusers could cost public employees their jobs, a 4-4 tie in the case of Dorothy Bailey confirmed the 1950 decision of the Washington, D.C., Court of Appeals that security considerations overrode her right to confront her accusers and allowed the government to fire people without giving them a fair hearing.[24]

SECURITY AND PARTISAN POLITICS

Unjust procedures were only part of the story, however. Because the drive to eliminate communism from American life was ultimately fueled by partisan politics, even the strongest devotion to due process and most rigorous standards of evidence would not have eliminated the serious inequities involved. By early 1947, when Alger Hiss left the State Department to take up a position as head of the Carnegie Endowment in New York, most of the communists and other leftists who had joined the civil service during the New Deal and World War II had also surrendered their government positions or else, like Hiss, had been forced to resign. From the start, many of the political leaders who went along with the anticommunist crusade recognized that it was designed more to gain partisan advantage than to protect America's security. Harry Truman, for example, did not take any serious steps to revise the government's administration's loyalty program until after the Republicans won control of Congress in November 1946. Fearing that the GOP might attack that omission, he hustled to protect his administration by establishing the 1947 Loyalty-Security Program (for an overview, see Harper 1969).

The maneuver did not succeed. With the behind-the-scenes help of J. Edgar Hoover, the Republicans continued to demand further measures and to accuse the Democrats of being soft on communism. The forthcoming presidential election was one reason why the hearings on Elizabeth Bentley's charges took place in the summer of 1948. As HUAC chair Parnell Thomas explained later, the head of the Republican National Committee "was urging me in the Dewey campaign to set up the spy hearings. At the time he was urging me to stay in Washington to keep the heat on Harry Truman" (Donovan 1982, 414). The president and his advisors recognized their vulnerability, as one of them noted, "it is a major Republican issue . . . the Administration's weakest link. . . . There is pay dirt here, and the Republicans had no intention of being diverted by appeals from anguished liberals who see the Bill of Rights transgressed."[25] Ironically, Truman's upset victory over Dewey, instead of dampening down the communists-in-government issue, intensified it. The Republicans recognized that, given the popularity of the New Deal's domestic program and their own adherence to Truman's bipartisan foreign policy, focusing on the communist threat would most effectively challenge the administration.[26]

Charges of communist subversion within the United States Foreign Service were particularly politicized. Even before McCarthy brought the "loss of China" scenario to the front pages, administration supporters worried about their vulnerability. "I do want you to see the position we are in," a Southern Democrat explained in 1949, "crudely expressed, from the standpoint of critics of the administration and critics of the [State] Department—severe critics. They are ready to believe almost anything— that maybe there is a Communist cell over there that is operating day by day. Of course, I don't think that is true, but nevertheless the state of the public mind is a fact that one just cannot quite overlook" (Donovan 1982, 38). Once Joe McCarthy got into the picture, the situation worsened. Though obviously a loose cannon, the Wisconsin senator was so adept at unsettling the administration that the Republican leadership egged him on. "If one case doesn't work out," Robert Taft advised him, "bring up another" (Oshinsky 1983, 133). When some of McCarthy's main critics went down to defeat in the 1950 congressional elections, he seemed just about invincible.[27] In response, the administration eased its criteria for dismissing federal employees and scrambled to purge the State Department.

The purges continued even after the Republicans took over the White House under Eisenhower. As is well known, Ike detested McCarthy, but initially refused to stand up to him. His secretary of state, John Foster Dulles, capitulated as well, reopening old loyalty investigations and firing almost every China hand who had survived the earlier inquisitions. Eager to show that it was tougher on communism than its predecessor, the Republican administration yet again revised the loyalty-security program to make it even easier to eliminate public servants as security risks (Broadwater 1992). Although administration insiders realized that there would be little danger in allowing contrite former party members to retain their jobs, they flinched from adopting such a policy, because, as Attorney General Herbert Brownell explained in March 1954, "there are many in our populace who are so rabid on this subject that they would want to lynch us if we were to hold that a man who ever held a Communist ticket at any time should get by."[28]

By that point, however, Eisenhower had made a covert decision to bring McCarthy down (see Adams 1983; Greenstein 1982). The automatic invocation of national security to justify eliminating alleged communists from positions of influence within American society had begun to wear thin. The anticommunist crusade continued, but its political force was waning. The nation's governing elites had come to recognize that the drastic measures devised in the late 1940s to handle communist subversion, espionage, and sabotage had fulfilled their function. Domestic communists no longer posed a threat to the nation's security. As he examined McCarthy's charges that the army had endangered the country by promoting Captain Irving Peress, UN Ambassador Henry Cabot Lodge reflected, "Let us not lose our sense of proportion. The United States is not going under because there is a reserve dentist in the Army who is a communist."[29]

The Supreme Court soon followed—albeit with some backsliding. Invoking procedural, rather than substantive, reasons for restoring constitutional protections, it cautiously began to undo some of the damage it had condoned but a few years before. Its decisions of the late 1950s—*Cole v. Young, Yates, Watkins, Nelson, Jencks, Sweezy, Parker v. Lester*, among others—made it increasingly difficult for the government to openly pursue a wide-ranging anticommunist campaign that denied its targets basic procedural rights. Optimists see progress here. After all, the worst excesses of the anticommunist crusade were rolled back and apologies soon followed. Civil servants were reinstated; blacklisted entertainers made movies again; and the government dropped many of its remaining cases against communist defendants.

Even so, despite the obvious gains for civil liberties that these late 1950s decisions entailed, the political repression continued. To begin with, these decisions turned out to be so unpopular that, as L. A. Powe notes, the Court backtracked for several years. In addition, because he realized that the constraints these decisions placed on legal proceedings might make it impossible to mount successful prosecutions of communist offenders, J. Edgar Hoover created the secret and illegal COINTELPRO program to harass the politically unpopular groups and individuals that the government could no longer put on trial (Theoharis 1978, 133–40; O'Reilly 1983, 198–207; Donner 1980, 178–94). Political repression, as Geoffrey Stone demonstrates in the chapter 5 essay, just took another form. Moreover, as the post-9/11 incursions against civil liberties reveal, the current administration still assumes that national security will (and should) trump individual rights. Whether that assumption is correct remains to be seen. Despite considerable lip service to the Bill of Rights, it is by no means clear that America's judges and political leaders, not to mention its ordinary citizens, learned enough from the massive injustices of the early cold war to adopt a critical perspective when national security comes into play.

NOTES

1. Douglas dissent, *Scales v. U.S.*, 367 U.S. 203 (1961), 275, quoted in Gellhorn, 82–83.
2. Harry S Truman, memo for Attorney General, James McGrath, May 19, 1950, Box 31, Internal Security File, National Defense-Internal Security (2 of 2), Stephen J. Spingarn Papers, Harry S Truman Library, Independence, Mo. (Spingarn Papers).
3. *Cole v. Young*, 351 U.S. 536 (1956), 547.
4. *Cole v. Young*, 351 U.S. 536 (1956), 570.
5. R. J. Keene, "The Story of Screening," pamphlet, Marine Cooks and Stewards Union, nd, Gladstein, Leonard, Patsey, and Anderson Papers, Box 29, Bancroft Library, University of California Berkeley (Gladstein Papers).
6. National Association of Manufacturers, amicus curiae brief in *Black v. Cutter Laboratories*, in personal possession of Doris Brin Walker.
7. The best accounts of the Communist Party's early days are still Theodore Draper's *The Roots of American Communism* (1957) and *American Communism and Soviet Russia* (1960), but a new study, using the party's records from the former Soviet Union, certainly needs to be done.
8. United States 1976, 392–405, 439, D. Milton Ladd, memorandum to Director, January 22, 1948; Director, memorandum to Tamm, Ladd, and Tolson, Oct. 30, 1947, Smith Act FBI File, #1123. Copy on file with author.
9. Smith Act, 54 Stat. 671, 18 U.S.C.
10. *Dennis v. United States*, 341 U.S. 494 (1951).
11. There is a considerable literature on the loss of China issue. See, for example, Klehr and Radosh 1996; Newman 1992; Kahn 1975; May 1979.
12. There is a massive literature on Soviet espionage during World War II, much of it produced since the collapse of the USSR allowed scholars to view

Soviet files. The most authoritative account is Allen Weinstein and Alexander Vassiliev, *The Haunted Wood* (1999), though the inability of other scholars to check out their sources is a problem. See also West and Tsarev 1998; Feklisov and Kostin 2001.

13. Truman to George H. Earle, former Pa. governor, February 28, 1947, HST-OF, Box 880 file 263, Spingarn Papers; Bernstein 1989, 197–8.

14. U.S. House, 1947a. The evidence that Budenz fabricated his remarks comes from the transcript of his initial debriefing by the FBI, in which he was asked what he knew about political strikes and did not mention Allis-Chalmers. SAC, New York, to Director, October 23, 1951, Budenz, New York, FBI file, #404; list of questions drawn up for Budenz in J. C. Strickland to Ladd, December 3, 1945, Budenz, HQ file, #149x; summary of interviews with Budenz in Winterrowd to Strickland, February 7, 1947, Budenz, HQ file, #211. Copy on file with author.

15. *American Communications Association v. Douds*, 339 U.S. 382 (1950).

16. Emanuel Celler, quoted in United States 1957, 195, 331; Merlin O'Neill, affidavit, May 16, 1951, Box. 30/2030.74-1c-a, Gladstein Papers.

17. R. J. Keene, "The Story of Screening," Gladstein Papers; George R. Andersen to Ralph S. Brown, Jr., August 22, 1952, Box 20/2030.74-I, Gladstein Papers.

18. Memo on *Bailey v. Richardson*, 1950 Term, no. 49, "JGB" W. O. Douglas notes, Box 198, O.T. 1950, William O. Douglas Papers, Library of Congress, Washington, D.C.

19. *Black v. Cutter Laboratories*, 351 U.S. 292 (1956).

20. Bontecou 1953, 137–40; Abram Flaxer to Truman, November 24, 1948, HST OF 252K (1948) Box 872, Spingarn Papers.

21. Press Release, November 11, 1947, Walter White to President Truman, November 26, 1948, Thurgood Marshall to Seth Richardson, n.d., NAACP Papers, part 13, Series C, reel 5. Frederick Md.: University Publications of America, 1982.

22. H. B. Montague to Samuel J. Scott, October 5, 1962, Senate Internal Security Subcommittee records, Post Office Department, Box 249, U.S. Senate, Committee on the Judiciary, Subcommittee on Internal Security, Records, Record Group 46, National Archives, Washington, D.C.

23. Yarmolinsky (1955) offers examples of some of the charges that were made. See also Scientists' Committee on Loyalty and Security 1955.

24. *Bailey v. Richardson*, 182 F.2d 42.

25. George Elsey, "Random thoughts 26 August," Box 68, Internal Security— Congressional Loyalty Investigations (2), Elsey Papers, Harry S Truman Library, Independence, Mo.

26. Though an older study, Earl Latham's *The Communist Controversy in Washington* (1966) offers the most thoughtful discussion of the partisanship involved in the communists-in-government issue.

27. Robert Griffith offers a good overview of McCarthy's political impact in *The Politics of Fear* (1987).

28. Brownell, Memo, March 22, 1954, DDE (Ann Whitman) Administration
     File, Box 8, Herb Brownell Jr., 1952–54 (3). Brownell papers, Dwight David
     Eisenhower Library, Abilene, Kan.
29. Lodge to DDE, February 23, 1954, DDE (Ann Whitman) Administration
     series, Box 32, Lodge, Henry Cabot, 1954 (7), Eisenhower Papers, Dwight
     David Eisenhower Library, Abilene, Kan.

REFERENCES

Adams, John G. 1983. *Without Precedent: The Story of the Death of McCarthyism.*
    New York: W. W. Norton.
Albright, Joseph, and Marcia Kunstel. 1997. *Bombshell: The Secret Story of
    America's Unknown Atomic Spy Conspiracy.* New York: Times Books.
American Business Consultants. 1950. *Red Channels.* New York: American
    Business Consultants.
Benson, Robert Louis, and Michael Warner, editors. 1996. *VENONA: Soviet Espi-
    onage and the American Response.* Washington: National Security Agency, Cen-
    tral Intelligence Agency.
Bernstein, Carl. 1989. *Loyalties: A Son's Memoir.* New York: Simon & Schuster.
Bird, Kai, and Martin J. Sherwin. 2005. *American Prometheus: The Triumph and
    Tragedy of J. Robert Oppenheimer.* New York: Alfred A. Knopf.
Bontecou, Eleanor. 1953. *The Federal Loyalty-Security Program.* Ithaca, N.Y.: Cor-
    nell University Press.
Broadwater, Jeff. 1992. *Eisenhower and the Anti-Communist Crusade.* Chapel Hill,
    N.C.: University of North Carolina Press.
Brown, Ralph S., and John D. Fassett. 1953. "Security Tests for Maritime
    Workers: Due Process Under the Port Security Program." *Yale Law Journal*
    62(8): 1187.
Ceplair, Larry, and Steven Englund. 1980. *The Inquisition in Hollywood: Poli-
    tics in the Film Community, 1930–1960.* Garden City, N.Y.: Anchor Press/
    Doubleday.
Craig, R. Bruce. 2004. *Treasonable Doubt: The Harry Dexter White Spy Case.*
    Lawrence, Kan.: University Press of Kansas.
Donner, Frank J. 1980. *The Age of Surveillance: The Aims and Methods of
    America's Political Intelligence System.* New York: Alfred A. Knopf.
Donovan, Robert J. 1982. *Tumultuous Years: The Presidency of Harry S Truman,
    1949–1953.* New York: W. W. Norton.
Draper, Theodore. 1957. *The Roots of American Communism.* New York: Viking.
———. 1960. *American Communism and Soviet Russia, The Formative Period.* New
    York: Viking.
Duberman, Martin Bauml. 1988. *Paul Robeson.* New York: Alfred A. Knopf.
Dudziak, Mary L. 2000. *Cold War Civil Rights: Race and the Image of American
    Democracy.* Princeton, N.J.: Princeton University Press.

Emerson, Thomas, David Haber, and Norman Dorsen. 1967. *Political and Civil Rights in the United States*, vol. 1. Boston, Mass.: Little, Brown.

Feklisov, Alexander, and Sergin Kostin. 2001. *The Man Behind the Rosenbergs.* New York: Enigma.

Fordham, Benjamin O. 1998. *Building the Cold War Consensus: The Political Economy of U.S. National Security Policy, 1949–1951.* Ann Arbor, Mich.: University of Michigan Press.

Freeland, Richard. 1971. *The Truman Doctrine and the Origins of McCarthyism: Foreign Policy, Domestic Politics, and Internal Security, 1946–1948.* New York: Alfred A. Knopf.

Gellhorn, Walter. 1960. *American Rights: The Constitution in Action.* New York: Macmillan.

Greenstein, Fred I. 1982. *The Hidden Hand Presidency: Eisenhower as Leader.* New York: Basic Books.

Griffith, Robert. 1987. *The Politics of Fear: Joseph R. McCarthy and the Senate*, 2nd ed. Amherst, Mass.: University of Massachusetts Press.

Harper, Alan D. 1969. *The Politics of Loyalty: The White House and the Communist Issue, 1946–1952.* Westport, Conn.: Greenwood Publishing.

Harsha, E. Houston. 1952. "Illinois." In *The States and Subversion*, edited by Walter Gellhorn. Ithaca, N.Y.: Cornell University Press.

Haynes, John Earl, and Harvey Klehr. 1999. *Venona: Decoding Soviet Espionage in America.* New Haven, Conn.: Yale University Press.

Herken, Gregg. 2002. *Brotherhood of the Bomb: The Tangled Lives and Loyalties of Robert Oppenheimer, Ernest Lawrence, and Edward Teller.* New York: Henry Holt.

Hoover, J. Edgar. 1947. Memorandum to Tamm, Ladd, and Tolson, Oct. 30, 1947, Smith Act FBI File, #1123.

Iversen, Robert. 1959. *The Communists and the Schools.* New York: Harcourt, Brace.

Johnson, David K. 2004. *The Lavender Scare: The Cold War Persecution of Gays and Lesbians in the Federal Government.* Chicago, Ill.: University of Chicago Press.

Kahn, E. J., Jr. 1975. *The China Hands: America's Foreign Service Officers and What Befell Them.* New York: Viking.

Kimeldorf, Howard. 1988. *Reds or Rackets? The Making of Radical and Conservative Unions on the Waterfront.* Berkeley and Los Angeles, Calif.: University of California Press.

Klehr, Harvey. 1984. *The Heyday of American Communism: The Depression Decade.* New York: Basic Books.

Klehr, Harvey, and Ronald Radosh. 1996. *The Amerasia Spy Case: Prelude to McCarthyism.* Chapel Hill, N.C.: University of North Carolina Press.

Ladd, D. Milton. 1948. "Memorandum to Director, Jan. 22, 1948." In U.S. Congress, Senate, Select Committee to Study Governmental Operations with

Respect to Intelligence Activities. *Final Report,* Book III, "Supplementary Detailed Staff Reports on Intelligence Activities and the Rights of Americans." 94th Cong., 2d sess., April 23, 1976.

Latham, Earl. 1966. *The Communist Controversy in Washington: From the New Deal to McCarthy.* Cambridge, Mass.: Harvard University Press.

Levenstein, Harvey A. 1981. *Communism, Anti-Communism, and the CIO.* Westport, Conn.: Greenwood Press.

Lewy, Guenter. 1990. *The Cause that Failed: Communism in American Political Life.* New York: Oxford University Press.

Lichtenstein, Nelson. 1982. *Labor's War at Home: The CIO in World War II.* New York: Cambridge University Press.

May, Gary. 1979. *China Scapegoat: The Diplomatic Ordeal of John Carter Vincent.* Washington: New Republic Books.

Meyer, Stephen. 1992. *"Stalin Over Wisconsin": The Making and Unmaking of Militant Unionism, 1900–1950.* New Brunswick, N.J.: Rutgers University Press.

Moynihan, Daniel Patrick. 1998. *Secrecy: The American Experience.* New Haven, Conn., and London: Yale University Press.

Nelson, Bruce. 1988. *Workers on the Waterfront: Seamen, Longshoremen, and Unionism in the 1930s.* Urbana and Chicago, Ill.: University of Illinois Press.

Newman, Robert. 1992. *Owen Lattimore and the "Loss" of China.* Berkeley, Calif.: University of California Press.

O'Brien, F. S. 1968. "The 'Communist-dominated' Unions in the United States since 1950." *Labor History* 9(2): 191.

Olmsted, Kathryn S. 2002. *Red Spy Queen: A Biography of Elizabeth Bentley.* Chapel Hill, N.C.: University of North Carolina Press.

O'Reilly, Kenneth, 1983. *Hoover and the Un-Americans: The FBI, HUAC, and the Red Menace.* Philadelphia, Pa.: Temple University Press.

———, editor. 1989. *McCarthy Era Blacklisting of School Teachers, College Professors, and Other Public Employees: The FBI Responsibilities Program File and the Dissemination of Information Policy File.* Bethesda, Md.: University Publications of America.

Oshinsky, David. 1983. *A Conspiracy So Immense: The World of Joe McCarthy.* New York: Free Press.

Ottanelli, Fraser M. 1991. *The Communist Party of the United States: From the Depression to World War II.* New Brunswick, N.J.: Rutgers University Press.

Philbrick, Herbert. 1949. Testimony, April 8, 1949. United States of America, appellee, vs. Eugene Dennis et al., defendants-appellants. United States Court of Appeals for the Second Circuit, 1950, transcript of the trial, microfilm ed. Wilmington, Del.: M. Glazier, 1978, prepared by Fund for the Republic.

Polenberg, Richard, editor. 2002. *In the Matter of J. Robert Oppenheimer: The Security Clearance Hearing.* Ithaca, N.Y.: Cornell University Press.

Powers, Richard Gid. 1995. *Not Without Honor: The History of American Anti-communism.* New York: Free Press.

Radosh, Ronald, and Joyce Milton. 1983. *The Rosenberg File: A Search for the Truth.* New York: Holt, Rinehart and Winston.

Rosswurm, Steve, editor. 1992. *The CIO's Left-led Unions.* New Brunswick: Rutgers University Press.

Schrecker, Ellen W. 1986. *No Ivory Tower: McCarthyism and the Universities.* New York: Oxford University Press.

———. 1998. *Many Are the Crimes: McCarthyism in America.* Boston, Mass.: Little, Brown.

Scientists' Committee on Loyalty and Security. 1955. "Fort Monmouth One Year Later." *Bulletin of the Atomic Scientists* 11(April): 148–55, 158.

Stein, Bruno. 1963. "Loyalty and Security Cases in Arbitration." *Industrial and Labor Relations Review* 17(1): 105.

Stouffer, Samuel A. 1955. *Communism, Conformity, and Civil Liberties.* Garden City, N.Y.: Doubleday.

Tanenhaus, Sam. 1997. *Whittaker Chambers: A Biography.* New York: Random House.

Theoharis, Athan G. 1970. *The Yalta Myths: An Issue in U.S. Politics.* Columbia, Mo.: University of Missouri Press.

———. 1978. *Spying on Americans: Political Surveillance from Hoover to the Huston Plan.* Philadelphia, Pa.: Temple University Press.

Theoharis, Athan G., and John Stuart Cox. 1988. *The Boss: J. Edgar Hoover and the Great American Inquisition.* Philadelphia, Pa.: Temple University Press.

United States. 1957. *Report of the Commission on Government Security.* Washington: Government Printing Office.

———. 1976. *Final Report of the Select Committee to Study Governmental Operations with Respect to Intelligence Activities, United States Senate.* Book III, *Supplementary Detailed Staff Reports on Intelligence Activities and the Rights of Americans.* 94th Congr., 2nd Sess. Report No. 94-755. Washington: Government Printing Office.

———. 1977. *United States of America v. Eugene Dennis et al. United States Court of Appeals for the Second Circuit, 1950.* Transcripts of trials, microfilm ed. Wilmington, Del.: M. Glazier.

U.S. Congress. House of Representatives [U.S. House]. 1947a. Committee on Education and Labor. *Hearings, Amendments to the National Labor Relations Act.* 80th Cong., 1st sess. (March 13, 1947), 3609–13.

———. 1947b. Committee on Un-American Activities. *Hearings on H.R. 1884 and H.R. 2122.* 80th Cong., 1st sess. (March 26, 1947).

U.S. Congress. Senate [U.S. Senate]. 1952. Committee on Labor and Public Welfare. *Communist Domination of Unions and National Security.* Hearings before a Subcommittee. 82nd Cong., 2nd sess. (March 19, 1952).

Weinstein, Allen. 1997. *Perjury: The Hiss-Chambers Case,* rev. ed. New York: Alfred A. Knopf.

Weinstein, Allen, and Alexander Vassiliev. 1999. *The Haunted Wood: Soviet Espionage in America—The Stalin Era*. New York: Random House.

West, Nigel, and Oleg Tsarev. 1998. *The Crown Jewels: The British Secrets at the Heart of the KGB Archives*. London: HarperCollins.

Whitaker, Reg, and Gary Marcuse. 1994. *Cold War Canada: The Making of a National Insecurity State, 1945–1957*. Toronto, Ont.: University of Toronto Press.

Williams, Robert Chadwell. 1987. *Klaus Fuchs, Atom Spy*. Cambridge, Mass.: Harvard University Press.

Yarmolinsky, Adam, editor. 1955. *Case Studies in Personnel Security*. Washington: The Bureau of National Affairs.

CHAPTER 5

THE VIETNAM WAR: SPYING ON AMERICANS

GEOFFREY R. STONE

The Vietnam War triggered one of the most turbulent periods in American history, raising old—and new—questions about the nature and depth of the American commitment to civil liberties in wartime. Opposition to the war came from many quarters and employed a broad range of tactics to challenge the war, ranging from prayer vigils, teach-ins, mass public demonstrations, and nonviolent civil disobedience to mob violence and bombings.

During more than a decade of conflict, the war in Vietnam provoked bitter dissent and increasingly furious repression. It was an era marked by the Chicago Democratic Convention, the Kent State shootings, the Pentagon Papers, COINTELPRO, and the Days of Rage. During this era, many Americans believed that their nation was, quite literally, coming apart.

CRITICISM AND PROTEST

War critics posed fundamental questions about America's political, military, and strategic aims in Vietnam. They asked whether the United States should pursue unilateral military action in Vietnam or stay its hand in the absence of multinational cooperation. They questioned whether it was moral for the United States to inflict such suffering on the Vietnamese people to achieve its own military and strategic goals.

A major challenge for those who opposed the war was how to criticize the nation's policy without providing, or seeming to provide, "aid and comfort to the enemy." Like war protesters in other wars, opponents of the war in Vietnam were vilified as traitors or dupes who (intentionally or unintentionally) encouraged and emboldened the enemy. Lyndon Johnson feared that war opponents were harming American interests by raising false hopes among the enemy that the United States would weaken and disengage from the conflict. Senator Thomas Dodd of Connecticut castigated antiwar demonstrations as "tantamount to open insurrection" and Senator Richard Russell of Georgia accused dissenters of disloyalty because "every protest will cause the Communists to believe they can win if they hold on a little longer" (U.S. Senate 1965).

By mid-1966, public approval of the president's handling of the war had fallen below 50 percent, and one in three Americans felt that intervention in Vietnam had been a mistake. In April 1967, hundreds of thousands of antiwar demonstrators marched peacefully in protest rallies across the nation. By this time, however, the more radical elements of the antiwar movement had already begun to lose patience with efforts to change the government's position by building public opinion. They had learned from the civil rights movement that there was power in polarization and that polarization requires direct confrontation and resistance. Thus, the refrain We Won't Go began to echo across college campuses. Over the next several years, more than 25,000 men were indicted for draft offenses, infuriating those who supported the war.

In October 1967, some 50,000 antiwar demonstrators convened at the Lincoln Memorial and headed to the Pentagon. Several thousand demonstrators broke through lines set up by federal troops and then refused to leave the Pentagon grounds. After a lengthy standoff, hundreds of heavily armed soldiers formed a wedge and sliced through the demonstrators, who were sitting, arm in arm, in rows. The troops used tear gas, rifle butts, and cudgels to scatter and beat the protesters. By the end of the night, 647 demonstrators had been arrested and forty-seven hospitalized. Lyndon Johnson began referring to protesters as storm troopers and publicly accused the antiwar movement of being directly linked to communist subversion.

Stop the Draft protests occurred in thirty cities, leading to the arrest of more than 600 people. Increasingly, the police indiscriminately used nightsticks and blackjacks on demonstrators and onlookers alike. The next twelve months saw the continued escalation of the war, the tragic assassinations of Martin Luther King Jr. and Robert F. Kennedy, the withdrawal of Lyndon Johnson from the Democratic campaign for the nomination, the dramatic riots at the Chicago Democratic Convention, and the election of Richard Nixon as president of the United States.

Antiwar protests intensified in violence as the decade drew to a fractious end. From the fall of 1969 to the spring of 1970, at least 250 bombings, about one per day, were directed at ROTC buildings, draft boards, induction centers, federal offices, and the headquarters of multinational corporations. The goal of these bombings was to "bring the war home." At Kent State University, national guardsman shot and killed four students who were protesting their presence on campus.

Student protests erupted on more than half the nation's campuses. Within a few days, 1.5 million students walked out of classes, shutting down a fifth of the nation's colleges and universities. It was the most massive protest in the history of the United States. Thirty ROTC buildings were burned or bombed in the first week of May, and National Guard units were mobilized in sixteen states.

A SENSE OF PANIC

The Johnson and Nixon administrations were shocked and appalled by the magnitude and intensity of the opposition to the war in Vietnam. After the events at Kent State, "a sense of panic enveloped Richard Nixon and the men around him" (Evans and Novak 1971, 285). Henry Kissinger recalled that "the fear of another round of demonstrations permeated all the thinking about Vietnam" (1979, 968–9). Understandably, both the Johnson and Nixon administrations wanted desperately to suppress or at least defuse the critics of their policies in Vietnam.

The most natural thing, of course, is to put such critics in prison. After all, in wartime it is essential that the nation be united in support of its men and women in uniform. Once the nation has committed itself to a war, and the lives of American soldiers are on the line, it is the responsibility of all citizens to put aside their differences and to help the nation achieve victory as quickly and painlessly as possible. Dissent and dissension can serve only to obstruct the war effort, undermine the morale of citizens and soldiers, discourage enlistment, increase draft evasion, desertion, and insubordination, and strengthen the resolve of the enemy.

Despite the command of the First Amendment that Congress shall "make no law . . . abridging the freedom of speech, or of the press," this view of the exigencies of wartime had dominated national policy from the very founding of the republic. Early in our history, when the United States was on the brink of war with France, Congress enacted the Sedition Act of 1798, which effectively made it a crime for any person to criticize the president, the Congress, or the government of the United States. Among those prosecuted was Vermont Congressman Matthew Lyon, who had publicly chastised the Adams administration. During the Civil War, the Lincoln administration shut down some 300 opposition newspapers and imprisoned or exiled many critics of its policies, including former Congressman Clement Vallandigham, a national leader of the Peace Democrats.

During World War I, the Wilson administration prosecuted more than 2,000 individuals for their opposition to the war or the draft, often sentencing them to terms of ten to twenty years in prison. Among those convicted was the national leader of the Socialist Party, Eugene Debs, who had received a million votes for president in the election of 1912. During World War II, President Roosevelt demanded and got the prosecution and conviction of William Dudley Pelley, a fascist troublemaker, for criticizing the president's war policies. And during the cold war, many Americans, including Eugene Dennis, the leader of the Communist Party of the United States, were prosecuted for what were termed their un-American views.

It was inevitable, then, that Lyndon Johnson and Richard Nixon, following in the footsteps of Adams, Lincoln, Wilson, Roosevelt, Truman, and Eisenhower, would want to prosecute and imprison those dissenters whose criticism harmed the war effort. Certainly, they believed that war critics were wrong on the merits, that they were either dupes or agents of the communists, that the incessant opposition was demoralizing Americans, discouraging enlistment, obstructing the draft, fostering insubordination in the military, and encouraging the enemy to stiffer resistance.

Nonetheless, neither Johnson nor Nixon seriously contemplated prosecuting war critics for the crime of seditious libel. This restraint reflected a fundamental change in America's political and constitutional culture. By 1966, it had become impossible to imagine the United States government systematically prosecuting American citizens, to say nothing of Eugene McCarthy or George McGovern, merely for expressing their opposition to the war. Gradually, over the course of almost two centuries, America's understanding of free speech and its commitment to free and open public debate, even in wartime, had changed profoundly.

This is not to say, however, that the Johnson and Nixon administrations took no steps to squelch their critics. To the contrary, both administrations, particularly the latter, prosecuted individuals for a wide variety of acts related to their opposition to the war, including trespass, resisting arrest, flag desecration, draft card burning, and conspiracy to incite riots and draft evasion. The most important of the government's methods to neutralize dissent, however, was its aggressive use of domestic surveillance to disrupt, expose, and subvert the antiwar movement.

INVESTIGATING DISSENT

During the Red Scare after World War I, in the years leading up to World War II, during World War II, and throughout the cold war, J. Edgar Hoover and the Federal Bureau of Investigation played a major role in investigating dissident political activity. In some instances, the FBI's actions were clearly authorized; in others, Hoover disobeyed direct orders to terminate his activities. In the 1950s, the FBI initiated a counterintelligence program (COINTELPRO) against the Communist Party of the United States (CP). Hoover instituted this program without the knowledge or authorization of either the attorney general or the president. The goal was to go beyond surveillance to active political harassment and disruption.

Under its initial COINTELPRO, the FBI attempted to undermine the CP. It actively encouraged the media to publish information that would embarrass or humiliate members of the party, fostered animosity and division among party members by fabricating rumors of disloyalty and betrayal, secretly arranged for meeting places to be denied the party, set organized crime against the CP by sending forged letters, and undermined the political campaigns of candidates who challenged or criticized the government.

As antiwar protests escalated in the mid-1960s, the FBI, with prodding from the Johnson administration, expanded its domestic intelligence activities. At the 1964 Democratic National Convention, the FBI kept tabs on all so-called dissident groups within the Democratic Party and kept the president informed of their plans. In early 1965, the government installed wiretaps on both Students for a Democratic Society (SDS) and the Student Non-Violent Coordinating Committee. In April, President Johnson personally asked Hoover to investigate alleged communist infiltration of the antiwar movement.

Hoover was confident that the investigation would prove that the Communist Party had played an aggressive role in generating opposition to the war in Vietnam. The ensuing FBI report found Johnson's and Hoover's suspicions unfounded. Undaunted, the FBI expanded its surveillance to campus antiwar activities. A teach-in in Philadelphia, for example, resulted in a forty-one-page FBI intelligence report, incorporating remarks by ministers, professors, and other participants. The report, compiled by undercover informants, was distributed widely to military intelligence, the State Department, and the Internal Security Division of the Justice Department.

Lyndon Johnson also requested and received FBI reports on antiwar senators, congressmen, journalists, and academics. At his instructions, the FBI investigated the philosopher Hannah Arendt, newsman David Brinkley, and columnist Joseph Kraft, among others. As his anxiety about dissent grew, Johnson directed Hoover to investigate citizens who had sent antiwar letters or telegrams to the White House.

In 1968, the FBI turned its COINTELPRO tactics against the antiwar movement. After the student protests at Columbia University, the bureau formally launched a new COINTELPRO in order to hasten the collapse of the so-called New Left. The key directive stated that the goal was to "expose, disrupt and otherwise neutralize the activities of the various New Left organizations, their leadership and adherents." FBI agents were instructed to frustrate "every effort of these groups . . . to recruit new . . . members," to disrupt the activities of these groups, to spread misinformation about meeting places and times, to exploit "organizational and personal conflicts," and to promote suspicion, distrust, and dissension within the leadership. Hoover exhorted his agents to approach these new responsibilities with "imagination and enthusiasm" (see "Intelligence Activities: Senate Resolution 21" in United States 1976, 393).

In its efforts to destabilize and incapacitate the Left, FBI agents sent anonymous letters to the parents of antiwar protesters, accusing them of drug abuse, homosexuality, or other vices; wrote anonymous letters to employers to cause the firing of antiwar activists; distributed bogus newspapers on college campuses defaming peace activists; sent fraudulent letters to campaign contributors and other supporters of antiwar candidates to sabotage their campaigns; mailed anonymous letters to the spouses of antiwar activists, suggesting that their partners were having extramarital affairs; and spread false rumors that individuals were embezzling funds or secretly cooperating with the FBI.

In other COINTELPRO actions, FBI agents infiltrated antiwar organizations to spy on members and disrupt their activities; caused antiwar activists to be evicted from their homes; disabled their cars; intercepted their mail; wiretapped and bugged their conversations; planted derogatory information about them in the press; prevented them from renting facilities for meetings; incited police to harass them for minor offenses; sabotaged and disrupted peaceful demonstrations; and instigated physical assaults against them.

The FBI's COINTELPRO was not the only government program directed against the antiwar movement. The Central Intelligence Agency also entered the picture. In 1956, it began opening international mail to pursue foreign intelligence. In 1966, it expanded this program to include mail sent to or from individuals involved in the antiwar movement, even where the inquiry was directed toward domestic rather than foreign intelligence. Over the next few years, the CIA turned over to the FBI information resulting from more than 20,000 such mail openings, including material—often highly personal—about individuals involved in antiwar demonstrations, teach-ins, and similar activities.

The CIA also engaged directly in wholly domestic spying. In 1967, it initiated Project MERRIMAC, which was designed to protect CIA facilities and personnel against antiwar protests by infiltrating and monitoring an array of antiwar organizations. That same year, the CIA created Project RESISTANCE, an aggressive effort to gather information about radical activities in the United States. This program compiled material on more than 12,000 individuals, particularly those active on college campuses.

The most drastic domestic CIA program was Operation CHAOS, which was initiated as a result of pressure from President Johnson. Its purpose, in clear violation of the CIA's legislative charter, which expressly prohibited the CIA from undertaking any internal security role, was to investigate possible communist or other subversive involvement in the antiwar movement. Although the CIA consistently reported that foreign involvement was minimal, presidents Johnson and Nixon continued to insist on further investigation. As the Rockefeller Commission on the CIA later reported, Operation CHAOS became a repository for large quantities of information about the lawful activities of American citizens, ultimately accumulating material on more than 300,000 people. Much of this information was routinely shared with the FBI and the White House.

At roughly the same time that the CIA established CHAOS, army intelligence began its own large-scale domestic spying operation. The purported goal was to enable the army to plan effectively for domestic disorders. Directed initially at possible urban race riots, CHAOS expanded quickly. By October 1967, some 130 army intelligence agents were actively infiltrating, photographing, and reporting on an antiwar march at the Pentagon. The following year, the army expressly directed its domestic intelligence program at the antiwar movement.

Army intelligence assigned 1,500 undercover agents to collect information about virtually every group seeking significant change in the United States. The army gathered information on more than 100,000 opponents of the Vietnam War, including Senator Adlai Stevenson of Illinois, Congressman Abner Mikva, Georgia State Senator Julian Bond, Martin Luther King Jr., and Joan Baez. Among the organizations investigated were the ACLU, Americans for Democratic Action, the Anti-Defamation League, the American Friends Service Committee, and *Ramparts* magazine. Army intelligence agents monitored private communications, infiltrated antiwar organizations, participated in antiwar protests and demonstrations, and posed as press representatives. The army disseminated the material it gathered, including information about the private political, financial and sex lives of tens of thousands of individuals, to a broad range of government agencies, among them local police, the FBI, the CIA, and the National Security Agency (NSA).

At the behest of the White House, the NSA in 1969 began to intercept telephone communications involving the antiwar movement. Because this program was directed at American citizens, it was clearly illegal. To ensure security, NSA devised separate filing systems for these intercepts and classified the records as top secret. On July 1, 1969, it formalized this program under the code name MINARET, and expressly directed the program to restrict the knowledge that such information was being collected.

When Richard Nixon assumed the presidency in January 1969, he had in place a formidable apparatus to implement a program of political repression. His administration took full advantage of this machinery. From the outset, Nixon pressed the FBI to expand its domestic surveillance activities. In 1969, the Justice Department directed the FBI to gather information about individuals who participated in campus antiwar protests, and J. Edgar Hoover instructed his agents to record all "inflammatory" speeches. Over the next two years, the Justice Department asked the FBI for information on the income sources of antiwar groups, the FBI instructed its agents to investigate all members of SDS or other New Left campus organizations, and Hoover directed his agents to record the identities of all speakers at antiwar demonstrations. FBI reports on these matters were disseminated to the White House, the CIA, the State Department, the military intelligence agencies, the Secret Service, and the Department of Justice.

The administration prodded the FBI to expand its New Left COINTELPRO and pushed the CIA to intensify its domestic surveillance activities. During the Nixon administration, the CIA furnished the FBI with more than 1,000 domestic intelligence reports each month. This information was gathered by undercover agents, break-ins, wiretapping, and mail openings. Eventually, 300,000 names were indexed in the CIA's computers. The CIA was fully aware of the illegality of these activities. In passing one report on to the White House, CIA Director Richard Helms noted, "This is an area not within the charter of this Agency, so I need not emphasize how extremely sensitive this makes the paper" (Lukas 1976, 29).

Army intelligence developed a new plan in April 1969, calling for the identification of all persons involved, or expected to become involved, in protest activities. Attorney General John Mitchell went so far as to claim that the president had the authority to authorize electronic domestic intelligence surveillance without court order.

The Nixon administration enlisted the Internal Revenue Service on a massive scale. In 1969, it informed the IRS of the president's concern that tax-exempt funds might be supporting activist groups. Eight days later, the IRS established the Activist Organizations Committee to "collect relevant information on organizations predominantly dissident or extremist in nature and on people prominently identified with these organizations" (Theoharis 1978, 188–9; Lukas 1976, 22). This committee was later renamed the Special Services Staff (SSS) to disguise its real purpose.

By 1974, the SSS had compiled files on 2,873 organizations and 8,585 individuals. The IRS routinely furnished this information, including lists of contributors to SDS and other antiwar organizations, to the FBI, the Secret Service, army intelligence, and the White House. The goal was to strike critics of the administration with targeted tax audits and tax investigations. The SSS investigated such individuals as the columnist Joseph Alsop, folk singer Joan Baez, journalist Jimmy Breslin, New York City Mayor John Lindsay, actress Shirley MacLaine, and Senator Charles Goodell. The organizations it investigated included the ACLU, the American Jewish Committee, the National Organization of Women, the National Council of Churches, and the Americans for Democratic Action. This program was kept strictly secret because of its "political sensitivity" (Berman and Halperin 1975, 90–92).

By 1970, the White House began compiling an enemies list, under the direction of Charles Colson, special assistant to the president. Some 200 individuals and eighteen organizations were targeted for "special" government attention. Among them were former Attorney General Ramsey Clark, Congresswomen Bella Abzug and Shirley Chisholm, Senators Edward Kennedy, Edmund Muskie, and Walter Mondale, the presidents of Harvard, Yale, the Ford Foundation, and the Rand Corporation, the actors Gregory Peck and Carol Channing, and the journalists James Reston, Marvin Kalb, Daniel Schorr, and Joseph Kraft.

A month after the Kent State killings, Nixon moved to centralize domestic intelligence in the Oval Office. At his request, the White House assistant Tom Charles Huston proposed a new White House unit to oversee the investigation of political dissent. In July 1970, Huston prepared a memorandum, which came to be known as the Huston Plan, recommending intensified electronic surveillance, monitoring of international communications, "mail coverage" (that is, opening and reading mail), expanded use of undercover informants and "surreptitious entry" on college campuses, and the creation of a central agency on domestic intelligence, with representatives from the White House, FBI, CIA, NSA, and the military. The Huston Plan has been fairly characterized as a "blueprint for a police state in America" (Wise 1976, 154–5).

DISCLOSURE

The government's secret machinations to "expose, disrupt and otherwise neutralize" the antiwar movement were not known to the public until March 8, 1971, when an antiwar group—the Citizens' Commission to Investigate the FBI—broke into an FBI office in Media, Pennsylvania, and stole approximately 1,000 confidential documents. The group released excerpts to members of Congress, journalists, and organizations who were named in them. One of the documents, dated September 16, 1970, was mysteriously captioned "COINTELPRO-New Left." The first public intimation of the existence of this covert program, this document recommended intensified FBI interviewing of dissidents to "enhance the paranoia" and underscore the fear that "there is an FBI agent behind every mailbox" (Theoharis 1978, 148–9).

The administration's response to these disclosures was to warn that any further disclosure "could endanger the lives or cause other serious harm to persons engaged in investigation activities on behalf of the United States" ("Mitchell Issues Plea on F.B.I. Files," *New York Times*, March 24, 1971, 24). The *Washington Post* countered that these revelations showed that the FBI had been implementing a form "of internal security appropriate for the Secret Police of the Soviet Union." The *Post* argued that "the American public needs to know what the FBI is doing" and "needs to think long and hard about whether internal security rests especially upon official surveillance and the suppression of dissent or upon the traditional freedom of every citizen to speak his mind on any subject, whether others consider what he says wise or foolish, patriotic or subversive, conservative or radical" ("What Is the FBI Up To?" March 25, 1971, A20).

Over the next several weeks, as more of the FBI's COINTELPRO activities came to light, several major newspapers and congressmen called for J. Edgar Hoover's resignation. Under intense public pressure, Hoover announced on April 28, 1971, that he had officially terminated COINTELPRO. At that time, the FBI had some 2,000 agents engaged in domestic intelligence activities, and they were supervising an additional 1,700 domestic intelligence informants and 1,400 "confidential" sources who were not on the FBI payroll. By April 1971, the antiwar movement had been the target of almost 300 "disruptive" FBI actions, 40 percent of which were intended to prevent citizens from "speaking, teaching, writing or publishing."

After the public disclosure of these activities, Congress authorized investigating committees to probe more deeply. The Senate Select Committee to Study Governmental Operations with Respect to Intelligence Activities made the following findings:

> The Government has often undertaken the secret surveillance of citizens on the basis of their political beliefs, even when those beliefs posed no threat of violence or illegal acts. . . . The Government, operating primarily through secret informants . . . has swept in vast amounts of information about the personal lives, views, and associations of American citizens. Investigations of groups deemed potentially dangerous—and even of groups suspected of associating with potentially dangerous organizations—have continued for decades, despite the fact that those groups did not engage in unlawful activity. . . . FBI headquarters alone has developed over 500,000 domestic intelligence files. (U.S. Senate 1976, 5–6)

In March 1971, the army announced that it was banning any further collection of information about individuals and organizations unaffiliated with the military, except where essential to the military mission, and that it was destroying all material it had previously gathered. The Senate Judiciary Subcommittee on Constitutional Rights, which conducted hearings into the army's surveillance program, concluded that it had served no legitimate governmental purpose, but had seriously infringed "the rights of the citizens it was supposed to be safeguarding" (U.S. Senate 1971, 97).

In 1976, President Gerald Ford formally prohibited the CIA from using electronic or physical surveillance to collect information on domestic activities of Americans and banned the NSA from intercepting any communication made within, from or to the United States. Two years later, Congress enacted the Foreign Intelligence Surveillance Act (FISA), which was designed to prevent many of these abuses from recurring by placing sharp limits on when and how the government could pursue foreign intelligence investigations.

In 1976, the new FBI director, Clarence Kelly, publicly apologized for FBI excesses under J. Edgar Hoover, conceding that the bureau had engaged in activities that "were clearly wrong and quite indefensible" and that must "never" be repeated (*San Diego Union,* May 23, 1976, quoted in Goldstein 1983, 540–2).

That same year, Attorney General Edward Levi, following the example of Attorney General Harlan Fiske Stone after the 1919 to 1920 Red Scare, imposed stringent limitations on the investigative authority and activities of the FBI. In these "guidelines," Levi expressly prohibited the FBI from investigating, discrediting, or disrupting any group or individual on the basis of protected First Amendment activity. The guidelines declared that the FBI could investigate only criminal conduct and that it would no longer be permitted to monitor protected First Amendment activity, except in a legitimate and narrowly tailored effort to enforce the criminal law. The guidelines provided further that the FBI could not initiate an investigation of any organization engaged in protected First Amendment activity in the absence of "specific and articulable facts" justifying a criminal investigation. Finally, the guidelines adopted a series of procedural requirements to implement these restrictions. The Levi guidelines were hailed as a major advance in law enforcement and a critical step forward in protecting the rights of American citizens against zealous and misguided government officials.

The Levi guidelines represent good government at its best. Without regard to whether the limitations were required by the Constitution, and without waiting for legislative action, Levi imposed them on the FBI as a matter of sound public policy. The protection of civil liberties demands not only compliance with the Constitution, but also thoughtful, restrained use of government power.

UNCONSTITUTIONAL?

Were the activities implicated in COINTELPRO, the Huston Plan, and the army, CIA, and NSA domestic intelligence programs of the late 1960s and early 1970s unconstitutional? Some plainly were. For example, it is settled that, as a general rule, the government cannot constitutionally break into a person's home, open her mail, bug her office, or tap her telephone without probable cause and a warrant. Such activities clearly violate the Fourth Amendment, which forbids "unreasonable searches and seizures."

During the Vietnam War, the Nixon administration argued that, in order to protect the nation from attempts to attack and subvert the existing structure of government, the president was constitutionally entitled to engage in electronic surveillance of American citizens without comply-ing with the requirements of the Fourth Amendment. In *United States v. United States District Court* (Keith),[1] decided in 1972, the Supreme Court unanimously rejected this assertion, holding that that even in national security investigations the president has no lawful authority to conduct electronic surveillance of American citizens on American soil without a judicially issued search warrant based on a finding of probable cause.

The constitutionality of some of the other activities employed in this era is less certain. Consider government surveillance of public meetings and demonstrations. Suppose an antiwar group sponsors a public event at which speakers will question the wisdom and morality of a war. May the FBI send a government agent to attend the meeting in order to photograph participants and record the names of those in attendance? Under current law, this surveillance would not violate the Fourth Amendment, because the Court has held that individuals have no "reasonable expectation of privacy" in not being observed when they are voluntarily in a public place, so there is no "search" within the meaning of the Constitution.[2]

On the other hand, this practice would clearly violate the Levi guide-lines. But would it violate the First Amendment? The First and Fourth Amendments protect different values. The former protects free expression, association, and religion; the latter, one's general sense of privacy. The argu-ment that this practice violates the First Amendment, even though it does not violate the Fourth, finds support in the Supreme Court's compelled dis-closure cases of the late 1950s and early 1960s. In cases like *NAACP v. Alabama*[3] and *Gibson v. Florida Investigating Committee*,[4] the Court held that for the government to invade the privacy of protected First Amend-ment activities in at least some circumstances violates the Constitution. This is so because the freedoms of speech, association, and religion are pro-tected "not only against heavy-handed frontal attack, but also from being stifled by more subtle governmental interference."[5]

In the situation of the public meeting, knowledge that government agents (whether undercover or in uniform) are, or may be, taking names and photographs would undoubtedly chill the willingness of some people to attend the event. The fear of ending up on a government list or in an FBI or IRS or INS file merely for participating in a public rally or attend-ing a public lecture will inevitably cause some, perhaps many, people to stay away. We have seen this throughout our history. Thus, unless the government has a clear, articulable, legitimate, and evenhanded justifica-tion for engaging in such surveillance, this practice should be held to violate the First Amendment.[6]

What of the use of informers and secret agents? The Court has held that the government's use of undercover agents to deceive individuals into revealing information about themselves or inadvertently granting informers access to nonpublic meetings, places, and conversations is not a search within the meaning of the Fourth Amendment. The Court's rationale is that in day-to-day life individuals must assume the risk that those with whom they deal are not who they purport to be. Thus, if your friendly neighborhood drug dealer turns out to be a snitch or your inquisitive meterman is snooping in your basement for the government, you have no basis for complaining that this is an unreasonable search.

Whatever the merits of this conclusion in the Fourth Amendment context, it should not govern the use of such deceit to infiltrate a political or religious organization. For the government to put such organizations in a position where they have to suspect every member of secretly being a government spy would empower the government to undermine the mutual trust that is essential to effective political or religious association. As Attorney General Harlan Fiske Stone noted after World War I, "a secret police may become a menace to free government and free institutions." This practice should be held to violate the First Amendment unless the government has reasonable grounds to believe that the political or religious organization is involved in criminal activity and the investigation is narrowly tailored to that end. And for the government to plant an agent in such an organization with the express purpose of disrupting its protected First Amendment activities should be deemed a violation of the Constitution.[7]

TOLERATING DISSENT

As in the Vietnam War, the government in the war on terrorism has not attempted to prosecute its critics. Just as it would have been unthinkable during the Vietnam era for the government to have prosecuted Eugene McCarthy or George McGovern for their dissent, it would be unthinkable during the war on terrorism for the Bush administration to prosecute former Governor Howard Dean or Congressman Jack Murtha for their criticisms of the war in Iraq.

The change in the extent to which the United States has learned to tolerate dissent in wartime is quite dramatic. Compared to the repression of earlier eras, exemplified by the Sedition Act of 1798, the Espionage and Sedition Act prosecutions during World War I, and the prosecutions and blacklisting of the McCarthy era, the restraint of the past forty years is remarkable. John Yoo argues in this volume that this shift is due less to a change in our political and constitutional culture than to differences in the nature of the threats to the nation. Certainly, differences in the nature of the threats matter. But it is simply wrong not to recognize that both public attitudes and legal doctrine have evolved. We have come to understand better both the importance of individual liberties and the dangers of their suppression. This is not to say that, in the face of a much greater threat to our security, we would not again panic and revert to the overt suppression of dissent. It is to say, though, that we would be much less likely to embrace such measures today. It is one of the greater features of a self-governing society—and of the rule of law—that we are capable of learning from our mistakes.

On the other hand, sadly and dangerously, in disregard of the lessons of the Vietnam era, the government has once again launched aggressive domestic surveillance programs against the American people. Three examples, in particular, are worth noting. In the quarter century after Edward Levi formulated the FBI guidelines, two of his successors, William French Smith and Richard Thornburgh, attorneys general under Presidents Reagan and George H. W. Bush, weakened the restrictions, but left their essential core intact. In 2002, however, Attorney General John Ashcroft effectively dismantled the Levi guidelines. Ashcroft expressly authorized the FBI to enter any place or attend any event open to the public to gather information that may be relevant to criminal activity, thus enabling the FBI once again to monitor a wide range of constitutionally protected political and religious activities without any showing that unlawful conduct might be afoot.

Second, section 215 of the PATRIOT Act authorizes executive branch officials investigating terrorism to demand records from businesses and other institutions and organizations without any showing of probable cause. This includes not only business records, but personal medical records, financial records, educational records, and library and bookstore records. At first blush, one might think this would violate the Fourth Amendment. But the Supreme Court has held that an individual has no "reasonable expectation of privacy" in information he voluntarily exposes to strangers, including those who work for banks, hospitals, universities, Internet companies, bookstores, and libraries.[8] Hence, section 215 does not violate the Fourth Amendment.

As noted earlier, however, that a law does not violate the Fourth Amendment does not mean that it doesn't violate the First. The issue here is somewhat similar to the question posed about government surveillance or infiltration of political organizations. If FBI agents can create a file on an individual merely because she bought or borrowed a book on, say, the history of terrorism or terrorist practices, and this file might turn up sometime in the future when she applies for a government job, she will think twice before reading such a book.

Although reasonable minds can differ on whether the application of section 215 to libraries and bookstores violates the Constitution, that is not the only question. The Constitution provides only the minimum protection of individual liberty in our society. For the most part, we rely on common sense, a commitment to traditional American values, and a decent respect for the fundamental freedoms of the American people to protect our liberty. Although librarians and others have identified legitimate concerns about section 215, and although members of Congress, including some Republicans, have supported changes in the act to address those concerns, the Bush administration has fiercely opposed any significant change in the PATRIOT Act that would substantially mitigate the dangers to free expression posed by this provision. As in its repeal of the Levi guidelines, the Bush administration has disregarded the lessons of the past and failed in its responsibility to protect not only American's safety, but its freedoms as well.

Third, one of the most important laws resulting from the Vietnam era abuses was the Foreign Intelligence Surveillance Act of 1978. FISA was designed to strike a careful balance between protecting civil liberties and enabling the government to protect the nation against foreign enemies. It established special rules dealing with foreign intelligence surveillance, and set up a special "secret" court, the Foreign Intelligence Surveillance Court, to handle these matters, but it retained the probable cause and warrant requirements of the Fourth Amendment. FISA criminalizes any electronic surveillance not authorized by statute, and sets forth the exclusive means by which foreign intelligence surveillance may be conducted.

In January 2006, the *New York Times* disclosed that in early 2002 President Bush had secretly authorized the National Security Agency to circumvent FISA by conducting foreign intelligence surveillance of American citizens on American soil without any showing of probable cause and without first obtaining a warrant from the FISA Court. This program directly violated FISA and very likely violated the Constitution. The president's response to the disclosure was to initiate a Justice Department investigation to identify the sources of the leak and to condemn the *New York Times* for reporting the story, which he labeled a shameful act that undermined the nation's security.

The Bush administration offered three arguments in defense of this program, which has resulted in the secret surveillance of thousands of American citizens. First, it argued that foreign intelligence surveillance is not governed by the Fourth Amendment. During the Vietnam War, the Nixon administration had argued that national security surveillance was not subject to the Fourth Amendment. As we saw earlier, in the Keith decision the Supreme Court unanimously and unequivocally rejected this argument. The Court set aside the question of foreign intelligence surveillance, however, as posing an issue not then before it. Although this therefore remains an open question, the logic and reasoning of Keith powerfully apply to foreign intelligence as well as national security investigations, especially when they involve American citizens on American soil and when the program is as loosely defined as the Bush spy program.

Second, defenders of the Bush program argue that it does not violate FISA because Congress's enactment of the Authorization to Use Military Force (AUMF) implicitly overrode FISA. The AUMF authorized the president "to use all necessary and appropriate force against those nations, organizations, or persons he determines planned, authorized, committed, or aided the terrorist attacks of September 11, 2001 . . . in order to prevent any future acts of international terrorism against the United States."[9] Although the AUMF certainly gave the president certain powers, for example, the power to invade Iraq, it did not in any way amend FISA. When there is an apparent conflict between a specific law and a general law, the specific law governs. Clearly, FISA is the specific law in this context. More fundamental, though, is that FISA expressly anticipated what would happen in the event of a declared war, and provided that in such an event the president could lawfully use warrantless foreign intelligence surveillance for a maximum of fifteen days, after which he would have to comply with FISA or formally seek a specific congressional amendment of the law. The AUMF, of course, falls far short of a declaration of war, but even if we were to treat it as the equivalent of a declaration of war, the NSA program does not in any way purport to address the fifteen-day provision of FISA. In short, nothing in the AUMF expressly or impliedly authorized the president to violate FISA.

Finally, defenders of the Bush program argue that the president, as commander in chief of the army and navy, has the inherent authority to implement warrantless electronic surveillance of American citizens on American soil, without probable, and without going to the FISA Court, if he deems it necessary.

The Supreme Court recently dealt with this issue in its 2004 decision in *Hamdi v. Rumsfeld*,[10] which dealt with the president's authority to detain an American citizens captured on the battlefield in Afghanistan. On the one hand, the Court found that the detention of such individuals was a "fundamental and accepted incident to war," and thus was within the president's authority. On the other hand, the Court made clear that the president does not have inherent constitutional authority to hold such individuals indefinitely or to deny them due process in deciding whether they are in fact enemy combatants. As Justice O'Connor proclaimed, "a state of war is not a blank check for the President when it comes to the rights of the Nation's citizens."[11]

Moreover, the Court has long recognized that the president's inherent authority as commander in chief is at its lowest ebb when, as here, the Congress has expressly prohibited the action he seeks to take. Whatever the commander in chief power may say about other circumstances, it does not give the president the authority to override both the Fourth Amendment and express congressional legislation to wiretap American citizens on American soil without either probable cause or a warrant. This is an excessive and unjustified assertion of the president's inherent authority, and is not by any means "a fundamental and accepted incident to war."

This is not to say that the president had no recourse if he believed that FISA unduly restricts his ability to protect the nation. What he could and should have done is to urge Congress to amend FISA by enacting new legislation, which could then be properly tested in a court of law. Instead, he sought to elide the constitutional process entirely and surreptitiously ordered the NSA spy program without either congressional affirmation or judicial review.

Only time will tell whether Congress, the courts,[12] and the American people will act on the lessons of the Vietnam era and eliminate these violations of individual liberty before, rather than only after, the conflict is over.

NOTES

1. *United States v. United States District Court*, 407 U.S. 297 (1972).
2. *Katz v. United States*, 389 U.S. 347 (1967).
3. 357 U.S. 449 (1958).
4. 372 U.S. 539 (1963).
5. *Bates v. City of Little Rock*, 361 U.S. 516, 523 (1960). See also *Shelton v. Tucker*, 364 U.S. 479 (1960), holding unconstitutional a state law requiring teachers to disclose all organizations with which they were affiliated.
6. If the government has a clear, legitimate, and evenhanded justification for being present at the public event, its conduct may be warranted. For example, the government has a responsibility to provide reasonable police protection

at mass public demonstrations. The presence of the police for that purpose is constitutionally permissible. But this would not justify "taking names" or photographs of individuals engaged in constitutionally protected First Amendment activity. On the other hand, if the government has reasonable grounds to believe that criminal activity is afoot, it may engage in surveillance, including "taking names," as long as its purpose is to investigate criminal activity and its investigation is narrowly tailored to that end.

7. In *Laird Secretary of Defense v. Tatum*, 408 U.S. 1 (1972), the Court declined to rule on the constitutionality of Army domestic intelligence activities, including the monitoring of public meetings, because the complainants lacked "standing." That is, they could not show that information gathered by the Army had actually been used to harm them. The Court held that the mere fact that their First Amendment activities would be "chilled" by the continuation of such activities was not sufficient to allow them to challenge the constitutionality of the surveillance. See *New Alliance Party v. Federal Bureau of Investigation*, 858 F Supp 425 (SD NY 1994) (same with respect to a challenge to FBI surveillance activities).

8. See *United States v. Miller*, 425 U.S. 435 (1976) (no "reasonable expectation of privacy" in banking records).

9. Pub. L. No. 107-40, 111 Stat. 224 (2001).

10. *Hamdi v. Rumsfeld*, 542 U.S. 207 (2004).

11. Ibid. at 516, 531

12. In *ACLU v. NSA*, 438 F. Supp. 2d. 754 (E.D. Mich.), a federal district judge held that the NSA program violated both FISA and the Fourth Amendment. On appeal, however, the United States Court of Appeals for the Sixth Circuit, in a two-to-one decision, invoked *Laird v. Tatum* for the conclusion that the plaintiffs did not have standing to challenge the constitutionality of the program.

REFERENCES

Berman, Jerry J., and Morton H. Halperin, editors. 1975. *The Abuses of the Intelligence Agencies*. Washington: Center for National Security Studies.

Evans, Rowland, Jr., and Robert D. Novak. 1971. *Nixon in the White House: The Frustration of Power*. New York: Random House.

Goldstein, Robert J. 1983. *Political Repression in Nineteenth-Century Europe*. Lanham, Md.: Rowman and Littlefield.

Kissinger, Henry. 1979. *White House Years*. New York: Little, Brown.

Lukas, J. Anthony. 1976. *Nightmare: The Underside of the Nixon Years*. New York: Viking.

Theoharis, Athan. 1978. *Spying on Americans: Political Surveillance from Hoover to the Huston Plan*. Philadelphia, Pa.: Temple University Press.

United States. 1976. *Hearings Before the Select Committee to Study Government Operations with Respect to Intelligence Activities of the United States Senate*, vol. 6, *Federal*

Bureau of Investigation. 94th Cong., 1st Sess. Washington: Government Printing Office.

U.S. Congress. Senate [U.S. Senate]. 1965. *Congressional Record.* 89th Cong., 1st sess., 1965. Vol. 111, Part I. Washington: Government Printing Office.

————. 1971. Committee on the Judiciary. *Army Surveillance of Civilians: A Documentary Analysis by the Staff of the Subcommittee on Constitutional Rights.* 92nd Cong., 2nd Sess. 97.

————. 1976. Select Committee to Study Governmental Operations with Respect to Intelligence Operations. *Intelligence Activities and the Rights of Americans,* Book II, *Final Report.* 94th Cong., 2nd Sess. (April 26, 1976).

Wise, David. 1976. *The American Police State: The Government Against the People.* New York: Random House.

PART II

THE MODERN EXPERIENCE IN CONTEXT

CHAPTER 6

DEFINING THE NATION: 1790 TO 1898

JAN ELLEN LEWIS

National security, like beauty, is in the eye of the beholder. The term is fraught with emotion yet devoid of specific meaning. This proposition may seem exceedingly provocative, but consider how difficult it is for nations to separate the actual conditions of national security from feelings and perceptions of that elusive state.[1] Any discussion of the connection between national security and civil liberties must confront this dilemma: national security is, to a significant degree, a subjective term, itself the object of political conflict and argumentation, intimately connected, moreover, to the nation's sense of itself as a nation.

This problem is readily apparent when we consider the first century of the history of the United States. Seyla Benhabib has recently observed that there is "an irresolvable contradiction . . . between the expansive and inclusionary principles of moral and political universalism, as anchored in universal human rights, and the particularlistic and exclusionary conceptions of democratic closure" (Benhabib 2004, 19; Zolberg 2006). In no modern nation is the contradiction more evident than in the United States.[2] As many scholars have noted, the United States came into being with a very weak sense of national identity. The nation was created by a revolution that posited that indeed there was a nation, even before there was a strong and distinctive sense of national identity to sustain it, yet it was, supposedly, a nation based not on particularistic or exclusionary conceptions of the nation, but on more universal principles, such as the ones articulated in the Declaration of Independence. The Revolution offered several propositions about what the character of the nation was, but these were propositions only, little more than wishful thinking about the suitability of the American people for government based upon universal principles. It was left to later generations to define the nation and to forge an American nationalism, one that attempted to reconcile universal principles with the sort of boundary setting that is intrinsic to the modern democratic state (Wood 1969; Miller 1961; Walzer 1983).

Not only was American nationalism protean in this formative period, but the very shape of the nation was literally in flux. For the first half of the nineteenth century, the national borders to the north, west, and south kept shifting as the United States acquired additional territory by warfare, treaty, and annexation, in the process incorporating new peoples with other national loyalties into the nation. National borders were both unfixed and permeable, which encouraged independent citizens to attempt to appropriate additional territories to be annexed to the nation as well as fears that outsiders would invade the nation or detach parts of it to turn over to rival countries (Thomson 1994).

Given the unstable nature of both American nationalism and national boundaries in this formative period of the country's history, it should not be surprising that national security was a highly contested topic, involving questions not only of security per se but also ones about the definition of the nation. National identity and national security were defined reciprocally, typically against perceived enemies, external and internal; this was intrinsic to the process of boundary setting. To identify a threat to national security was also to define an enemy, and to define an enemy was to identify a threat to national security. At the same time, because all the terms in these equations—national security, enemy, the nation itself—were so slippery and because they were defined in relationship to each other, such acts as taking up arms against the United States or its citizens or advocating armed rebellion or terrorist activity did not necessarily render one an enemy, an alien, or a threat to national security and hence a person whose civil liberties might lawfully be abrogated. Rather, the security of a person's civil liberties depended more upon whether he (or occasionally she) was, at that moment, considered a member in good standing of the bounded world of the political community.

This chapter examines several periods in the nation's history when civil liberties were imperiled. The first was during the Quasi-War with France in 1798, when Congress passed the Alien and Sedition Acts. The second was during the War of 1812, when New England Federalists opposed the war and mobs destroyed Federalist newspaper offices but the administration declined to pass a new Sedition Act. The third was in the mid-1830s, when Southerners and their sympathizers suppressed the mails and attacked abolitionist newspapers in order to prevent the spread of abolitionist ideas. The fourth was during the Civil War, when, in several well known cases, civil liberties were suppressed. The fifth was in the post–Civil War South, both during Reconstruction and after the removal of federal troops, when an insurgency movement took aim at the civil liberties of the former slaves.

Even a cursory comparison of these four periods, however, reveals significant differences. During the Quasi-War, Federalists clearly believed that national security was in peril; the Alien and Sedition Acts were their response. A number of men were tried and convicted under the provisions of the Sedition Act, but because the convictions of the men were not challenged and the acts either expired or were rescinded, the trials have left no constitutional trace. Most historians and jurists treat them as an embarrassment and an aberration. During the War of 1812, some New Englanders traded with the British enemy, interfered with militia recruitment, and even, in some cases, appeared to welcome a British victory. Mobs attacked opponents of the war, especially in Baltimore; government officials either would not or could not intervene. Nonetheless, the Madison administration chose not to renew the Sedition Act. In the antebellum period, particularly after the Nat Turner rebellion, Southerners and their sympathizers in the North expressed increasing fear of slave revolt. With the consent of the federal government, abolitionist mail to the slave South was embargoed, and, in the gag rule, Congress refused all petitions against slavery. In addition, mobs attacked abolitionist presses and publishers in the North as well as the South, sometimes with the encouragement and even participation of government officials.

During the Civil War, the nation, quite obviously, was at war. Abraham Lincoln suspended habeas corpus, and the government restricted the right to free speech. These actions, however, led to several notable court cases in which the government was overruled. Historians and jurists continue to debate whether, or how far, Lincoln overreached. Less notice has been taken of the abrogation of civil liberties in the South, which included a domestic passport system and an Alien Enemies Act. After the formal conclusion of the Civil War, white Southerners mobilized to keep former slaves from exercising their political and civil rights. The national government responded to this insurgency movement by imposing military rule and passing several pieces of legislation designed to protect the civil liberties of the former slaves; in addition, Ulysses S. Grant temporarily suspended habeas corpus. After the withdrawal of federal troops, however, episodic terrorist activity, from which neither the federal or state governments offered any protection, effectively deprived blacks of their civil liberties. Although this terrorist activity was the continuation of the postwar insurgency, it was defined, by and large, as local political action or lamentable random violence, rather than as warfare or a threat to national security.

This brief survey of the connection between national security and civil liberties suggests not only that the very term *national security* is remarkably malleable but that threats to civil liberties have emanated both from governmental action and from the failure of the government to offer protection. It also suggests that an invasion by a foreign army need not lead to the abrogation of civil liberties by the state. A more thorough examination of these periods of American history will be necessary, however, before we can offer an explanation for why some attacks and threatened attacks have led the federal government to abrogate civil liberties (or look the other way when they were abrogated by others) and others have not.

THE QUASI-WAR

What we today call the Alien and Sedition Acts were, in fact, four separate pieces of legislation passed by Congress in the early summer of 1798: the Naturalization Act, the Alien Friends Act, the Alien Enemies Act, and "An Act for the Punishment of Certain Crimes against the United States," known as the Sedition Act. All of them sought to protect the United States from enemies on their own soil at a time when war with France seemed imminent. The congressional debates over these pieces of legislation reveal conflicting ideas about citizenship and national security and, in particular, how threats to the nation might be manifested.

In this context, it is important to note that the Naturalization Act of 1798 was the third American naturalization act in less than a decade. The terms of the first, passed in 1790, had been quite liberal. Citizenship was available to any "free white person" who had resided in the United States for two years, provided that he was "a person of good character" and swore to support the Constitution (*Statutes at Large* 1851, Act of March 26, 1790, ch. 3, 1 Stat. 103). Here we see the nation's first formal act of boundary setting. Without any discussion, nonwhite people[3] were marked as outside the political community. Other provisions of the Naturalization Act of 1790, however, were contested. The waiting period of two years, remarkably liberal for its time, was the product of compromise not only between those who wanted an even shorter period of residence and those who preferred a longer one, but also between different theories of citizenship. Indeed, the two issues were closely related. Rogers M. Smith has suggested that the debate was between those who thought that citizenship was a matter of volition and consent and those who thought that it should derive from character, which was a product of habit, training, experience, and culture (Smith 1997). In the congressional debates on the Naturalization Act of 1790, this debate was framed not so much in terms of abstract theories of citizenship as in a discussion about the meaning of the American Revolution. Here we see the contradiction between universalist, inclusionary principles and more particularist and exclusionary conceptions of the nation. Those who favored a restrictive naturalization policy believed that the United States was exceptional and that the Revolution had made the Americans a distinctive people, markedly different from the inhabitants of other nations. In the debate over the Naturalization Act, Michael Stone, representative from Maryland, explained that the current inhabitants of the United States "have been engaged in a long, hazardous, and expensive war. They . . . feel . . . a laudable vanity in having effected what the most sanguine hardly dared to contemplate. . . . The admission of a great number of foreigners . . . may tincture the system with the dregs of their former habits, and corrupt what we believe the most pure of all human institutions" (United States 1789, 1st Cong., 2nd sess., 1157–58).

At issue in this formative period of American nationhood was the question of just what made a person an American. Given the novelty—in both senses of the word—of the United States, this was a pressing question. If the United States were to admit to citizenship those who had not experienced the Revolution, then at least it should require a period of probation long enough, as Pennsylvania's Thomas Hartley put it, to "give a man an opportunity of esteeming the Government from knowing its intrinsic value." The capacity for republican government came not from a "bare oath" to the Constitution but from a residency in the United States, during which a person might "have an opportunity of knowing the circumstances of our Government, and . . . have acquired a taste for this kind of Government" (United States 1789, 1st Cong., 2nd sess., 1147, 1157). Surely, this was the principle that the other nations of the world followed. It was unheard of to put new immigrants on the same footing as those who were born in the country, and great harm could come from admitting immigrants too quickly to citizenship. Was it not possible, one congressman asked, that without a significant residency requirement, on election day ship captains would round up their crews and take them to the polls, in order to throw the election to their favorite faction? (1161). Perhaps, several representatives even suggested, the United States should do as "the old nations of Europe" had done and draw "a line between citizens and aliens." Because the "great object of emigration is generally with the view of procuring a more comfortable subsistence, or to better the circumstances of the individuals," the United States might admit foreigners and let them purchase and work on the land without giving them the right to participate in government (1148, 1159–60). Here was the vision of American citizenship at its most particularist.

If some feared for the fragility of the new nation, others saw in the novelty of the new nation and its universalist ideals a remarkable strength. Virginia's John Page, for example, argued against a long period of probation. Instead "a more liberal system ought to prevail." He warned that "we shall be inconsistent with ourselves, if, after boasting of having opened an asylum for the oppressed of all nations, and established a government which is the admiration of the world"—on this particular he and Stone were in agreement—"we make the terms of admission to the full enjoyment of that asylum so hard as is now proposed." Page believed that the liberal ideal on which the United States was founded was so strong that the new country could easily absorb what might seem the most unpromising candidates for citizenship. "It is nothing to us, whether Jews or Roman Catholics settle amongst us; whether subjects of Kings or citizens of free States wish to reside in the United States, they will find it their interest to be good citizens, and neither their religious nor political opinions can injure us, if we have good laws, well executed" (United States 1789, 1st Cong., 2nd sess., 1148–49). Like the proponents of an extended period of probation, Page believed in the uniqueness of the American form of government and the transformative power of its ideals. The disagreement was about how fragile the new nation was, how vulnerable to unrepublican outsiders.

Although Congress compromised on a two-year period of residency, subsequent events that made the United States seem more vulnerable, at least to some, renewed the debates. This was by no means a settled question. The Naturalization Act of 1795 increased the probation period to five years. An influx of immigrants fleeing upheavals in France, Haiti, Germany, and Ireland had increased American anxiety (Kettner 1978, 239–40). The objective, according to Massachusetts' Fisher Ames, was "to make a rule of naturalization for the admission of aliens to become citizens, on such terms as may consist with our tranquility and safety" (United States 1789, 3rd Cong., 2nd sess., 1048).

By 1798, war with France seemed imminent, making the question of national security even more pressing. France was at war with Britain, and although only a few years earlier, France's support had been critical to the American revolutionaries' victory, now France was interdicting American trade with Britain, seizing ships and their cargoes as well as their crews, using the proceeds to help finance the war with Britain. France refused to recognize American neutrality. Moreover, a few years earlier, France's minister to the United States, the notorious Citizen Genet, had attempted to stir up support for his government by appealing to the American people directly, over the heads of George Washington and his administration. Although the government that Genet represented fell and he sought and was granted asylum in the United States, the memory, particularly of the willingness of Jefferson's Democratic-Republican party to entertain the agent of a foreign nation, remained.

In 1798, John Adams was president, and relations with France had become even worse. Adams sent a delegation to France to negotiate, but the French Foreign Minister Talleyrand's agents—subsequently referred to as X, Y, and Z—refused to negotiate with the Americans unless they paid off Talleyrand personally and provided a substantial loan to his nation; in addition, the United States must assume the debts owed to Americans by France. "You must pay money—you must pay a great deal of money," agent Y, Jean Claude Hottinguer, explained (Elkins and McKitrick 1993, 571). Whereas Talleyrand's demand for a bribe was unusual, the one for a loan to France was not; the Directory had embarked upon an aggressive foreign policy and needed the means to finance it. Although subsequent accounts suggest that the American envoys took umbrage at the demands for bribes, at the time, the chief concern seemed to be that even if the Americans acceded, the French would not stay bought, and, as John Marshall, one of the envoys, put it, France's "depredations on us would be continued" (Ziesche 2006, 174). The American agents left France, and war seemed imminent.

Certainly, war was what a powerful faction within the Federalist Party wanted. As Philipp Ziesche has recently argued, they saw war as an instrument of nationalism and they "looked to war as a panacea that would purge the nation of its enemies on the inside and unite it against those on the outside."[4] George Cabot, a prominent Federalist, thought that "we have much more to fear from peace than war" and that "war, open and declared, would not only deprive our external enemy of his best hopes, but would also extinguish the hopes of internal foes." The Federalists were deeply suspicious of the cosmopolitanism of their Francophile Democratic-Republican opponents, which, they feared, would "undermine the ties of nationhood that preserved social order and open the nation to foreign subversion" (Ziesche 2006, 184–5). To the Federalists, hence, subversion was not only a matter of clear, identifiable acts, for example French privateers preying on American shipping or Citizen Genet appealing to the people over the heads of their elected officials, but also something murkier and less tangible, such as words and deeds that might undermine the attachment of the American people to their nation.

This was the context in which the Alien and Sedition Acts were passed. With their new government barely ten years old, Americans were acutely aware of the novelty of their experiment in republican government (Freeman 2003). To the Federalists, the collapse of the French Revolution into horrific violence was only further proof of the fragility of republics. The Democratic-Republicans, however, were more sanguine. They thought that the Directory, its flaws notwithstanding, had at least brought stability to France, and were loath to enter into a war with a sister republic. In the spring of 1798, even before word of the failure of the American emissaries even to secure a formal meeting with Talleyrand made its way back to the United States, the Federalists, who held a slight majority in Congress, were making preparations for war, by raising an army and levying the taxes to pay for it. The Alien and Sedition Acts were an integral part of the preparation for war.

The Federalist majority thought the very survival of the new United States was in peril, and the subsequent debates were phrased in terms of national security. Jonathan Dayton believed that "the time was arrived when we ought to take measures for our own security," and Harrison Gray Otis thought "this country to be in a very hazardous situation" and that consequently "it would be prudent to guard against it before it comes." It is almost impossible to exaggerate the anxiety of the Federalists. Otis saw "an irruption in Europe more to be dreaded than the irruption of the Goths and Vandals. . . . everything great and good destroyed," and he feared that "our country [may] meet with a similar fate" (United States 1789, 5th Cong., 2nd sess., 1696, 1736). Federalist congressmen spun out feverish scenarios by which France would invade and conquer England and move on to the United States, or, perhaps, France would try to get at England by sending "thirty or forty thousand men, to come out and invade our country first." Another scenario had England, "a nation, whom, it is frequently said, would rejoice in our destruction," watching happily as France invaded and subjugated the United States (1696, also 1692).

The Federalists' Republican opponents insisted that the fears of a French invasion were absurd, as indeed they were. Albert Gallatin tried both reason and ridicule. He noted that France, which had been unable to secure a loan on the international markets, simply lacked the resources to support an invasion "twelve hundred leagues from home." He implied that those who argued that France would attack the United States instead of England, "the only enemy France has left," must think that their fellow congressmen were fools. In exasperation, he resorted to ridicule, saying that a South Carolina Federalist was so certain of invasion that he had "even pointed out the very spot at which the enemy was to land, the route they were going to take." Gallatin simply could not take seriously all of this "speaking of falling mountains, unfurled banners, &c" (United States 1789, 5th Cong., 2nd sess., 1693, 4, 2). Republicans, however, could indulge in their own sort of fanciful thinking. Nathaniel Macon did not believe that the French would invade the United States, but even if it did, he thought "the militia would be able to kill them as fast" as they landed, and in any event "did not believe all the Powers of Europe united could subjugate the United States" (1699).

The prospect of war with France released deep anxieties about the security of the United States, not just its capacity to withstand a foreign invasion, but the viability of its republican form of government. When John Dennis warned that "there was great danger in conceiving ourselves too secure" (United States 1789, 5th Cong., 2nd sess., 1697), he encouraged his fellow congressmen to imagine the worst possible outcome. Unable to catch their Republican opponents up in their fantasies of destruction, they turned on them, imagining them an internal enemy. David Brooks of New York warned that "we have those within our bosom who would give up our country too." He implicitly accused his congressional opponents of disloyalty. "Were France herself to speak through an American mouth, I cannot conceive what we would say more than what we have heard from certain gentlemen to effect her purposes." Their reservations were only so many "Constitutional questions, theories, doubts, nice distinctions, learned metaphysical disquisitions, and long speeches to excite divisions, to encourage their party, occupy time, and protract the debate to an interminable and provoking extent" by "men who have been long devoted to" the cause of France (1481–2). Connecticut's John Allen responded to those who urged caution by asking, "Is this the language of an American who loves his country? No, sir, it is the language of a foreign agent" (1483). Nathaniel Macon was incredulous at the Federalists' wild fantasies. "Is there an American who believes that one half of the people of this country are devoted to France?" Did his colleagues truly think that "men who had fought and won the Revolution" would now "relinquish the prize to any nation?" (1699).

Nathaniel Smith in fact had no doubts. He imagined that France wanted to "subjugate" the United States, and it would do so "through the medium of a revolution." The only thing stopping the French, he thought, was that the opinions expressed by the Republican opposition were not more widely shared. "If they were, he should count upon nothing less than revolution and subjection" (1700). Smith came close to charging his political opponents with treason.

These were strong accusations to make against fellow congressmen, not to mention Revolutionary war veterans such as Macon. This was the climate in which the Alien and Sedition Acts were passed. The first of these pieces of legislation, the Naturalization Act of 1798 (*Statutes at Large* 1851, An Act to Establish an Uniform Rule of Naturalization, June 18, 1798, ch. 54, 1 Stat. 566–69), was designed to keep out of the country the sort of men who might foment a revolution against the new government. Under its terms, the period of probation was extended to fourteen years, the highest it has ever been at any time. Once again, the debate in Congress was between those who were skeptical that outsiders could ever become true Americans and those who thought that a republican frame of mind was all that was necessary. In the intervening decade, however, the center of the discussion had shifted perceptibly to the right. The most conservative of the Federalists now argued against admitting any aliens, even those living in the United States at the time, to full citizenship. Instead, they advocated a two-tier system, under which aliens might become residents and hold property but not be allowed to vote or hold office. Robert Goodloe Harper thought that the foreign-born "could not have the same views and attachments with native citizens" (1568; Kettner 1978, 244–5).

The Republican advocates of a more liberal naturalization policy had shifted to the right, as well. They retreated in the face of the Federalist assault on their patriotism, and there was no opposition to the principle of a significant waiting period, perhaps the five-year probation mandated by the current law. Nathaniel Macon was forced to agree that for the past several years, "people of all sorts of politics had come to this country, from the highest aristocrat to the greatest Jacobin." Having ceded the Federalists their main point—that unrepublican foreigners were taking advantage of the United States' liberal naturalization policies—Macon could only warn "that gentlemen . . . will go too far in this business" (United States 1789, 5th Cong., 2nd sess., 1780).

With the Federalists holding a majority in Congress and the Republicans conceding that some aliens were undesirable, the way was paved for legislation to deal with the threat supposedly presented by aliens already residing in the country and disloyal American citizens. Over the course of the decade, the Federalists had seen their abstract notions of assimilable foreigners take living form as thousands of immigrants from Ireland, France, and Germany found refuge in the United States. Many of them were political radicals, fleeing oppressive governments, and they aligned themselves with the emergent Republican party, some of them editing opposition newspapers. It is impossible, hence, to separate Federalist fears of invasion from without and revolution from within from their animosity toward their Republican opponents. The debates on the Alien and Sedition Acts reflect this conflation of threats to national security with political opposition.

The first of the Alien Acts, the Alien Enemies Act, was passed with relatively little opposition. It empowered the president, in the event of a declared war, to apprehend, confine, or deport any (adult male) aliens who were natives of the enemy country (*Statutes at Large* 1851, An Act Respecting Alien Enemies, July 6, 1798, ch. 66, 1 Stat. 577–78; Stone 2004, 30). Much more controversial was the Alien Friends Act, which authorized the president to order out of the country any alien he deemed "dangerous to the peace and safety of the United States." It was irrelevant which nation the immigrant came from. And making even more clear the political purposes of the act, it was set to expire in two years, at the end of John Adams's presidency, whether the United States was at peace or war[5] (*Statutes at Large* 1851, An Act Concerning Aliens, June 25, 1798, ch 58, 1 Stat. 570–72).

The debate on the Alien Friends Act proceeded much like that on the Naturalization Act. The opponents protested that the Federalists intended to create a two-tiered system of citizen and denizen, with the latter not "entitled to the protection of our laws" or basic civil liberties such as habeas corpus and trial by jury.[6] They warned too, that if such protections could be taken from aliens, they could be removed from citizens as well, for, as Albert Gallatin noted, the Bill of Rights spoke "not of citizens but of persons" (United States 1789, 5th Cong., 2nd sess., 2012, 1982). The Federalists responded that in such dangerous times, "uncommon measures were justifiable" to protect national security (1986). The Republicans demanded proof of the threat to the nation that the Federalists perceived. Robert Livingston insisted that "we must legislate upon facts, not on surmises; he must have evidence, not vague suspicions. . . . What facts have been produced?" He did not believe that any "plots have been detected, or are even reasonably suspected here" (2006). Albert Gallatin issued a challenge: "If there are gentlemen possessed of facts of this kind, it their duty to lay them before the House" (1980). The Federalists thought that the threat was self-evident and that no further facts were necessary. Robert Goodloe Harper did not believe that the laws already on the books were sufficient. "Are we to wait . . . until a judicial process can be entered upon? To stay until the dagger is plunged into our bosoms . . . ?" Once again, he flung the charge of disloyalty at his political opponents. Only "the worst of traitors and assassins" to their country would fail to "resist those attempts which are made to bind us hand and foot, until our enemy comes upon us" (1992).

Although no one was ever deported under the Alien Friends Act, it achieved its purpose nonetheless by cutting off the flow of immigration to the United States and causing aliens within the country to flee (Stone 2004, 33). In considering the Alien and Sedition Acts, as well as legislation that curtailed civil liberties in later periods such as the Espionage Act of 1917, the Sedition Act of 1918, as well as the PATRIOT Act of 2001, it is important to look beyond the prosecutions they engendered to the effect on political life more generally. The Sedition Act thus accomplished its ends both directly and indirectly, both by criminalizing criticism of the government and by its chilling effect. This act made it illegal to "write, print, utter or publish . . . any false, scandalous and malicious writing against the government of the United States, or either house of the Congress of the United States, or the President . . . with intent to defame [them], or to bring them . . . into contempt or disrepute; or to excite against them . . . the hatred of the good people of the United States." Violators were to be punished by imprisonment of up to two years and a fine of up to $2,000 (*Statutes at Large* 1851, An Act for the Punishment of Certain Crimes Against the United States, July 14, 1798, ch. 74, 1 Stat. 596–97). The target was newspaper editors, in particular those whose papers were critical of Adams and his administration. Little attempt was made to argue that the legislation was necessary to protect the nation from a French invasion; rather, the perceived danger was an internal enemy, the Republican opposition.

The Republicans understood that the bill was a political one. As Albert Gallatin, the most vigorous of the opponents of this entire rash of legislation, noted, the Sedition Act should "be considered only as a weapon used by a party now in power, in order to perpetuate their authority and preserve their present places" (United States 1789, 5th Cong., 2nd sess., 2110). The Federalists, however, deemed their opponents enemies of the state, outside the body politic, at the same time that they insisted that they were the true protectors of republican government. "The people I venerate," John Allen claimed. "They are truly sovereign; but . . . a mob, I know them not; if they oppose the laws, they are insurgents and rebels; they are not the people" (2096). The Republicans tried every means of argument at their disposal—logic, ridicule, demands for evidence, history, political philosophy, constitutional exegesis, and warnings of worse things to come—in order to defeat this obnoxious piece of legislation. Their anger and anxiety fairly leap off the pages of the congressional debates almost two centuries later. Why, Albert Gallatin wanted to know, was such a law necessary now? How could the nation have survived so long without it? He demanded that the Federalists "prove that the necessity now exists which heretofore did not exist." He accused them of what we would call McCarthyite tactics— promising "to unfold a plot in which not one member on this floor did believe" (2161). The lack of evidence, however, did not bother Federalist Robert Goodloe Harper. "Because proof is not produced in a fortnight, it does not follow that it will not be produced" at some later time, perhaps in a month, perhaps by the beginning of the next session. Then again, "legal proof was one thing, and he did not know that he should ever be able to produce it" (2166). The Federalists tended to fall back, also, on the kind of tautology often used by those who blithely restrict civil liberties. As Samuel Dana put it, "no honest man wanted the liberty of malicious falsehood—and this law would operate against no other publications" (2156). By definition, only the guilty would be punished; the innocent had nothing to fear.

The story of the prosecutions under the Sedition Act has been told often and told well. The government obtained fourteen indictments under the act. Both the timing and the targets of the prosecutions demonstrate that the objective was to secure Adams's reelection by silencing the president's critics. Timothy Pickering, Adams's secretary of state, led the administration's efforts. He read the Republican newspapers carefully, looking for opportunities to prosecute. At the same time, voluntary informants gladly recommended targets to him. Prosecutions were initiated against four of the top five Republican newspapers as well as a number of smaller presses. Individual newspapers were either suppressed or put out of business altogether. Urged on by the Federalist press, citizens sometimes took matters into their own hands, once almost tarring and feathering the editor William Duane until he was rescued by sympathizers and another time, beating him until he was unconscious, the latter performed by a group of soldiers (Stone 2004, 48–65; Pasley 2001, 125, 189–90; Smith 1956, 176–87, 285). Vermont Congressman Matthew Lyon, long a thorn in the Federalists' side, was in the middle of his campaign for reelection in a swing district. He was indicted and convicted for publishing a letter in a local newspaper that accused Adams of "unbounded thirst for ridiculous pomp, foolish adulation or selfish avarice" and several related character flaws (Smith 1956, 230); he was sentenced to a fine of $1,000 and four months in jail (Stone 2004, 51). Thomas Cooper, a Pennsylvania editor and essayist, was indicted and convicted for listing what he believed to be Adams's chief failures as president, such as incurring "the expense of a permanent navy" (Smith 1956, 314) and reducing the credit of the United States. He was sentenced to six months in prison and a $400 fine. Supreme Court Justice Samuel Chase presided over the trial, in the process committing what one constitutional scholar has recently termed "memorable improprieties" (Stone 2004, 58). He effectively played the part of judge and prosecutor both. He told the jury that Cooper was trying to "arouse the people against the President so as to influence their minds against him on the next election" (Stone 2004, 59). As Chase's comments make clear, the Federalists were trying to criminalize political opposition.

Today some of the prosecutions look ridiculous. In Newark, New Jersey, Luther Baldwin was sentenced to prison for getting drunk and indiscreetly joking that he wished the ceremonial cannon that was saluting John Adams's arrival in Newark would shoot the president in his posterior (Smith 1956, 270–1). Some historians have pointed to such moments in an attempt to suggest that that there was something comic about the Sedition Act itself. According to Stanley Elkins and Eric McKitrick, for example, "even more striking" than "the brutal high-handedness" that others have noted, "is the almost comic clumsiness, the sheer political ineptitude, with which the Federalists went about their work of trying to silence the opposition press" (1993, 703–4). There is nothing funny, however, about six months in a late-eighteenth-century prison or being beaten to unconsciousness by a bunch of soldiers. Nor is there anything amusing about incarcerating a sitting congressman for saying that someone else had said that the president should have been sent "to a mad house" (Smith 1956, 227). It is hard, too, to see the humor in a presiding judge's taking over the role of the prosecutor, or of the secretary of state combing through the nation's newspapers to look for prosecutable insults to the president.

Still, it is sometimes argued too that the Federalists won the battle but lost the war: they achieved the temporary advantage of making dissent odious but at great cost to their popularity, not to mention their historical reputation. Moreover, if their objective was to return Adams to the White House, they failed miserably. Jefferson won the election, and the Federalists never regained the presidency or even a majority in Congress. In addition, despite the setbacks caused by the prosecutions, the Republican press came back stronger than ever (Freeman 2003, 23–24; Pasley 2001, 124–31).

In a powerful new article, however, Seth Cotlar has argued that the Federalist repression of the late 1790s had a significant impact on American democracy. The Federalists, he argues, successfully demonized their most radical Republican opponents by tarring them as Jacobins. This was not an accidental byproduct of political discourse but instead the result of a carefully orchestrated and effectively executed political campaign made to appear as if it were a groundswell of public opinion.[7] For example, in the summer of 1798, Federalists organized 300 or so local meetings, at which the attendees adopted prepared statements in support of Adams, which were then sent to Adams and subsequently printed in the newspapers. The *Gazette of the United States* published eighty-seven of them. "This barrage of patriotic print," Cotlar explains, "took these hundreds of discrete, well-orchestrated public moments of local patriotism and reflected them back to an American audience as evidence of a preexisting spirit of national unity" (2004, 279). Such remarkably sophisticated political tactics were in support of a distinctive version of American nationalism. Whether anyone seriously believed that the French were about to invade or that a version of the French revolution was about to be reenacted in the United States is hard to tell. Even John Adams—sounding almost like Albert Gallatin—thought a French invasion unlikely. "Where is it possible for her to get ships to send thirty thousand men here? . . . What would 30,000 men do here?" (Elkins and McKitrick, 1993, 596). But these comments were made in private.

It is clear that the Federalists thought their opponents, including Jefferson, dangerous radicals, purveyors of a cosmopolitan universalism. In contrast, they believed that, as Noah Webster put it, "America alone seems to be reserved by Heaven as the sequestered region, where religion, virtue, and the arts may find a peaceful retirement from the tempests which agitate Europe." Universal notions of liberty, equality, and justice threatened to undermine attachment to the American nation. Instead, Cotlar notes, Federalists such as Webster urged their fellow Americans to identify themselves as part of a particular historical community. According to Webster, "Our fathers were men—they were heroes and patriots—they fought—they conquered—they bequeathed to us a rich inheritance of liberty and empire. . . . We have an excellent system of religion and of government—we have wives and children and sisters to defend; and God forbid that the soil of America should sustain the wretch, who wants the will or the spirit to defend them" (Cotlar 2004, 280–1). Here was the conservative vision of America that the Federalists offered as an antidote to the Republicans universalist one: a nation whose identity was rooted in history, religion, family, empire, and blood.

The Federalist assault had its desired effect. One need only consider the fate of James Thomson Callender, a Scottish pamphleteer who had fled Britain to avoid prosecution for sedition. In the United States, he made himself useful to the Republicans by his scathing attacks on the Federalists. When Callender tottered on the edge of bankruptcy—newspaper writing was an ill-paying and low-prestige occupation, making its practitioners dependent on the patronage of the politicians they served—Thomas Jefferson led a subscription drive that kept him afloat and even gave him money out of his own pocket. After Callender's incarceration for violating the Sedition Act, however, Jefferson avoided him like the plague. He disingenuously told Abigail Adams that "nobody sooner disapproved of his writing than I did" (Durey 1990, 112).[8]

More generally, as a result of the Federalist onslaught, the Republican party lost its left wing, and even though Jefferson was elected, he was a more moderate Republican than he otherwise would have been. And although the Alien Friends Act expired at the end of Adams's administration, the Sedition Act was repealed under Jefferson's, and the probation period for aliens was soon rolled back to five years, the effects of these pieces of legislation and the political currents that fed them have been long lasting. The Federalists demonstrated the political usefulness of exaggerating the threat of an enemy attack. When challenged for evidence, they warned that if the nation waited for proof, it might be too late. They demonstrated, too, the effectiveness of branding their political opponents as subversives, or, at the very least, the allies or dupes of subversives, and of eliding the distinction between external and internal foes. They showed how far a political party might go in rendering all opposition illegitimate, to the point not only that political opponents could be called dangerous radicals and disloyal Americans, but also that the leading members of the opposition press could be tried, convicted, and imprisoned for merely voicing their opposition. The Federalists also put forth a distinctive notion of American nationalism, one that detached it from universal notions of liberty and justice and identified it with characteristics that were supposedly distinctively American: religion, family, heritage, history. This notion of American nationality and the political tactics that have been used to advance it constitute the unhappiest part of the Federalist legacy to the United States.

THE WAR OF 1812

The War of 1812 offered the Republicans an opportunity to turn the tables on the Federalists and drum up nationalism by marginalizing their political opponents, if not eliminating them altogether. The threat to the nation this time was far from imaginary. Britain and the United States were engaged in a real war. At its height, the British not only burned the nation's capital at Washington and the much smaller town of Buffalo, New York, but they also occupied the eastern portion of Maine (until 1820 part of Massachusetts). The Republicans assumed that once war was declared, opposition to administration policies would cease. One Republican newspaper predicted that the war would unify the nation and *"weed our country of traitors"* (Hickey 1989, 55; italics in original). Tennessee Congressman Felix Grundy predicted—and warned—that "the distinction of Federalists and Republicans will cease . . . the inquiry shall be, are you for your country or against it?" (United States 1789, 12th Cong., 1st sess., 1410). Such predictions notwithstanding, a significant portion of the population, particularly in New England, was at best lukewarm to the war. With much of the economy dependent on trade with Britain, opposition to the war in that region was only to be expected. Moreover, Republicans had made gains in recent elections, and the Federalists saw in the war an opportunity to gain a partisan advantage. The Federalist governors of Massachusetts, Rhode Island, and Connecticut refused to call out their militias, claiming that the Constitution forbade it unless the nation were in imminent danger of invasion, which determination they would make. New Englanders used a variety of methods to impede the war, ranging from sermons and fast days to beating up Republican congressmen who had voted for the war. In Connecticut, the state and local governments both attempted to prevent the United States Army from recruiting and even from playing military music within town limits. How serious the New England secessionist movement was—ultimately the Hartford Convention asked for reforms to the Constitution rather than the dissolution of the union—is debatable, but some New Englanders did happily consort with the enemy. Smuggling was a persistent problem; the trade in livestock alone across the northern border effectively provisioned the British army. When the British seized the eastern part of Maine and offered any who took an oath to maintain the peace the same commercial privileges as British citizens, one Massachusetts paper reported that "it is scarcely possible to conceive the joy of the inhabitants" (Hickey 1989, 195). Wealthy landowners in the Maine District thought their property would be more valuable if it were British soil. From the administration's perspective, Massachusetts Governor Caleb Strong was a particular problem. When officially asked to help finance an expedition to oust the British from Maine, not only did he decline, but, it was suspected, he leaked the plans to a local newspaper, which printed them—for the British to see (Hickey 1989, 264; Stagg 1983, 476–7). Without question, the combination of foot-dragging and outright resistance retarded the war effort in the North.

Congress and the administration wrestled with the challenge of waging an unpopular war. How far could—and should—it push a recalcitrant public? When the army failed to meet its recruitment goals, the secretary of the army recommended drafting militia into the regular army. Congress opted instead for doubling the bounty it offered enlistees. On the other hand, Congress enhanced the power of military courts to deal with refractory members of the militia. Some Republican congressmen suggested giving such courts authority over civilian spies as well—to cover contingencies that seem eerily familiar from our current war on terror: American citizens caught aiding the enemy on foreign soil and apprehended traitors who successfully applied for writs of habeas corpus from civilian judges. Federalists were outraged by what they perceived to be attacks on fundamental constitutional principles, the right to trial by jury and habeas corpus. Both New Jersey's Richard Stockton and Massachusetts' Daniel Webster called the proposal "monstrous." They thought that the laws governing treason were fully adequate and that making civilians subject to military law was uncalled for. "The resolution," Stockton raged, "goes to subvert every principle of civil liberty."[9] "The simple question," Webster explained, was whether prosecution of treason was to be taken from the "courts of law, where the Constitution has placed it" and conferred on the military. As for the charge that judges were too quick to issue habeas writs, "the Constitution contains no provision more valuable; it makes no injunction more direct and imperative than those respecting trials for treason, and the benefits of habeas corpus." If the proposal were enacted, it would be "a most enormous stride of usurpation." Alexander Hanson of Maryland likewise detected ulterior motives. "A war was now to be commenced against our own citizens" (United States 1789, 13th Cong., 2nd sess., 881, 883–86). Although the resolution passed, it was never enacted into law. Much of the Republican support seemed half-hearted, as if it were enough to go on record against treason—which all of the speakers pointedly did—without actually tampering with the Constitution.

Like Congress, Madison resisted pressure to limit the civil liberties of the war's opponents. Vice President Elbridge Gerry, who as the former Republican governor of Massachusetts knew New England's war opponents intimately, thought they had to be punished. He recommended an array of measures to suppress the "internal foe": loyalty lists, vigilance committees, federal legislation to punish "refractory governors," and a state law to punish seditious editors. Convinced that the Federalists wanted to sever

New England and replace republican government with "a Hanoverian monarchy," he warned that "if we do not kill them, they will kill us" (Stagg 1983, 254). He fantasized a civil war that would have republicans wading "knee deep in blood" (Stagg 1983, 261). Supreme Court Justice Joseph Story and Attorney General William Pinkney advocated a new sedition law. Story complained that "offenders, conspirators, and traitors are enabled to carry on their purposes almost without check" (Hickey 1989, 70). Motivated by both political calculation and principle, Madison instead decided, in the words of historian J. C. A. Stagg, "to ignore as far as was possible any opposition to the war" (1983, 258). When the New England governors declined to raise their militias, Madison—one of the authors of the Constitution—proclaimed their interpretation of it "novel and unfortunate" but declined to press the issue. The war was so unpopular in New England that anything more than half-hearted measures and cajoling might only have strengthened the Federalists.

Madison believed that the resistance from New Englanders—he called it a "wicked project" (Stagg 1983, 265)—was "the source of our greatest difficulties in carrying on the war" and the chief reason that the British had not yet, at the end of 1814, ended it. He thought, however, that the opposition would fall of its own weight, and in the meantime, "the best may be hoped." His only other alternative was to rally the war's supporters, hoping that they would drown out the opposition (Rakove 1999, 706–7).

There was a fine line, however, between rallying the war's supporters and countenancing mob violence, particularly in a nation that still considered such violence a legitimate form of popular political action. At the beginning of the war, Jefferson counseled Madison that the Federalists were "poor devils . . . not worthy of notice." He thought that a "barrel of tar to each state South of the Potomac" would "keep all in order, and that will be freely contributed without troubling the government." In the North, however, "rougher drastics" might be necessary: "hemp [for nooses] and confiscation" (Smith 1995, vol. 3, 1699). Jefferson meant to reassure Madison that, for the most part, the public would police the war's opponents and federal action would be unnecessary. And just as Federalist opponents of the war roughed up its supporters in New England, so the war's supporters took action against its opponents in areas where support for the war was strong.

The most severe instance of mob violence took place in Baltimore, where Alexander Hanson—the same Hanson who raged against threats to civil rights from the floor of House of Representatives—edited a newspaper, the *Federal Republican*, which was strident in its opposition to the war.

Rumors circulated that the paper's offices would be attacked, and indeed, one night a crowd destroyed the building and its contents. When the newspaper's Federalist supporters appealed to city officials to intervene, a constable replied that the mob "ought to put a rope around his neck, and . . . hang him." The city's mayor walked among the rioters ineffectually pleading, "my dear fellow, you ought not to do so" (Hickey 1989, 59). Undeterred, Hanson and his supporters returned a month later, intent not only on resuming publication of the *Federal Republican* but also "wresting Baltimore from the tyranny of the mob." In his absence, the mob had continued to police those perceived to be opponents of the war, destroying ships thought to be trading with the enemy and the home of a black man "charged with the expressions of affection for the British nation." "Our country is at war," one citizen noted, "and we will shed our blood to put down all opposition to it" (Royster 1981, 158–60). Fearing—and, in fact, provoking, an attack—Hanson and his supporters asked the Revolutionary War hero Light Horse Harry Lee to organize the defense of their headquarters.

The paper resumed publication on the morning of July 27, 1812, and predictably, by evening the mob had gathered. As it grew in size and menace, the Federalists inside the building fired a warning shot, and then, when the mob—which eventually numbered 2,000—forced its way into the building, the Federalists shot at it, killing one man and wounding several others. Still city officials and the militia commander refused to intervene. The militia's commander said, "I am no disperser of mobs" (Hickey 1989, 63). Eventually, the Federalists were persuaded to retreat to the city jail, for their own protection.[10] The mob stormed the jail, however, severely beating the nine Federalists who had taken refuge, including Hanson and Lee. With women and children cheering them on, members of the mob stabbed the Federalists with pen knives and poured hot wax into their eyes. They taunted Lee—one of the Revolution's greatest heroes—as a "d—old Tory general" and left him for dead. He never recovered fully from his wounds. Another elderly Revolutionary veteran, General James Lingan, was stabbed to death (Royster 1981, 164).

The excesses of the Baltimore riot worked ironically to the Federalists' benefit. The Federalists took control of the Maryland legislature at the next election, and everywhere commentators recoiled from the violence, associating it with the French Revolution. The conventional wisdom holds that the Federalists' opposition to the war hastened their demise, but in the short term, at least, their fortunes rose. The Republicans' dream of nation united in opposition to a common foe—even one that had burned down the nation's capital—proved chimerical. Whatever other lessons might be drawn from the nation's experience in the War of 1812, it should be instructive that the United States was able to survive so serious an assault upon its security without fundamentally curtailing civil liberties. The administration and Congress resisted the impulse to alter the laws, and though neither they nor local officials interfered with mobs who punished, sometimes quite violently, war opponents, those mobs had a limited political effect.

THE ABOLITIONIST MOVEMENT

The presence in the United States of a large number of enslaved persons—an eighth of the nation's population and more than half in several Southern states—necessarily raised questions about the security of the nation. For the most part, these questions could be addressed without reference to civil liberties. Slaves, by definition, had no civil rights, and the punitive measures necessary to maintain order and police the slave population could be taken without triggering debates about civil liberties. Abolitionism, however, was another matter, and slavery's protectors perceived it as a threat to national security, one serious enough to warrant restrictions on whites' civil liberties. Moreover, what Stephen Holmes in the conclusion to this volume calls "the insidious influence of partisan politics on the way national security is defined and defended" enabled Southerners to curtail the liberties of slavery's critics.

Although the number of abolitionists was relatively small, the movement had been picking up strength over the course of the 1830s, growing from forty-seven local organizations in 1833 to around 1,300 in 1839 (Richards 2000, 136). Moreover, advances in both printing technology and the postal system gave the abolitionists the ability to reach far beyond their communities by printing and mailing thousands of pamphlets and petitions. During the summer of 1835, for example, abolitionists mailed 175,000 tracts to the South, and in 1837 and 1838, they sent Congress more than 130,000 petitions requesting the abolition of slavery in the District of Columbia (John 1995, 261; Richards 2000, 136). In both cases, as we shall see, the federal government took action; the objective of both the suppression of the mails and the gag rule, which prevented congressional discussion of the petitions, was, as one Congressman put it, to "silence debate" (U.S. Congress 1970, Vol. XII, 24th Cong., 1st sess., 1980).

The growth in the abolitionist movement coincided with a moment of crisis in the second party system. The enormously popular and reliably pro-slavery Andrew Jackson anointed his vice president, Martin Van Buren, as his successor, but as a New Yorker, Van Buren was suspect to slave owners. Simultaneous faction fights within both the Democratic and Whig parties led the most ardent proslavery Southern Democrats to demand proof from Van Buren and his supporters that they would combat the abolitionists and protect slavery. The problem here was that there was little that either the federal or free state governments could do to protect slavery that they were not already doing. The Southerners were not making specific demands as much as looking for rhetorical and symbolic forms of loyalty. And as for combating the abolitionists, here the Southerners asked for nothing less than the elimination of a group of people they considered fanatics and incendiaries. Southern newspapers advised Northerners to start hanging abolitionists if they wanted to continue trading with the South, and one North Carolina congressman sent the prominent abolitionist Arthur Tappan a piece of rope. Rhetorical excess, perhaps, but in a private letter to a friendly New York newspaper editor, South Carolina Congressman James Henry Hammond insisted that the abolitionists "can be silenced in but one way. *Terror and Death*" (Grimsted 1998, 22, 29).

Such extravagant demands on the part of pro-slavery Southerners created a dilemma for those political leaders who wanted to maintain their parties' interregional appeal without renouncing the rights to free speech, assembly, and petition. Few in number, the abolitionists were generally unpopular, and few others were willing to defend them or to argue, in Congress at this point, at least, for the immediate end to slavery. Political leaders were, however, willing to make rhetorical concessions and to consent to some restrictions upon the abolitionists' rights. The result was a series of compromises that preserved the ideal of free speech, in the North, while effectively curtailing it in the South and setting limits to what could be discussed in Congress.

There are four discrete episodes to be discussed, all of which occurred almost simultaneously: the suppression of abolitionist tracts mailed to the South; the gag rule on debate about petitions asking for the abolition of slavery in the District of Columbia; antiabolition riots in both the North and the South; and a seditious libel prosecution in the District of Columbia. In each of these, the same themes appear: branding abolitionists as fanatics; alleging foreign involvement; trying to suppress all discussion of slavery; and suggesting that even discussing the future of slavery would lead necessarily to servile insurrection. Southerners argued that abolitionism threatened the security of the nation in two ways: first, by inciting the slaves to revolt, and, second, by undermining the compact that held the nation together. Proslavery Southerners said that the Southern states would never have entered the union had not slavery been protected and threatened that they would leave the nation if that protection were not guaranteed. Andrew Jackson struck both these themes in his 1835 message to Congress. He warned that the abolitionists were making "inflammatory appeals . . . to the passions of the slaves . . . calculated to stimulate them to insurrection, and to produce all the horrors of a servile war." Moreover, "Our happiness and prosperity essentially depend upon peace within our borders—and peace depends upon the maintenance, in good faith, of those compromises of the Constitution upon which the Union is founded" (U.S. Congress 1970, Vol. XII, 24th Cong., 1st sess., Appendix, 11).

Let us consider the suppression of the mails first. In late July 1835, Alfred Huger, the postmaster of Charleston, South Carolina, found his post office filled with abolitionist tracts sent from the North and addressed to whites. Holding the tracts in the post office, he simultaneously wrote Postmaster General Amos Kendall asking for instructions and tried to broker a deal with local moderates: He would place all the pamphlets in a separate, well-labeled sack and await a reply from Washington. Perhaps hoping for this result, Kendall delayed his response, and in the meantime, late on the night of July 29, a mob led by Charleston's leading citizens broke into the post office, seized the bag of offending mail, and burned its contents in front of a cheering crowd of 2,000 people, one-seventh of the white population of the city (Grimsted 1998, 22–23; John 1995, 257–9; Wilentz 2005, 410–2).

Although the break-in was clearly a violation of federal law, and the abolitionists themselves had broken no national laws, the Jackson administration lined up in support of the South Carolinians. The secretary of state reported to Vice President Van Buren that "all parties unite to write Postmaster Huger in fixed resolve to prevent the circulation of those papers the laws of the United States to the contrary notwithstanding" (John 1995, 269). There was the rub. The administration knew it was on the wrong side of the law, which left it two options: trying to keep things quiet and changing the law. They tried both approaches.

Kendall was explicit about his motives. He told Jackson that he wanted to prevent the distribution of the abolitionist tracts with "as little noise and difficulty as possible" and that he wanted to do whatever was required to "pacify the South" (John 1995, 269). At the same time, both Kendall and Jackson, determined to ease Van Buren's candidacy by placating Southern Democrats, urged Congress to make illegal the mailing of abolitionist literature. A few days after the Charleston riot, Jackson privately raged against the abolitionists, musing that they "ought to be made to atone for this wicked attempt with their lives." He also suggested to Kendall that the names of everyone who subscribed to abolitionist publications should be published, thereby shaming them publicly—and perhaps exposing them to the rage of local mobs (John 1995, 269–70). By the time that he sent his formal message to Congress in December, Jackson had moderated his tone, if not his belief, that abolitionist tracts should be barred from the mails. Asserting the importance of "peace within our borders," Jackson called the abolitionists "wicked" and suggested that they had been encouraged by foreigners. He urged Congress to make illegal the mailing to the South of "incendiary publications intended to instigate the slaves to insurrection" (U.S. Congress 1970, Vol. XII, 24th Cong., 1st sess., Appendix, 11). In his own message, Kendall struck the same themes, concluding in a states-right argument that is as strained as it is remarkable. Only a few years earlier, Jackson had faced down South Carolina when it asserted its right to nullify the federal tariff within its borders. Now Kendall was insisting that, when it came to slavery, "the States are still independent, and may fence round and protect their interest in slaves" by any laws they wanted. Moreover, if a state chose to "limit the carrying on discussions" or "distribution of printed papers" by their own citizens within their own borders, then surely, citizens from other states could not claim those privileges. Here Kendall invoked the privileges and immunities clause to limit the First Amendment right to free speech. Surely, states could limit free expression to ensure "the safety of their people," and just as surely, they could not "confer on the citizens of one State higher privileges and immunities in another, than the citizens of the latter possess." Moreover, the federal government was obligated to protect the states against domestic violence, and hence it could not be a party to the dissemination of "papers calculated to produce domestic violence" (U.S. Congress 1970, Volume XII, 24th Cong., 1st sess., Appendix, 24).

The constitutional logic was circuitous, the connection between suppressing free speech and protecting national security indirect. Perhaps understanding that Northerners in particular would resist wholesale limitations upon their rights to speech, Kendall did not claim that the abolitionists threatened the security of the entire nation. Rather, by encouraging slave insurrection, they threatened the security of the slave states, which were entitled to ban abolitionist talk as a matter of self-preservation. And, because of their obligation to assist in the suppression of domestic violence, the other states must offer their support. Kendall provided a constitutional justification for the creation of what Richard John has called a cordon sanitaire around the South, insulating the Southern states from criticism of slavery (1995, 264).

In spite of the urgings of Jackson and his administration, Congress declined to forbid the delivery of abolitionist mail to the South. Jackson and Kendall had gone too far for some Northern Democrats, but when the *New York Evening Post* criticized the administration—by pointing out, for example, that Kendall's policy would, in the words of historian David Grimsted, make "every postmaster his own nullifier" (Grimsted 1998, 25), the administration retaliated by cutting off patronage to the *Post*. The administration had gone too far for Congress, as well, and the Post Office Act of 1836 threatened punishment of any postmaster who did not deliver the mail. Congress upheld the principle of freedom of the mail. Nonetheless, Southern postmasters continued to detain abolitionist literature and none of them was ever subjected to federal prosecution. To the contrary, Southern states prosecuted those postmasters who refused to comply with the orders of local communities (John 1995, 273–5; U.S. Congress 1970, Vol. XII, 24th Cong., 1st sess., Appendix, 76-7). The outcome, then, of the conflict over the mailing of abolitionist pamphlets to the South was a tacit agreement by the executive branch to permit Southern states to prevent their citizens from receiving abolitionist literature. This was a compromise that maintained the cordon sanitaire while permitting Northerners to believe that their governments and the national government as well remained untainted (Freehling 1990, 310).

The compromise, however, left both abolitionists and Southern extremists dissatisfied. Finding that their pamphlets could no longer penetrate the South, abolitionists decided to flood Congress with petitions aimed at the limited and presumably constitutional goal of abolishing slavery in the District of Columbia. Moreover, even though the right to petition has in modern times become, as Gregory Mark has noted, "vestigial," it was "at the core of the constitutional law and politics of the early United States" (1998, 2157). Hence it would be difficult to turn away petitions from the citizenry.

Congress customarily received petitions and put them on the table, and that is what it did with the first two abolitionist petitions that arrived in December 1835. When the third such petition in three days arrived, South Carolina's Representative James Henry Hammond proposed that it and all successors be rejected "peremptorily." He "could not sit there and see the rights of the southern people assaulted day after day, by the ignorant fanatics from whom these memorials proceed" (U.S. Congress 1970, Vol. XII, 24th Cong., Appendix, 1st sess., 1966–67). The invocation of rights and the branding of the petitioners as fanatics signaled that Hammond's was a calculated political move, and indeed it was. His immediate objective was to strengthen the pro-slavery wing of the Democratic party by cutting out the ground from underneath moderates in his own party. He forced Northern congressmen into a particularly tight corner. Either they insist on receiving the petitions (which had no prayer of achieving their objective), satisfying their own constituents and surrendering the hope of maintaining national political coalitions, on the one hand, or they appease the South and infuriate their constituents, on the other.[11] With little national support for abolition, almost all of the Democrats from both sections and most of the Southern Whigs competed to see who could best satisfy the most extreme Southerners' demands for condemnation of abolitionism without going so far as to offend those Northerners who balked at capitulation to pro-slavery apologists. The House and the Senate arrived at slightly different compromises, both of which gagged any discussion of the future of slavery without denying slavery's opponents the right to petition. The Senate adopted (future president) James Buchanan's proposal that the petitions be received and immediately rejected. The House opted for a nominally less extreme procedure supported by soon-to-be president Martin Van Buren: the petitions would be referred to a select committee where they would die (Freehling 1990, 308–52; Fehrenbacher 2001, 75–76).

As with the controversy over the mails, the Southerners' ostensible demand was that slavery be kept out of national politics, but in fact what they insisted on was the right to agitate the issue themselves and demand rhetorical concessions from the North. The chief concession they gained was the branding of abolitionism as fanaticism, a threat to the security of the South and the perpetuity of the Union.[12] Buchanan, eager to mollify the South, let his imagination run riot. He decried the abolitionists as "fanatics, led on by foreign incendiaries" and warned they were spreading fear of "servile war" throughout the South. He conjured up a picture of "many a mother clasp[ing] her infant to her bosom, when she retires to rest, under dreadful apprehensions that she may be aroused from her slumbers by the savage yells of the slaves by whom she is surrounded." Buchanan also imagined the consequences of complying with the petitions and freeing the few hundred slaves who lived in the nation's capital. "You would thus erect a citadel in the very heart of these States . . . a central point from which trains of gunpowder may be securely laid . . . which may, at any moment, produce a fearful and destructive explosion" (United States 1833, 24th Cong., 1st sess., 77). But even those Northern Democrats who were willing to uphold the right to petition still excoriated the abolitionists. "We all, North and South, abhor abolition incendiarism," New Jersey's Garret Wall declared. "It is the attempt . . . to put the dagger and the torch in the hands of *infuriated* madmen . . . to involve our fellow-citizen in the horrors of rapine, murder, and a servile war" (134).

Even those Northerners such as John Quincy Adams who opposed the gag rule did so on the basis of the right to petition, not the justice of the petitions themselves. Although personally opposed to slavery, he thought that discussing the matter in Congress would only lead to more ill will (Fehrenbacher 2001, 72). Hence pro-slavery Southerners gained something more than mere rhetorical concessions about the fanaticism of the abolitionists. They effectively silenced debate in Congress about the future of slavery itself for almost a decade by depicting the countenancing of even limited reform as tantamount to inciting servile insurrection. Although Adams challenged it in every Congress, the gag rule remained in place until 1844, when Northern opponents of slavery finally had enough strength to defeat it—and Southern defenders of the institution shifted their focus to the more pressing issue of extending slavery into newly acquired territories. In the interim, the Democratic Party, North and South, had become effectively proslavery, in thrall to its Southern wing, and any discussion by Southerners of the gradual emancipation of slavery had been rendered wholly illegitimate.

Limitations of space do not permit a full accounting of the antiabolition mob actions of the antebellum period. A brief description of their pattern and cursory accounts of several of the most prominent of them will have to suffice. There were at least 100 antiabolition riots in the United States between 1833 and 1838, with more than two-thirds of them taking place in 1835 and 1836 (Richards 1970, 12). These riots were deeply political, coming in response to the demands in the Southern press, reaching a crescendo in the late summer of 1835 with the insistence that the abolitionists be "put down." Some of the riots were in major Northern cities— New York, Boston, Utica—where abolitionism was strong and local Van Buren Democrats wanted to show their Southern friends that they were eager to eradicate it. Lest there be any doubt that this was the intent, the Utica riot, which broke up a meeting of the New York Anti-Slavery Society, was led by the New York congressman who was Van Buren's closest ally in the House. The point was not lost on the Jacksonian press, which said that the riot proved that the Van Burenites were not soft on abolitionism. On the same day as the Utica riot, there were antiabolition riots in Boston, Newport, Rhode Island, and Montpelier, Vermont, the latter instigated by leading Jacksonians (Grimsted 1998, 26–27).

David Grimsted has argued that such mobbing "propitiated" Southerners, who did not notice the ritualistic character and limited destructiveness of the riots. Northerners, he suggests, were willing to break up a few abolitionist meetings, but further than that they would not go. This analysis needs some qualification. Although it is true that there were elements of play-acting in some mob riots, such as the one in 1836 in Granville, Ohio, in which the rioters and the abolitionist James G. Birney taunted each other, others crossed over into genuine violence. The best known of these is the one in which the abolitionist editor Elijah Lovejoy was killed. In fact, the fatal confrontation was the culmination in a series of mob actions against Lovejoy. Lovejoy had already been driven out of St. Louis in 1836 after denouncing a local judge—the improbably named Luke Lawless—who had advised a grand jury not to indict the white men who had burned alive a free black man who had killed a deputy in an altercation. Lovejoy moved his press across the Mississippi to Alton, Illinois, but even though he was now in a free state, he still met with opposition. Neither the threat of a tar and feathering nor the repeated destruction of his press deterred Lovejoy from his abolitionist organizing and editorializing. When his adversaries attempted to set fire to the warehouse in which he had secured his fourth press, shots were exchanged, leaving both Lovejoy and one of his attackers dead (Gilje 1996, 81–82; Richards 1970, 100–11). Such violence was generally not the objective of Northern mobs, but it was certainly always a possibility, particularly when a town's leading figures encouraged mob action, as was the case in Alton. Moreover, by arming himself and his allies, Lovejoy refused to play his part in the ritual of mobbing. The confrontation in Alton proved that the line separating political theater from outright violence in antiabolitionist riots was very thin indeed.

Moreover, that line disappeared entirely in the slave South and regions close to it, where, as Grimsted has shown, slavery's defenders insisted on the suppression of abolitionist talk and not simply intimidation. Mobs destroyed thirteen abolitionist presses, all but one of these in the South or regions bordering it and drove abolitionist publications out of the South (Grimsted 1998, 35, 53). If Northern antiabolitionist riots reached their peak in the mid-1830s, as an expression of partisan politics, they continued throughout the antebellum period in the South. There are two reasons for this difference in regional patterns. First, attacks on abolitionists in the North only strengthened the movement, both by creating attractive martyrs such as Lovejoy and by casting antislavery rioters as the enemies of liberty and tools of the Southern "slave power." Second, Southerners continued to use mobs as an instrument of policing, making victims not only of the occasional abolitionist brave enough to remain in the South but also anyone who seemed out of place or unreliable on the question of slavery. A few examples will have to suffice. In 1831, when his Georgia neighbors heard that John Lamb subscribed to the *Liberator*, they dragged him from his house, tarred and feathered him, doused him in oil and set him on fire, carried him out of town on a rail, dunked him in the river, tied him to a post, whipped him, and then ordered him out of town (Grimsted 1998, 121–2). Holding that abolitionism itself was foreign—"stimulated by an impulse derived from abroad," as the writer James Kirke Paulding put it (Davis 1971, 136)—Southerners targeted foreigners, sometimes simply because they were foreign. A Virginia mob beat up an Englishman named Robinson who had the bad judgment to mention, in a private conversation a month after the Nat Turner rebellion, that he thought that blacks deserved their freedom. Four years later, another Virginia mob threatened an Englishman named Robertson, apparently because they mistook him for the similarly named Robinson, and five years after that, another Englishman, this one named Roberts, was arrested in Georgia for "insurrectionary activity," though at his trial none could be proved. The seeming arbitrariness of such attacks was, in fact, as Grimsted has pointed out, "a central aspect of their social utility." They served to put people on notice that at any time, an idle comment or even a mistaken identity might make them the target of a mob. "Terror as a political system works best when rules are vague, and Southern mobs acted often and arbitrarily enough to make terror visible and felt" (Grimsted 1998, 117).

Mobs, newspaper editorials, and political pressure were the favorite and most effective tools that pro-slavery Southerners used to attempt to silence all discussion of slavery. When they could, they arrested and prosecuted suspected abolitionists, but this tactic depended on both their capacity to apprehend the suspect and there being enough evidence to make a trial plausible. As in the case of the hapless Roberts, sometimes suspected abolitionists were incarcerated on flimsy evidence. More common was the indictment of prominent abolitionists in absentia and the demand that such men be extradited to stand trial. The only federal prosecution of a suspected abolitionist took place in 1836; it was part of the Jackson administration's campaign to appease Southern Democrats to pave the way for Van Buren's election. Dr. Reuben Crandall was arrested in Washington, D.C., on charges of seditious libel after it was discovered that he had abolitionist publications in his possession. The prosecutor, Francis Scott Key, a Jackson appointee better known as the author of "The Star-Spangled Banner," argued that mere possession of such literature constituted intent to publish it, particularly since the pictures in the pamphlets "could be meant only for the illiterate [that is, slaves], and tended only to insurrection and violence" (Crandall 1836, 47). Crandall's defense lawyer insisted that mere possession of the pamphlets in question in the absence of any "overt act against the community" was not unlawful. If it were, then "any individual in this community might be arrested, his papers seized and examined, his most private correspondence exhibited to the public gaze" (42–43), and prosecuted for sedition. Moreover, so far as Crandall's attorney knew, no one had ever been prosecuted for seditious libel in the United States, except under the provisions of the Sedition Act, and that law had subsequently been "denounced as tyrannical, oppressive, unconstitutional, and destructive of the liberty of speech and of the press." (41). It took the jury less than an hour to return a verdict of not guilty, but after eight months in jail, Crandall's health had been destroyed, and he died of tuberculosis two years later (Fehrenbacher 2001, 74). Once again, a compromise of sorts had been struck—prosecution, but not conviction.

Except for the occasional mobbing, the abolitionist controversies had pretty much run their course by 1838. As with the Alien and Sedition Acts episodes, American politics had been pulled perceptibly to the right. Abolitionists in the North could generally speak and write with freedom, though they still risked the occasional beating. The South, however, was now surrounded by a cordon sanitaire that protected it from abolitionists and their message. It was no longer safe to preach abolition—or even to be suspected of it—in the South. In the slaveholding regions of the nation, the right to free speech was no longer secure. In addition, if slavery's defenders had not silenced debate on the issue of slavery in Congress, they had quieted it for about a decade, when it would be reopened after the acquisition of the Mexican territory. By then, the gap between North and South had grown significantly, with the principle of free speech valued in the North, and conformity on the issue of slavery more important in the South.

THE CIVIL WAR

The troubled history of civil liberties during Abraham Lincoln's presidency is too well known to require a full accounting here. Less familiar is the repression of civil liberties by the Confederate government. If we are interested in the history of the American people, and not that of the federal government alone, then we must consider the experience of the North and South both. The difference in the patterns of repression is instructive.

Historians and constitutional scholars continue to debate whether Abraham Lincoln's suspension of habeas corpus and the numerous arrests for disloyal speech were lawful. Even those most sympathetic to Lincoln often conclude that he or other members of his government went too far, particularly in prosecuting newspaper editors, politicians, and even individual citizens who spoke out against the war. The purpose here is not, however, to evaluate whether Lincoln exceeded his authority but instead to assess the fate of civil liberties during perceived threats to national security. In this context, there can be no denying that during the Civil War, the security of the nation was in grave peril. The eventual triumph of the Union sometimes makes the survival of the government seem inevitable, a foregone conclusion. Lincoln and his government, however, faced not only the Confederate army, but substantial opposition at home, particularly in the border states of Maryland, Missouri, Kentucky, and Delaware, as well as among the members of the Democratic Party who opposed the war and favored reconciliation with the South. Such resistance raises the uncomfortable question of when opposition to the policies of the government crosses the line separating legitimate disagreement from treason. Moreover, making such determinations is, and was, a political challenge, and not simply a legal and constitutional one: Lincoln had to try to preserve the Union and overcome disloyalty without, at the same time, creating more resistance by punishing disloyalty too harshly.[13]

Thus, rather than focusing on the well-known cases such as Ex Parte *Merryman* and Ex Parte *Milligan*, it may be more useful to look at the pattern of prosecutions and dissent. For example, the Merryman case turned on Lincoln's right unilaterally to suspend the right of habeas corpus. (With Maryland under martial law early in the war, Union officers had arrested John Merryman, a Maryland militia officer who had prevented Massachusetts troops from passing through the border state on their way to the District of Columbia. L. A. Powe also discusses this episode in chapter 7 of this volume.) Supreme Court Justice Roger Taney ruled that only Congress could suspend habeas. Lincoln refused to obey the order and instead defended his actions vigorously. There was no substantial criticism from the Northern public, and Merryman was released a few weeks later (Farber 2003; Neely 1991; Stone 2004). Many of the wartime arrests seemed to follow this pattern of thrust and retreat. Perhaps the most notorious of these was the near-arrest of a former president, Franklin Pierce, after a fraudulent accusation of disloyalty. An exchange of letters with the administration cleared the matter up. Then there were the foreign sailors, captured in the blockade, who were kept in custody until their consuls could secure their release or oaths of loyalty could be administered (Neely 1991, 24–27).

Lincoln himself often seemed to calculate the potential political consequences of an action before taking it. Thus, he imposed martial law in

Maryland to protect troop movements—leading to the arrest of Merryman—but refused to prevent the meeting of the Maryland legislature as it considered secession. The latter decision proved wise, as the legislature, even though dominated by Democrats, declined to secede. Lincoln sometimes countermanded his army officers, sometimes not. When John Frémont imposed martial law in St. Louis and freed the slaves of those loyal to the Confederacy, Lincoln overruled the part of Frémont's order that freed the slaves, but let stand the martial law. He advised his general, however, not to execute any of his prisoners, purely on prudential grounds: "Should you shoot a man . . . the Confederates would very certainly shoot our best man in their hands in retaliation; and so, man for man, indefinitely" (Neely 1991, 33–34).

Lincoln declined, however, to overrule Ambrose Burnside, the commander in Ohio (who had been removed as head of the Army of the Potomac after his failures in the East). In his zealousness, Burnside created several embarrassments for the administration. The best known of these was the arrest of Clement Vallandigham, a former congressman and an outspoken Democratic peace advocate who had recently denounced the March 1863 Conscription Act, the first draft in the nation's history. The draft met with considerable resistance, culminating in the New York City draft riots of July 1863, in which thousands of predominantly Democratic, Irish immigrants rose up against draft officers but eventually turned against the free black inhabitants of the city, whose neighborhood was destroyed and some of whom were lynched. Lincoln defended Vallandigham's arrest, insisting that his crime was not speech per se but the act of interfering with the raising of the army. "Must I shoot a simple-minded soldier boy who deserts," Lincoln asked, "while I must not touch a hair of the wily agitator who induces him to desert?" The arrest led to a riot in Vallandigham's home town of Dayton and demonstrations in most of the Northern cities, and Lincoln, attuned to the politics as always, decided to exile him to the Confederacy rather than imprison him (Farber 2003, 170–2; Stone 2004, 98–107; Neely 1991, 65–68; McPherson 1988, 596–8). Vallandigham slipped out of the South by running the Union blockade, eventually making his way to Canada, where he campaigned, unsuccessfully, for the governorship of Ohio. A year later, he came back to the United States, where he helped lead the Democratic opposition to Lincoln in the 1864 election. Although Lincoln could have had him arrested for violating the terms of his release to the South, he chose instead to ignore him, calculating—correctly—that having so notorious a figure campaigning for the Democrats would do them more harm than good (Stone 2004, 118–9).

We see a similar pattern of clamping down on dissidents and then letting up in the way that the federal government handled the opposition press. Throughout the war, Lincoln faced a vigorous political opposition, and the Democratic press was its mouthpiece. Yet censoring it or shutting it down flew in the face of widespread public support for freedom of the press. That was the result when the overzealous Burnside seized the offices of the *Chicago Times*, a persistent critic of administration policies. Both a mob of 20,000 and the leading citizens of Chicago, including Republicans, called on the president to relent. He did (Stone 2004, 109; Farber 2003, 229 n. 68). The editor of the *Dubuque Herald* was arrested for discouraging enlistments, but when prominent supporters interceded with the secretary of state, he was released. The editor promptly wrote a book about his experiences and entitled it *The Prisoner of State* (Neely 1991, 58). Obviously, rather than silencing the opposition, such arrests only fueled it. Perhaps the most extreme case of suppression of the press came after the New York *World* published a false article in 1864 claiming that Lincoln was instituting a new draft of 400,000 men. In fact, this fake report was part of a scheme by two newspapermen to make a fortune by forcing up gold prices. Fearful that the story was a Confederate plot, and that not only the newspapers but also the telegraph wires (which relayed the report) were insecure, Lincoln ordered the newspaper shut and the arrest of its editors and publishers. But once again, having achieved their desired immediate effect, these actions were subsequently rescinded, and Gideon Welles, Lincoln's secretary of the navy, later reflected that they were "hasty, rash, inconsiderate, and wrong, and cannot be defended" (Neely 1991, 104; Farber 2003, 173–4).

The point here is not to exonerate the Lincoln administration from its excesses but to describe the pattern, which was highly responsive to political pressures. It should be noted that the vast majority of civilians prosecuted by the administration were, as Mark Neely points out, true enemies of the state: Confederates caught behind Northern lines, blockade runners, purveyors of contraband goods, informers, and the like, and the public had little objection to their incarceration (1991). But any time a newspaper was shut down or a Democratic critic of the administration arrested, no matter how outspoken, there was sure to be an outcry. After one of his generals arrested a St. Louis newspaperman in 1863, Lincoln implored, "please spare me the trouble this is likely to bring" (Neely 1991, 28). This was the context in which the North fought the Civil War—a loud internal opposition that could not be silenced.

Should it have been? Again, that is not the point. Instead, we should note that the Confederacy was defeated even as Lincoln had to contend with outspoken domestic critics, ones who—to pick a few examples—called him a Caesar, tyrant, dictator, and half-witted usurper, and who, arguably, may even have crossed the line separating legitimate dissent from active disloyalty. The *Dubuque Herald* asked rhetorically whether soldiers were "bound by patriotism, duty or loyalty" to fight a war to emancipate slaves, and it printed, implicitly with approval, letters written by family members to their kinsmen in the army decrying an "unholy, unconstitutional and hellish war" and imploring them "to come home, if you have to desert, you will be protected." While he was in exile in the South, Vallandigham suggested to a Confederate agent that the peace Democrats would triumph in the 1864 election and then, if the South were not amenable to reconciliation, he might support independence (Stone 2004, 109; McPherson 1988, 595–8). Lincoln defended his administration's suppression of civil liberties, explaining that the Confederacy was taking advantage of the Union's liberties to undermine it: "under cover of 'liberty of speech,' 'liberty of the press,' and *habeas corpus* [the rebels] hoped to keep on foot among us a most efficient corps of spies, informers, suppliers, and aiders and abettors of their cause" (Fehrenbacher 1989, 45–63). Lincoln thought that the civil courts were "utterly incompetent" to deal with this threat, which was why the Constitution provided for the suspension of habeas corpus in the case of rebellion (McPherson 1988, 598).[14]

These were strong measures, but, as Lincoln put it, "ours is a case of Rebellion . . . in fact, a clear, flagrant, and gigantic case of Rebellion" (Fehrenbacher 1989, 457). Perhaps in some instances they were too strong, but if test is the threat they were meant to counter, then the comparison with the response to the political opposition during the Quasi-War is instructive. Then, with the threat of invasion somewhere between remotely possible and pure fantasy, the national government passed a series of stringent laws and incarcerated editors, political leaders, and town drunks. Nor were there massive riots against suspected Confederate sympathizers; though such riots were not unknown, the worst of them—one of the worst in American history—protested the draft and made victims of free blacks.

How might we explain this discrepancy? The experience of the nineteenth century suggests that the suppression of civil liberties has been easiest when those who have been targeted were or could be depicted as radicals and foreigners. Both tactics were used against the Democratic-Republicans and the abolitionists.[15] Indeed, these cases suggest that characterizing political adversaries as dangerous, foreign or foreign-inspired radicals— not true Americans—has been an effective strategy for pulling politics to the right. Such tactics could not be used as successfully when dealing with the Confederacy, for several reasons. First, theirs was a genuine rebellion, not an imaginary one—and the branding of adversaries as dangerous radicals was a strategy for silencing them and rendering them illegitimate by suggesting that they were a much more serious and different kind of threat than they actually were. Second, in certain critical respects, the Confederates were already on the conservative side of the political spectrum: they were powerful white men, fighting to maintain their property in other human beings; they were the very people who had successfully depicted abolitionists as the radical threat.

In addition, as Mark Neely has observed, the North could not characterize Southern rebels as aliens and anti-Americans because it was waging a war whose very premise was the opposite: that the South was an inalienable part of the Union (1999, 171). As the Supreme Court ruled in the Prize Cases in 1862, Southerners were "enemies though not foreigners" (The Amy Warwick, 67 U.S. 635, 674). This way of looking at Southern rebels—as true Americans, even when waging a rebellion—continued to shape the government's actions after the Civil War, when unrepentant Confederates waged an insurgency. During congressional debates on Reconstruction, moderates recoiled from defining Southerners as aliens. Congressman Lewis Winans Ross urged reconciliation. Southern whites "have got to live in this country. Do you want an Ireland, a Hungary, a Poland in your midst?" Likewise, John Bingham rejected any suggestion that Southerners were like "alien enemies" (United States 1833, 39th Cong., 1st sess., 1867, 502; Foner 1988, 273).

The contrast with the South is instructive. As Neely also shows, the South still had available to it the ideological weapon of choice for those who want to suppress dissent: the capacity to characterize its opponents as aliens. Hence, in 1861, early in the war, the Confederacy passed an Alien Enemies Act that defined as alien enemies and hence subject to arrest, incarceration, and deportation all males fourteen and older who were not citizens of the Confederate states.[16] The Confederacy used the law to police its population, first by evicting from the South Northerners who might otherwise have ended up as political prisoners and second, by giving the Confederacy another tool for arresting long-time Southern residents of dubious loyalty who happened to have been born in the North or residents of contested regions such as West Virginia who refused to serve in the Confederate Army or otherwise appeared loyal to the Union (Neely 1999, 145–6, 171; Athey 1996). The Alien Enemies Act was thus an instrument of mobilization. It simultaneously defined clearly who was a member of the nation—and who was not, and pushed those in the middle to choose. Incomplete attachment to the Confederacy was unacceptable.

Although the Confederacy prided itself on its greater commitment to personal freedom than the North, which, Jefferson Davis alleged, was filled with "Bastilles" (McPherson 1988, 434), in significant ways, civilian life in the South was more tightly circumscribed. Unlike the North, the South restricted travel by means of a system of domestic passports. Because it was enacted unilaterally by the War Department, rather than by statute, the only historical trace is left by the apparatus of enforcement. The system was initiated in the summer of 1861, and within three years, those who wanted to travel almost anywhere in the South had to obtain in advance a passport for that particular trip. Roads and railroad lines were policed, sometimes with a soldier in each train car; all travelers, regardless of status, had to provide their passes, and all baggage and goods were subject to inspection, as well. Unlike the Alien Enemies Act, the passport system applied to women. Once, two young women who were traveling with South Carolina Senator James Orr were ejected from a car at three in the morning. Such restrictions on freedom of movement were unprecedented in what had been the United States—except, of course, for slaves and free blacks in the South, who also had to have passes to enable them to travel. This precedent was not lost on the few white Southerners who complained about having "to show a pass, like some negro slave" or "getting a pass like a negro" (Neely 1999, 1–7).

The passport system provoked other complaints. The lines to get passes, particularly in large cities such as Richmond, could be very long, causing some people to miss their trains. Business people said that the cumbersome system impeded trade, and reporters said it effectively muzzled the press. Congressmen resented the inconvenience, so finally, in 1864 they reformed it—but for themselves only. Henceforth, congressmen could travel with a single pass. In spite of the occasional protests, what is most remarkable about the domestic passport system is how willingly white Southerners complied with it. Some even thought that it did not go far enough. The *Charleston Courier* was concerned about "strangers, who come to us or go from us" and wondered "whether some additional and stringent regulations are not required" (CSA 1904, May 25, 1864, 7:97; Neely 1999, 6, 4).

From one perspective, the restrictions on civil liberties in the South were no worse than in the North. Indeed, Mark Neely has concluded that "the two societies were more alike than unlike in the way that they handled civil liberties" (1999, 172), and if one focuses only on the suspension of habeas corpus and the making of political prisoners, this conclusion is largely true. However, these restrictions on civil liberties in the South came on top of existing legal and customary restrictions that already significantly hampered the freedom of the region's residents. In the antebellum period, for example, several states had explicitly banned antislavery publication and speech (Stone 2004, 95).[17] Likewise, Southern newspapers were already in the habit of self-censorship; hence, no additional measures were necessary to silence them. Significant as these restrictions were, they pale in comparison to those placed upon slaves. As Neely notes, "slavery effectively put under permanent arrest the people of the South with the most potential for disloyalty" (91–92).[18] Among other things, slavery defined as permanent aliens those persons who were enslaved (171). Because the South was less free than the North even before the beginning of the Civil War, it was necessarily less free during the Civil War as well. Although this episode in the history of civil liberties in wartime is often overlooked,[19] surely it has bearing on our present dilemmas. Indeed, the almost complete expunging of this unhappy chapter of history from the historical record is an important part of the story, particularly if we want to understand the circumstances under which some Americans have treated others as alien enemies and required their own citizens to secure passes from the military before traveling, even within their own states.

RECONSTRUCTION AND THE POSTWAR INSURGENCY

The fate of liberty in the South during the Civil War is the necessary prelude to the Reconstruction and post-Reconstruction eras. Space does not permit a full account of the history of this period. Moreover, at first glance, it might seem an odd chapter in a history of civil liberties and national security. Although the denial of civil liberties to the emancipated slaves brought about Reconstruction, national security, and the post–Civil War South are usually not mentioned in the same breath. That is the point: this period in American history gives us an opportunity to examine the suppression of civil liberties in a context where national security did not seem to be a concern. With the Union victorious in the Civil War, the nation now seemed secure. Radical Republicans often thought that the defeated Southerners were unrepentant; they did not think that they were undefeated.

At the end of the Civil War, white Southerners hoped to return to the Union much as it had been. Mississippi even refused to ratify the Thirteenth Amendment, abolishing slavery (afraid that it would just provide opportunities for "radicals and demagogues"). The Southern states enacted Black

Codes, which severely restricted the most basic rights of the freedmen and women, for example, to marry, own property, enter into contracts, and sue and be sued. Moreover, in much of the South, "violence," in Eric Foner's words, "raged almost unchecked." Ex-slaves were killed for the slightest provocation—failing to doff a hat or share a whiskey flask—or no provocation at all. One white man said he just wanted "to see a d—d nigger kick" (1988, 199, 119–20). In response, Congress passed a series of Reconstruction Acts that put the former Confederate states (except for Tennessee) under military rule until they met certain conditions. In the meantime, civilians could be tried by military commissions whenever the military commander thought it "necessary," although the military was used primarily to protect the freedmen and women and not as a substitute for local courts where they existed (An Act to provide for the more efficient government of the rebel states, ch. 153, 14 Stat. 428; Neely 1999, 178).

Yet even with the former Confederacy under military rule, white Southerners continued to terrorize blacks and their white allies. Terror was the instrument of a white Southern insurgency movement whose objective was not to resist federal control per se but to maintain white supremacy. Its immediate political goal was reestablishing the hegemony of the Democratic Party. With the emergence of the Ku Klux Klan, which was the Southern insurgency's military force, the level of violence rose to levels unprecedented in American history (Foner 1988, 425). In this context, Reconstruction may be considered as a counterinsurgency effort, an attempt to quash what Congress, in the Ku Klux Klan Act of 1871 recognized as a conspiracy "to overthrow, or to put down, or to destroy by force the government of the United States" and "to prevent, hinder, or delay the execution" of the laws of the United States." The Klan Act attempted to secure the liberties of former slaves by, for the first time in American history, making conspiracies to deprive people of certain civil liberties—for example, voting and serving on juries—federal crimes. It also empowered the president to suspend habeas corpus if he deemed it necessary (An Act to enforce the Provisions of the Fourteenth Amendment to the Constitution of the United States, and for other purposes, ch. 22, 17 Stat. 13–15). The Klan Act was an extraordinary measure but, as Attorney General Amos Akerman concluded, the Southern resistance "amount[ed] to a war, and cannot be effectually crushed on any other theory." At Akerman's urging, in 1871 President Ulysses S. Grant found nine South Carolina counties to be in a "condition of lawlessness," suspended habeas, and sent federal troops to occupy the region. This use of federal force demonstrated that the Klan could be subdued, and violence dropped dramatically (Foner 1988, 454–5,

457–9). Quashing the Southern insurgency would have required repeated applications of federal force, however, and this the national government proved unwilling to do.

The turning point in the retreat from Reconstruction came in 1875. Democrats had determined to retake control of the state governments in Louisiana and Mississippi. In Louisiana, when they installed five of their members in disputed seats to seize control of the legislature, federal troops forcibly removed them and replaced them with Republicans. Because blacks constituted a majority in Mississippi, Democrats could take control only by suppressing the black vote. As the 1874 election approached, whites began to terrorize blacks. In Vicksburg, armed gangs patrolled the streets and murdered perhaps 300 blacks in the surrounding countryside. Outside of Clinton, they shot another thirty or so blacks "just the same as birds" (Foner 1988, 560). Routinely they broke up political meetings and assaulted political leaders. The Republican governor said that "they are going around the streets at night dressed in soldiers clothes and making colored people run for their lives" (Foner 1988, 560). He might have added that the attacks took place in broad daylight as well. Grant ordered General Philip Sheridan to New Orleans to investigate. Sheridan promptly concluded that "terrorism" existed in Louisiana, Mississippi, and Arkansas as well, and he recommended that Congress declare the white insurgents "banditti" and try them "by a military commission" (Lemann 2006, 93).

Sheridan, however, had gone too far. The specter of trying whites—even white "terrorists"—before military commissions was offensive to "respectable citizens" in the North (Foner 1988, 554). Hence, when Mississippi's governor asked Grant for troops, the president lamented that "the whole public are tired out with these annual autumnal outbreaks in the South" (560). His new attorney general suggested that the Republicans raise a militia and "*fight* for their rights" (which would have meant a race war). The intimidation and violence in Mississippi worked, and the Democrats seized power (Foner 1988, 554–63). That, effectively, was the end of Reconstruction. Without federal troops to protect black voters, one by one the Southern states returned to Democratic, all-white rule, the deep South almost immediately, and the upper South by the 1890s. Once the Democrats regained power, they sharply curtailed blacks' economic and political rights, rolling back many of the most important gains of the previous decade.

Democrats called this takeover of state governments Redemption. In another age, and from another perspective, one might say instead that the federal government had decided to cut and run. Although these events are often discussed as if they are a chapter in the history of African Americans only, they had a profound effect on American politics more generally. As Eric Foner has noted, "the removal of a significant portion of the nation's laboring population from public life shifted the center of gravity of American politics to the right, complicating the work of reformers for generations to come" (1988, 604). Moreover, this removal was accomplished by an insurgency movement that used terror—so recognized at the time—to accomplish its ends. For a time the federal government attempted to fight it, even calling it for what it was, an insurrection.

What we call things matters. Consider the episode that is still called, even by those who know better, the Wilmington Race Riot. Yet, as the recent report of the Wilmington Race Riot Commission, a group established by the North Carolina State Assembly in 2000, makes abundantly clear, this event may more properly be denominated a coup d'état, the culmination of a concerted effort by the Democratic elite to seize control of the government in a city where blacks still had a modicum of power (Umfleet 2006, 5). On the morning of November 10, 1898, a mob of 2,000 led by Alfred Moore Waddell, burned down the offices of the black-owned *Wilmington Daily Record*, using as a pretext an editorial that appeared to cast aspersions on white womanhood. Waddell was a former Confederate officer and United States congressman; before the day was out, he had become Wilmington's mayor. The mob targeted specific political leaders, shooting them or driving them out of town. The white mayor was given a day to gather his effects and get out of town. Other prominent Republicans were "told in forcible language that if ever again they set foot in Wilmington they would be shot on sight" (Umfleet 2006, 166). To this day, no one knows how many black people were killed, maybe twelve, maybe sixty. Blacks ran for their lives, and when some of them got as far as New Bern, there they found whites atop the water tower waiting to shoot them. Four hundred women and children took shelter in the woods. More than 2,000 blacks left town permanently. The more prosperous of them rented their own cars to attach to passenger trains heading north and west. After they left, whites seized their property for nonpayment of taxes (Umfleet 2006, 5; Gilmore 1996, 111–4).

President William McKinley refused to send troops because the governor had not requested them, and the governor did not request them because his Democratic opponents threatened him with impeachment if he did. Besides, peace had been restored. In his first act as mayor, Waddell had called for an end to the violence. John Spencer Bassett, a history professor in Durham, noted the irony. "If he [Waddell] had any sense of humor he must have split his undergarments laughing at his own joke" (Umfleet 2006,

194–5). But the armed overthrow of the elected government of an American city, all members of the same political party as the president of the United States, and the terrorizing of its black population was no joke. This was not a riot. It was a coup. In other circumstances, it might even have been considered a threat to national security. But Waddell and his followers claimed for themselves the mantle of patriotism. In a speech only a few weeks before the coup, he rallied his followers by insisting that "we are the sons of the men who won the first victory of the Revolution at Moore's Creek Bridge . . . who stained with bleeding feet the snows of Valley Forge . . . and only left the service of their country when its independent sovereignty was secured." Sooner than surrender their "heritage" to a "ragged rabble of negroes led by a handful of white cowards," better "to choke the current of the Cape Fear with carcasses" (Umfleet 2006, 80). In this way, the ever-malleable sense of American national identity might once again be twisted to define others as outside the pale of citizenship, entitled neither to civil liberties nor even their own lives.

CONCLUSION

Does the experience of the nineteenth century have any bearing on our present dilemmas? The history of the restriction of civil liberties during this period reveals several patterns. First, though the histories of assaults on civil liberties in the nineteenth century and panics about national security intersect, they are not identical. We would expect civil liberties to be in jeopardy during wartime, and that was certainly the case during the Civil War, in both the North and the South, though perhaps to a remarkable extent, not during the War of 1812, at least from the state. We might also expect an assault on civil liberties when a threat to national security might plausibly be invoked. This was the case with the Quasi-War with France and to, some extent, with the suppression of abolitionism in the 1830s. The issue here is not whether the threat to national security was real but whether some might persuade others that it was. On the other hand, civil liberties could be curtailed, and quite seriously, even without any claims of a threat to national security. Here, the most important example is the assault upon the liberties of black people and their supporters in the post–Civil War South. This attack was waged by an insurgency movement, a continuation of the Civil War that did not end until the black population had been driven almost completely out of public life.

If the connections between assaults on civil liberties and perceptions of threats to national security were so variable in the nineteenth century, what were the constants? Here is the second pattern. The most frequent targets were outsiders, those who could plausibly be depicted as outsiders, or radicals (defined here as those who were most inclusive in their vision of American democracy): the republicans of the 1790s, abolitionists in the 1830s, and Republicans black and white in the post–Civil War South. The critical context is the contingent and protean nature of American nationalism of the time. In this context, depriving certain Americans of their civil liberties was one instrument for mobilizing the nation and setting boundaries for membership in it. Moreover, if the nation is defined by the process of setting boundaries, then there is an internal logic to American nationalism that defines as outsiders those whose vision of the nation is more inclusive. Necessarily, this tactic could not be deployed effectively against those who were already particularist in their vision of the nation.

Finally, a third pattern: the process of limiting civil liberties was highly political, in both the partisan and general meanings of the term. Civil liberties were particularly vulnerable during periods of intense partisan political conflict, for example the Quasi-War, the transition between the Jackson and the Van Buren administrations, and the reestablishment of the hegemony of the Democratic Party in the post–Civil War South. In each of these cases, moreover, as political opponents were demonized, intimidated, or driven out of politics altogether, politics was pulled perceptibly to the right. Considering politics more generally, both the attempts to limit civil liberties and the resistance to these attempts have been sensitive to political forces. We see this process at work during the War of 1812, when the unpopularity of the war (and some of the Republicans' scruples) limited what the Madison administration could do to suppress the Federalist opposition. We see it, too, in the Civil War, when Lincoln faced limits in how far he could go in curtailing the rights of his Democratic opponents. At the same time, the Confederacy, established in a region that had already sharply curtailed the rights of blacks and their supporters, could go considerably further. Again, context is critical. It is much easier to deprive of their liberties those who are outside the narrowest boundaries of the nation, much more difficult to take them away from those who seem—because of their race, their status, or their particularist notion of citizenship—within the boundaries, even if they display sympathies with those who have taken up arms against the nation, even if they engage in a coup d'état.

If we would draw any lesson from the nineteenth-century experience, it might be a set of danger signs, warnings of situations in which we might be most concerned for the fate of civil liberties. First, there would not necessarily have to be an actual threat to national security; the capacity to claim such a threat would be equally if not more important. Second, a highly partisan political atmosphere, with a great deal of contention, increases the peril to civil liberties. Third, some groups are more vulnerable than others. Those who are more universalistic in their notion of citizenship, as well as those who because of their national origin or race appear to be outsiders, are most in jeopardy. Those whose notion of citizenship is more exclusive are less vulnerable. Then there is the greatest danger sign of all: the protean and open-ended nature of American democracy, with its inherent contradiction between inclusive and exclusionary tendencies, means that citizenship is always contested and that the civil liberties that give character to the democratic form of government are never wholly secure.

NOTES

1. As a case in point, consider John Yoo's argument in chapter 3 of this volume that restrictions upon Americans' civil liberties in wartime have been a function only of the threat to national security presented by an external foe, and he offers a formula for assessing threat: It "will depend on the *expected* harm to the United States posed by the enemy, which we can think of as the magnitude of the harm that *might* come about factored by the *probability* that it will occur" (emphasis added). Yet even in so simple a formula, Yoo cannot avoid piling up hypotheticals so that his formula necessarily rests upon a succession of subjective assessments.

2. "In the Old World, the people came with the territory," as Aristide Zolberg recently noted. "In contrast, from the very outset, by way of its state and federal governments, the self-constituted American nation not only set conditions for political membership, but also decided quite literally who would inhabit its land" (2006, 1).

3. Because there was no discussion of this provision, it is not clear whom Congress considered white and exactly which people it intended to exclude. As a number of scholars have demonstrated recently, the term *white* has proved remarkably malleable. Presumably, Congress intended to exclude Africans and perhaps Asians as well. What is most important is that Congress intended to use color and race as a means of setting the boundaries of the political community (Jacobson 1998).

4. This notion of war as an instrument of national unity has reemerged periodically, for example, during World War I, as Alan Brinkley shows in chapter 2 of this volume. An extreme version of this notion may also be seen in a *Philadelphia Daily News* column by Stuart Bykofsky, who welcomes another attack by al Qaeda because it "would sew us back together" as a nation ("To Save America We Need Another 9/11," August 9, 2007).

5. Curiously, the Alien Enemies Act applied only to males fourteen and older, while the Alien Friends Act made no distinctions as to age or gender. Because there is no discussion of it, it is hard to tell if this discrepancy between the two acts was intended or not.

6. No mention was made, however, of slaves, who obviously were inhabitants without the rights of citizens. Slavery did come up, however, when the representatives debated whether Article 1, Sect. 9, Para 1, of the Constitution ("migration or importation of such persons as any of the States now existing shall think proper to admit") was relevant (United States 1789, 5th Cong., 2nd sess., 1797).

7. Ellen Schrecker notes in chapter 4 of this volume that the anticommunist crusade of the cold war period too was "largely . . . a top-down phenomenon."

8. It was, of course, Callender's rejection by his former patron that turned Callender against Jefferson, leading to his most famous publication, the allegation that Jefferson was the father of his slave Sally Hemings's children.

9. Alan Brinkley, in chapter 2 of this volume, notes that Roger Baldwin, one of the founders of the ACLU, thought that he was responsible for making the term *civil liberties* commonplace. Although it is true that the discourse of civil liberties was not fully developed until after World War I, the term had resonance a century earlier. It meant, in particular, such fundamental rights as habeas corpus, trial by jury, and freedom from warrantless searches. For another example of common usage, consider the 1812 prediction of the *Federal Republican* that war with Britain "would put the Constitution and all civil rights to sleep" (Hickey 1989, 57).

10. To the best of my knowledge, these were the only war opponents who saw the inside of a jail during the war—and it was with their consent, for their own protection. In chapter 5 of this volume, Geoffrey Stone notes that "it was inevitable that Lyndon Johnson and Richard Nixon, following in the footsteps of Adams, Lincoln, Wilson, Roosevelt, Truman, and Eisenhower, would want to prosecute and imprison" the Vietnam War's opponents. The War of 1812, it would appear, was hence the odd war out, so to speak, at least until recent times, when, as Stone notes, surveillance has replaced incarceration as the chief means of policing dissent.

11. My analysis of the underlying political strategies derives from William Freehling, *The Road to Disunion* (1990).

12. Freehling suggests that by silencing all discussion of the future of slavery, Southerners were able to end all possibility of gradual emancipation.

13. Geoffrey Stone's *Perilous Times* (2004) does an excellent job of sketching in this necessary context.

14. These quotations are from Lincoln's famous letter to Erastus Corning and Others, June 12, 1863.

15. This comparison necessarily raises the questions of why the Federalist opposition during the War of 1812, seemingly allied with foreigners, did not

suffer a harsher fate. The chief reasons were their political strength in New England, which would have made it difficult to marginalize them entirely, and also their decidedly un-radical character. In fact, Republicans tried to characterize them as an internal enemy, but the label didn't stick.

16. Citizens of the border states and those who were in the process of becoming Confederate citizens were exempted. The language of the Confederate Alien Enemies Act was modeled after the 1798 act, which too had applied to males fourteen and older. Subsequent legislation provided for the confiscation of the property of alien enemies; restricted the rights of the "next kin" of alien enemies; and also declared as alien enemies all those who left the Confederacy to avoid conscription, with their property, too, subject to confiscation (CSA 1904, March 24, 1862, 5:139; November 15, 1864, 4:268; January 25, 1864, 3: 616).

17. My focus here is on the federal, rather than state, government. Although consideration of restrictions upon civil liberties in the states is beyond the scope of this article, it is common knowledge that abolitionist speech was proscribed in the slave states. John Dann's work suggests that the need to protect slavery retarded the development of humanitarian reform in the South. Slave owners feared that any discussion of reform would lead inevitably to critiques of slavery, a risk they were not willing to take. By implication, slavery prevented the development in the South of a vigorous public sphere (see Dann 1975).

18. Here Neely's argument resembles that of Edmund Morgan (1975) in his important *American Slavery, American Freedom:* the enslavement of the working class, a segment of the population that, based on the European experience, could be expected to be restive, yielded important political benefits to go along with the obvious economic ones.

19. Geoffrey Stone almost completely overlooks the Southern experience in his otherwise excellent *Perilous Times* (2004), and James McPherson downplays the suppression of civil liberties in the Confederacy in his magisterial *Battle Cry of Freedom* (1988).

REFERENCES

Athey, Lou. 1996. "Loyalty and Civil Liberty in Fayette County During the Civil War." *West Virginia History* 55(1996): 1–24.

Benhabib, Seyla. 2004. *The Rights of Others: Aliens, Residents and Citizens.* New York: Cambridge University Press.

Confederate States of America (CSA). 1904. *Journal of the Congress of the Confederate States of America, 1861–1865.* Washington: Government Printing Office.

Cotlar, Seth M. 2004. "The Federalists' Transatlantic Cultural Offensive of 1798 and the Moderation of American Democratic Discourse." In *Beyond the Founders:*

New Approaches to the Political History of the Early American Republic, edited by J. L. Pasley, A. W. Robertson, and D. Waldstreicher. Chapel Hill, N.C.: University of North Carolina Press.

Crandall, Reuben. 1836. *The trial of Reuben Crandall, M.D. charged with publishing seditious libels, by circulating the publications of the American Anti-Slavery Society, before the Circuit Court for the District of Columbia, held at Washington, in April, 1836, occupying the court the period of ten days.* New York: H. R. Piercy.

Dann, John C. 1975. "Humanitarian Reform and Organized Benevolence in the Southern United States, 1780–1830." Ph.D. dissertation, College of William and Mary.

Davis, David Brion, editor. 1971. *The Fear of Conspiracy: Images of Un-American Subversion from the Revolution to the Present.* Ithaca, N.Y.: Cornell University Press.

Durey, Michael. 1990. *"With the Hammer of Truth": James Thomson Callender and America's Early National Heroes.* Charlottesville, Va.: University of Virginia Press.

Elkins, Stanley M., and Eric McKitrick. 1993. *The Age of Federalism.* New York: Oxford University Press.

Farber, Daniel. 2003. *Lincoln's Constitution.* Chicago, Ill.: University of Chicago Press.

Fehrenbacher, Don E. 1989. *Abraham Lincoln: Speeches and Writings, 1859–1865.* New York: Library of America.

———. 2001. *The Slaveholding Republic: An Account of the United States Government's Relations to Slavery.* Completed and edited by Ward M. McAfee. New York: Oxford University Press.

Freehling, William W. 1990. *The Road to Disunion: Secessionists at Bay.* New York: Oxford University Press.

Freeman, Joanne B. 2003. "Explaining the Unexplainable: The Cultural Context of the Sedition Act." In *The Democratic Experiment: New Directions in American Political History,* edited by Meg Jacobs, William J. Novak, and Julian E. Zelizer. Princeton, N.J.: Princeton University Press.

Foner, Eric. 1988. *Reconstruction: America's Unfinished Revolution, 1863–1877.* New York: Harper and Row.

Gilje, Paul A. 1996. *Rioting in America.* Bloomington, Ind.: Indiana University Press.

Gilmore, Glenda Elizabeth. 1996. *Gender and Jim Crow: Women and the Politics of White Supremacy in North Carolina, 1896–1920.* Chapel Hill, N.C.: University of North Carolina Press.

Grimsted, David. 1998. *American Mobbing, 1828–1861: Toward Civil War.* New York: Oxford University Press.

Hickey, Donald R. 1989. *The War of 1812: A Forgotten Conflict.* Urbana, Ill.: University of Illinois Press.

Jacobson, Matthew Frye. 1998. *Whiteness of a Different Color.* Cambridge, Mass.: Harvard University Press.

John, Richard R. 1995. *Spreading the News: The American Postal System from Franklin to Morse.* Cambridge, Mass.: Harvard University Press.

Kettner, James H. 1978. *The Development of American Citizenship, 1608–1870.* Chapel Hill, N.C.: University of North Carolina Press.

Lemann, Nicholas. 2006. *Redemption: The Last Battle of the Civil War.* New York: Farrar, Straus and Giroux.

Mark, Gregory S. 1998. "The Vestigial Constitution: The History and Significance of the Right to Petition." *Fordham Law Review* 66(1998): 2153–231.

McPherson, James. 1988. *Battle Cry of Freedom: The Civil War Era.* New York: Oxford University Press.

Miller, Perry. 1961. "From the Covenant to the Revival." In *Religion in American Life,* edited by James Ward Smith and A. Leland Jamison. Princeton, N.J.: Princeton University Press.

Morgan, Edmund S. 1975. *American Slavery, American Freedom: The Ordeal of Colonial Virginia.* New York: W. W. Norton.

Neely, Mark E., Jr. 1991. *The Fate of Liberty: Abraham Lincoln and Civil Liberties.* New York: Oxford University Press.

———. 1999. *Southern Rights: Political Prisoners and the Myth of Confederate Constitutionalism.* Charlottesville, Va.: University of Virginia Press.

Pasley, Jeffrey L. 2001. *"The Tyranny of Printers": Newspaper Politics in the Early American Republic.* Charlottesville, Va.: University of Virginia Press.

Rakove, Jack N., editor. 1999. *James Madison: Writings.* New York: Library of America.

Richards, Leonard L. 1970. *Gentlemen of Property and Standing: Anti-Abolition Mobs in Jacksonian America.* New York: Oxford University Press.

———. 2000. *The Slave Power: the Free North and Southern Domination, 1780–1860.* Baton Rouge, La.: Louisiana State University Press.

Royster, Charles. 1981. *Light-Horse Harry Lee and the Legacy of the American Revolution.* New York: Alfred A. Knopf.

Smith, James Morton. 1956. *Freedom's Fetters: The Alien and Sedition Laws and American Civil Liberties.* Ithaca, N.Y.: Cornell University Press.

———, editor. 1995. *The Republic of Letters: The Correspondence between Thomas Jefferson and James Madison 1776–1826,* 3 vols. New York: W. W. Norton.

Smith, Rogers M. 1997. *Civic Ideals: Conflicting Visions of Citizenship in U.S. History.* New Haven, Conn.: Yale University Press.

Stagg, J. C. A. 1983. *Mr. Madison's War: Politics, Diplomacy, and Warfare in the Early American Republic, 1783–1830.* Princeton, N.J.: Princeton University Press.

The Statutes at Large of the United States of America, 1789–1873 [*Statutes at Large*]. 1851. Boston, Mass.: Little and Brown.

Stone, Geoffrey R. 2004. *Perilous Times: Free Speech in Wartime.* New York: W. W. Norton.

Thomson, Janice E. 1994. *Mercenaries, Pirates, and Sovereigns: State Building and Extraterritorial Violence in Early Modern Europe.* Princeton, N.J.: Princeton University Press.

Umfleet, LeRae, editor. 2006. *1898 Wilmington Race Riot Report.* Wilmington, N.C.: Wilmington Race Riot Commission. Accessed September 2, 2006 at http://www.ah.dcr.state.nc.us/1898-wrrc/report/report.htm.

United States, and Joseph Gales [United States]. 1789. *Annals of the Congress of the United States, 1789–1824,* 42 vols. Washington: Gales and Seaton.

United States, Francis Preston Blair, John C. Rives, Franklin Rives, and George A. Bailey [United States]. 1833. *The Congressional Globe.* Washington: Blair & Rives.

U.S. Congress. 1970. *Register of Debates in Congress, 1824–1837,* 14 vols. Washington: Gales and Seaton.

Walzer, Michael. 1983. *Spheres of Justice: A Defense of Pluralism and Equality.* New York: Basic Books.

Wood, Gordon S. 1969. *The Creation of the America Republic, 1776–1787.* Chapel Hill, N.C.: University of North Carolina Press for the Institute of Early American History and Culture.

Ziesche, Philipp. 2006. "Americans in Paris in Age of Revolution, 1788–1800." Ph.D. dissertation, Yale University.

Zolberg, Aristide R. 2006. *A Nation by Design: Immigration Policy in the Fashioning of America.* Cambridge, Mass.: Harvard University Press.

CHAPTER 7

THE ROLE OF THE COURT

L. A. POWE, JR.

Civil libertarians are looking to the courts—and especially the Supreme Court—to redeem the Constitution's ideals from what they believe are the Bush administration's illegal excesses. American history suggests, however, that the courts may not be the venue that best protects civil liberties. Yet civil libertarians have an answer: the Warren Court changed all that. Perhaps. I will begin with the Warren Court and why its decisions cause civil libertarians to place so much faith in courts and then offer a more complete historical picture to suggest that this faith may be myopic.

THE MCCARTHY ERA

The years just before Senator Joseph McCarthy gave his name to the era were the beginning of a dark age for civil libertarians. In 1947, President Harry Truman had succumbed to Republican pressure and issued an executive order initiating a loyalty-security program for federal employees. The attorney general, Tom Clark, followed up by creating an enumeration, soon labeled the "Attorney General's List," of organizations deemed communist dominated or oriented to assist in implementing Truman's program. In Congress, the House Un-American Activities Committee, staffed by some of the most reactionary members of both parties, basked in the spotlight of its hearings into communist infiltration of both the federal government and Hollywood. HUAC's one unambiguous success—the exposure of Alger Hiss as a communist spy—was derided by liberals who were convinced that someone like Hiss, who so perfectly symbolized the New Deal, had to be innocent and that his accuser, the ex-communist Whittaker Chambers, was a liar.

Suddenly, in the summer of 1949, both Frank Murphy and Wiley Rutledge, Supreme Court justices in their fifties, died. This halved the Court's liberal block—four men from the liberal wing of the Democratic Party appointed by the most liberal president in the twentieth century. In the years that followed, the phrase *Black and Douglas dissenting* signified that civil liberties issues had but two stalwarts on the Court, but gave those two justices enormous capital with civil libertarians for being willing to stand against the hysteria.

The dark age was exemplified by the Court's affirmation of the convictions of the leaders of the Communist Party for advocating violent revolution (but doing nothing to further it).[1] To justify the convictions, Chief Justice Fred Vinson had to gut the clear and present danger test, which he did by holding that Learned Hand's version from the court below was "as succinct and inclusive" as a court could devise. That test was really a balancing test (to prove negligence in tort law):[2] "In each case [courts] must ask whether the gravity of the 'evil' discounted by its improbability, justifies such invasion of free speech as is necessary to avoid the danger."[3] Hugo Black tersely hoped that "when present pressures, passions and fears subside [some] Court would restore the First Amendment liberties to the high preferred place where they belong in a free society."[4] William Douglas praised the New Deal for rendering the communists, "miserable merchants of unwanted ideas," irrelevant.[5] The communists' speech was being "outlawed because Soviet Russia and her Red Army are a threat to world peace."[6]

Douglas and Black truly spoke for a minority. Both the *New York Times* and *Washington Post* editorialized in favor of the Court's decision. The *Times* thought that "liberty shall not be abused to its own destruction" ("The Smith Act Upheld," *New York Times,* June 5, 1951, 30). The *Post* was enamored with the Court's able reconciliation of "liberty and security in our time" ("Freedom with Security," *Washington Post,* June 6, 1951, 12).

With the leaders of the Communist Party headed for prison, the government then commenced prosecutions of the next tier of party leaders. Then, after Dwight Eisenhower took office, the standards under the loyalty-security program were modified so that previously cleared government employees could be dismissed.

DISMANTLING THE DAMAGE

Two years later, some months after the Senate censured McCarthy, Black and Douglas were no longer dissenters. Dr. John Peters underwent two loyalty-security hearings under the Truman administration and twice the conclusion was that there was no reasonable doubt about his loyalty. Shortly after Eisenhower became president, the Loyalty Review Board on its own motion held its own hearing (where neither it nor Peters knew the names of the informants against him) and concluded that "on all the evidence there is a reasonable basis to doubt Dr. Peters' loyalty to the United States Government."[7] Whereas Black and Douglas wished to invalidate the conclusion because it was based on the faceless informer, the majority held that the Loyalty Review Board lacked the authority to conduct postaudit hearings on its own. This was the first setback for the federal program.

A year later, a second setback was created in *Cole v. Young*, 351 U.S. 536 (1956), when the Court held that summary dismissals from the civil service on loyalty grounds were limited to those employees who had access to sensitive information. More significant were two state cases, *Pennsylvania v. Nelson*, 350 U.S. 497 (1956) and *Slochower v. Board of Regents*, 350 U.S. 551 (1956). The former reversed the sedition conviction of Steve Nelson, the leader of the Communist Party in western Pennsylvania. Although the ground of reversal was that the state law was preempted by various federal laws, the solicitor general had stated there was no conflict (even though the proof in Nelson's state trial was identical to that of his Smith Act trial). Conservatives bemoaned that the sedition acts in more than forty states had been rendered inoperable. In Slochower, the Court invalidated New York's policy of treating the invoking of the right against self-incrimination when questioned about employment duties as a resignation. Seemingly ending the penalizing of Fifth Amendment communists, the Court ruled that because there were innocent reasons for taking the Fifth, a state could not so penalize its use. These decisions provoked outcries from Southerners and national security conservatives, but were greeted with satisfaction by civil libertarians as signaling the end of judicial acquiescence to the hysteria.

That signal was unmistakable a year later. During the 1956 term, the Court decided twelve cases dealing with communists or communism and the governments lost each time. A couple of the cases were truly significant—such as the gutting of the Smith Act[8] and the public lecture to Congress and HUAC that "exposure for exposure's sake," which was all that HUAC ever did in the 1950s, was unconstitutional.[9] Most of them weren't. Three reversed decisions because of perjured testimony.[10] One of those three, *Jencks v. United States*, 353 U.S. 657 (1957), allowed a defendant to see the FBI records on interviews of those who were testifying against him. The Court entered the debate on "who lost China" by finding the dismissal of John Stewart Service, one of the Old China Hands of the State Department, was improper, but the decision rested on a technicality.[11] In between the significant and not so significant decisions were a pair dealing with the relationship of past membership in the Communist Party and fitness to be a lawyer.[12] Whatever the significance of any particular decision, the cumulative weight, added to what had been decided in the two previous years, was unmistakable. There was one caveat. A close reading of the opinions revealed more lecture than law. The cases were infused with constitutional values, but only three state cases were actual constitutional holdings, and limited ones at that.

The caveat noted, Congress had censured McCarthy; the Court was operating to dismantle McCarthyism. The *New York Times* editorialized about "A Day for Freedom" (June 18, 1957, 32). It celebrated the Court as "by far the most courageous of our three branches of Government in standing up for basic principles." I. F. Stone, speaking to and for liberals, went further. The decisions "promise a new birth of freedom. They make the First Amendment a reality again" (1963, 203).

One of the cases involving perjury was the Subversive Activities Control Board's finding that the Communist Party was a communist action organization, a finding that would trigger registration requirements and civil disabilities for party members. It took almost five years for the SACB to issue a similar, but untainted finding, and for the case to finally be decided by the Court in an opinion affirming the SACB where only Black dissented on the First Amendment issue.[13] (Douglas held that because the Communist Party was funded and controlled by a foreign nation, it was not entitled to the presumption that it should be treated like a normal political party; he nevertheless found a Fifth Amendment violation.) The decision, *SACB v. Communist Party*, 367 U.S. 1 (1961), set the stage for the Court to complete the dismantling of the McCarthy era domestic security programs.

Eight opinions by Warren Court liberals—three by Douglas and two each by Earl Warren and William J. Brennan, the other by Arthur Goldberg—completed the constitutional demolition of both the federal and the remaining state programs. The state programs were simple, typically adopting some form of a loyalty oath that mythically would block subversives from teaching the young, and in a couple of states the creation of little HUACs. Douglas put an end to the last surviving little-HUAC when he stopped the questioning of a suspect about activities that were at least a decade in the past. Douglas found no showing that there was a present danger to the state.[14] Douglas also invalidated a loyalty oath for its failure to distinguish between people who joined the Communist Party with intent to overthrow the government and those who joined it without believing in its unlawful purposes and were therefore no threat to the state or its youths.[15] This was the Court's criminal standard and Douglas did not pause to explain why the state should not be entitled to more latitude where civil disabilities rather than jail time were at issue. The other state case involved New York's efforts to weed out subversive teachers. Brennan raced around the statute, which he called a "regulatory maze" and concluded that it lacked the necessary precision to avoid chilling freedom of speech and association.[16]

With two exceptions, the federal cases all dealt with the SACB's registration order. One exception was a noncommunist affidavit that labor leaders were required to file. In an explicable result with an inexplicable rationale, Warren held that the requirement constituted a bill of attainder.[17] The other was a requirement that anyone wishing to receive "communist propaganda" from certain countries—such as North Korea—had to go to the Post Office and sign a form requesting that the propaganda be delivered. Few citizens would do so even if they wished to receive the materials. With the chilling effect so obvious, Douglas tersely struck down the statute.[18]

The SACB cases all flowed from the consequences of the earlier decision upholding the finding that the Communist Party was a communist action organization. This was coupled with an order to the party from the SACB to register its members; if the party failed to do this, then individual communists had to register themselves. Furthermore, they could neither travel abroad nor work in defense facilities. The easiest provision to strike down was individual registration. Going to a government that is prosecuting communists and saying "I'm a commie" looks like a short-cut to jail. It also was a violation of the Fifth Amendment privilege against self-incrimination.[19] The ban on foreign travel—applied to one of the leaders of the party—was struck down in an opinion weaving back and forth between the right to travel and freedom of association both coupled with a hint that maybe the travel was for educational purposes instead of subversion.[20] If striking down the registration requirement was the easiest of the cases, the ban on defense employment surely was the hardest, because if there were jobs where sabotage would hurt the most, defense facilities would be the place. Nevertheless, Warren struck the ban entirely because it reached not only nonsensitive positions, but also members of the party who did not share its illegal aims.[21] At an earlier time, the Court might have saved the statute through some creative statutory construction. This time, however, it specifically refused to do so.

There it was, a total judicial dismantling of the domestic security program. Furthermore, it was occurring side by side with a protection of antiwar dissenters that was unique in American history. The first of the Vietnam cases came when the Georgia senate refused to seat civil rights activist Julian Bond, one of the first African Americans elected to the legislature in the twentieth century. Georgia's action was based on Bond's endorsement of an antiwar statement. He opposed the war and the draft. Had Bond's grandfather opposed World War I on similar grounds, he would have been prosecuted and the Court would have found no First Amendment violation (Powe, 2000, 323). But in 1966 a unanimous Court held that the speech was protected.[22] "The manifest function of the First Amendment in a representative democracy requires that legislators be given the widest latitude to express their views on issues of policy."[23] The World War I cases, thoroughly criticized by academics, were being interred. In the last year of the Warren Court the justices held that a man could not be convicted when, on receiving his draft notice, he stated that if he had a gun, "the first person I would want in my sights is LBJ." His statement, the justices ruled, was crude hyperbole.[24] And therefore harmless. So, too, were the black armbands worn by the Tinker children to the schools to protest the war. The school district, however, expelled them. Finding that the school district simply assumed that wearing an armband would cause disruption, the Court announced that "in our system, undifferentiated fear or apprehension of disturbance is not enough to overcome the right of freedom of expression."[25]

Although neither an antiwar nor a communist case, the contemporaneous *Brandenburg v. Ohio*[26] spoke powerfully to both situations as the Court fused Learned Hand's *Masses*[27] opinion with Louis Brandeis's separate opinion in *Whitney*.[28] Brandenburg held that speech advocating illegal action could be punished only in circumstances "where such advocacy is directed to inciting or producing imminent lawless action and is likely to incite or produce such action."[29] This is the most speech-protective test a majority of the Court has ever offered. It was not enough for Black and Douglas, each of whom concurred demanding more. Douglas acidly attacked the Dennis majority as "judges so wedded to the status quo that critical analysis made them nervous."[30]

Two years after Warren retired, the majority of the seven remaining members of the Warren Court decided *Cohen v. California*, 403 U.S. 15

(1971), and the Pentagon Papers cases, 403 U.S. 713 (1971). Cohen, with his jacket emblazoned with "Fuck the Draft," was not only challenging the war but also the generation that had engineered it because the F-word was, then, the most offensive word in the English language; indeed, there was no close second. The Court found Cohen's actions in wearing the jacket in a courthouse constitutionally protected.

The leak of the Pentagon Papers, some forty volumes of highly classified information, was the largest security leak in American history. After the *New York Times* refused to cease publication, the Nixon administration sought an injunction to prevent further publication. Although the *Times* was restrained so that the rocket-docket litigation could bolt forward, the *Washington Post* laid hand on some of the Pentagon Papers and began publishing them. Seventeen days after the first installment appeared in the *Times*, six justices ruled that prior restraints could be issued in only the most extraordinary circumstances, which these cases did not encompass. Even in time of war, top secret information, if obtained by the press, could be published (although perhaps subsequently applicable criminal law would be brought to bear on the papers). As Black, in his last opinion, explained: "The press was to serve the governed, not the governors. [It] was protected so that it could bare the secrets of government and inform the people. Only a free and unrestrained press can effectively expose deception in government."[31]

Thus words did more than summarize Black's views. They spoke to what the Court had been doing: "protecting those who challenged entrenched authority, removing government as an intermediary in establishing the acceptable level of style and criticism, and allowing citizen-critics the opportunity to challenge at will the established truth" (Powe 1991, 105). The First Amendment in 1971 was close to a civil libertarian's dream. It wasn't perfect, but it was close enough. Furthermore, it had been forged during turbulent times that historically had found the Court on the governments' side in attempts to promote stability.

THE FULL STORY

This is the liberal feel-good story. But it is not a complete one, of either Vietnam or domestic security. The full story is more nuanced and offers caveats about the abilities of even the most liberal of courts to protect civil liberties when the political branches do not wish them protected.

The domestic security decisions of 1957 caused the state attorneys general as well as the American Bar Association to join congressional national security conservatives in criticizing the Court (Powe 2000, 99–100). A number of bills were quickly introduced to curb the Court, including eleven to change the ways justices were selected. But in the summer of 1957 little could be done because Congress was focused almost entirely on what would become the Civil Rights Act of that year. Thus, though Congress was not in a position to do much more than verbally trounce the Court, it nevertheless hurriedly passed the Jencks Act at the demand of FBI director J. Edgar Hoover. Although the act basically codified Jencks, it was opposed by the Court's defenders and seen by all as a slap at the Court (Powe 2000, 101–2).

The second session of the Eighty-fifth Congress had time to consider Court-curbing bills.[32] Indeed the House passed H.R. 3, which created a presumption against finding a federal statute preempted state counterparts, rewrote the Smith Act provisions on organizing, and authorized summary discharges of nonsensitive government personnel for security reasons. Senate action focused on William Jenner's proposal to strip the Court of jurisdiction in all the areas where it had interfered with the anticommunist programs. There was too much opposition, and Senator John Marshall Butler offered an amendment to Jenner's bill that would limit jurisdiction-stripping to admissions to the legal profession, but also undo the HUAC holding, rewrite the Smith Act on organizing, and change the preemption doctrine. As modified, Jenner-Butler was voted out of the Judiciary Committee by a 10-5 vote (Powe 2000, 131).

Senate majority leader Lyndon Johnson tried to prevent any votes on anti-Court measures and was successful until the end of the session neared. Jenner-Butler was ultimately tabled by a 49-41 vote, but that was accompanied by a tremendous amount of anti-Court feeling. Immediately on the heels of that, a motion to table H.R. 3 failed 45-39. There was pandemonium in the Senate, but Johnson secured a recess until the next day and between his arm-twisting and that of organized labor enough votes were changed for the motion to recommit to pass 41-40. Even though no anti-Court measure had passed, a clear message had been sent.[33] And the Court, or at least a five-man bloc of the Court, got it (Powe 2000, 132–3).

A year later, in *Barenblatt v. United States*, 360 U.S. 109 (1959), the Court offered HUAC a carte blanche that resulted in affirming convictions in 1961 of two uncooperative witnesses who were called to testify solely because of their opposition to HUAC.[34] The state counterparts, too, were freed from their earlier boundaries.[35] The previous bar admission cases were gutted, and the Court ruled that someone who thought that "whenever the particular government in power becomes destructive of these [constitutional] ends, it is the right of the people to alter or abolish it and thereupon to establish a new government" could justifiably be asked if he were a communist and be denied admission if he refused to answer.[36] A Smith Act conviction using the membership provisions of the law was affirmed,[37] as was the order of the Subversive Activities Control Board to the party requiring it to register and list its members.[38] The Court also upheld a summary discharge of a short-order cook at the Naval Gun Factory.[39] Finally, in 1962, the Court voted to allow Florida to use HUAC hunting practices against the NAACP, a result that played right into the segregationists' claims that civil rights advocates were communists. The result was changed only by Charles Whittaker's timely retirement (Powe 2000, 155–6, 220).

The attacks on the Court by the Eighty-fifth Congress were successful in changing the Court's direction for four years. Congressman Wint Smith had stated that "the Court is simply blind to the reality of our time" (U.S. House 1958, 104 Cong. Rec. 2011). When the Court ultimately regained its eyesight and began to strike down aspects of the domestic security program it was 1964, the year of the Civil Rights Act and Lyndon Johnson's landslide victory over Barry Goldwater, and the issue had lost all of its political salience with only members of the John Birch Society likely to think in the terms Smith had used.

Vietnam, too, had a more checkered course than the earlier mention suggested. A principal legal issue, much mooted but never decided, was whether draftees could be sent to war against their will when Congress had not declared war. Even assuming that the war was unconstitutional—as Douglas believed and suggested—the "political questions doctrine" probably stood as a bar to a judicial declaration of unconstitutionality. The Court had several opportunities to decide on the constitutionality of the war and the applicability of the political questions doctrine. It ducked them all. More fundamentally, a majority of the Warren Court liberals—Earl Warren, Hugo Black, William Brennan, Abe Fortas, Thurgood Marshall—never cast a vote to even hear a case presenting the issues. On the central constitutional issue of the war—and the day—the Court was missing in action.

The liberals were no better when it came to the one piece of legislation specifically aimed at antiwar dissent—the ban on draft card burning. Everyone knew the purpose of the act—with its maximum five years in jail for burning three square inches of paper—was to pour cold water on the protest du jour. Warren's opinion held that the justices couldn't look at legislative motivation and the statute served important government interests—like telling draft eligible men their current status (as if we didn't know)—and so was valid. Only Douglas dissented.

Douglas was alone again four years later when a district judge in New York ordered a halt to the American bombing of Cambodia on the grounds that it was illegal. The Second Circuit quickly stayed the order and Justice Marshall refused to intervene. Using the operative assumption of the era, that if one Supreme Court justice refused a stay there was always the chance Douglas might go for it (a theory belied by reality), the ACLU flew to his vacation home in Goose Prairie, arranged a hearing the next day, and won when Douglas vacated the circuit order. The victory was short-lived. Within hours, Marshall arranged a conference call in which the eight justices overruled Douglas.[40]

Even *Brandenburg v. Ohio* with its incredibly speech-protective test is not without ambiguity. The Court did not overrule Dennis even though that decision was flatly inconsistent with Brandenburg. Indeed, the Court wrote as if Brandenburg were an application of Dennis' principles. Subsequently Brandenburg has been applied in only two cases[41] and Dennis' test has been cited as authoritative in one.[42]

My recapitulation is quite different from Geoffrey Stone's whiggish *Perilous Times.* Stone basically ends his discussion of domestic security in June 1957 when the Court seemingly had announced an end to McCarthyism. He follows with a few paragraphs critical of Barenblatt, but moves on to the happy note that Barenblatt was sharply limited four years later in a case involving the NAACP. There is not a whiff of the fury of the organized bar, the state attorneys general, or the Eighty-fifth Congress in his account, nor is there recognition of how fully the Court retreated for four years. In the case of Vietnam, it is understandable why he never discussed the constitutionality of the war and the Court's persistent ducking of the issue. But it may be surprising that he gives the Court a pass on draft card burning: "the better part of wisdom, if not valor, counseled in favor of the Court's resolution" (Stone 2004, 277). His overall conclusion about Vietnam was that the cases, "cut[ing] across many different facets of First Amendment jurisprudence . . . reflected an impressive commitment to protecting free expression—even in wartime" (519).

If the most liberal Court ever would not strike the ban on draft card burning or even tell draftees that the constitutionality of the war was a political question and not fit for judicial resolution, then what Court would? The full lessons of the Warren Court suggest that it protected civil liberties when it did not expect opposition from Congress, but was decidedly less protective when it had reason to fear a backlash. What differentiated the Warren Court from other periods in American history was its preference for civil liberties. What ties the Warren Court to other periods, both before and after, is that it would not attempt to stand up to the political branches when it appeared that they might strike back.

THE SEDITION ACT

Twice within the first two decades after ratification of the Constitution, the federal government went after dissenters. The Sedition Act controversy, when the Federalists tried to entrench themselves in power by silencing the Republican press at the end of the 1790s, is well known. Jefferson's attempt to use the blunt instrument of treason during his embargo is less so. Neither situation involved the Court per se because at the time the Court lacked appellate jurisdiction over criminal cases, but both involved Supreme Court justices because of circuit riding.

There were fifteen indictments under the Sedition Act, and all ten cases that went to trial resulted in convictions. All five of the leading Republican newspapers were prosecuted, three were forced to close, two of them never to resume publication. Albert Gallatin, the Republican house leader, subsequently observed: "How has it been executed? Only by punishing persons of politics different from those of the administration" (United States 1789, 6th Cong, 1st Sess., 952).

Justices James Iredell, William Paterson, and Samuel Chase, all Federalist appointees of Washington, presided at trials and each believed the act was constitutional. Iredell's views were fully representative: if you "take away from a Republic the confidence of the people . . . the whole fabric crumbles into dust" (Stone 2004, 68).

The justices were enthusiastic about applying the Sedition Act, Chase too much so. His handling of two trials, those of James Callender and Thomas Cooper, looked like he was part of the prosecution team. He informed the defendant that writing about the president was risky business, and in instructing the jury he went through Cooper's handbill line by line to explain why it violated the act. To Cooper's statement that Adams had called for a standing army, Chase noted that that was impossible because the Constitution limited an appropriation for the army to two years. Thus there could be no standing army unless "the Constitution is first destroyed."[43] In Callender's trial he refused to see a distinction between statements of fact and statements of opinion and was so abusive that Callender's attorneys withdrew. The remaining Republican press quite properly found his conduct "reprehensible" (Stone 2004, 62). Chase's aggressive proprosecution tactics left him as the Jeffersonian symbol of what was wrong with the federal judiciary. He would be impeached in 1804, but acquitted a year later.

To avoid going to war or paying for the necessary military build-up, Thomas Jefferson declared an embargo that forbid foreign trade. The embargo strangled the New England economies, and smuggling became so prevalent that Jefferson declared a state of insurrection. Several perpetrators were charged with treason. Justice Brockholst Livingston, a Jefferson appointee, would have none of it. "No single act in opposition to or in evasion of a law, however violent or flagrant when the object is private gain, can be construed as levying war on the United States."[44] This ruling echoed an earlier one by John Marshall that thwarted Jefferson's efforts to hang his former vice president, Aaron Burr. Between the two, the use of treason as a weapon to be wielded against political opposition ended.

With both the Sedition Act and the treason trials, the defendants got a trial before a judge sitting with a jury. The Civil War saw civil liberties threatened by the substitution of military commissions (or just plain detention) for jury trials.

THE CIVIL WAR ERA

After Fort Sumter, Marylanders sympathetic to the Confederacy believed that if they could prevent reinforcement of Washington, D.C., by rail, they might create conditions whereby the city might be captured quickly and with it independence for the South might be achieved relatively peacefully. Men like John Merryman, a prominent farmer, state legislator, officer in the state militia and ardent secessionist, were attempting to blow up the necessary bridges and track to accomplish that. Abraham Lincoln had declared martial law in Maryland, and at two o'clock in the morning Merryman was arrested, taken to Fort McHenry, and charged with treason for participation in the destruction of railroad bridges.

Because of his social and political standing, Merryman had immediate access to counsel, and his attorney petitioned for a writ of habeas corpus from Roger Taney in his capacity as chief justice. When General George Cadwalader ignored the writ, Taney sat down and wrote an opinion in the case for delivery to Lincoln.[45] The strongest part of Taney's opinion was that Lincoln was exercising a power that even George III did not have and never claimed. When the mayor of Baltimore congratulated him on preserving the integrity of the writ, Taney responded: "I am an old man, a very old man, but perhaps I was preserved for this occasion" (Swisher 1974, 848). Taney's opinion was applauded by Democrats in the North, loved by secessionists, and perhaps wisely ignored by Lincoln. It stands as a singular moment of a justice standing for civil liberties at the height of a crisis. This is perhaps marred by the fact that Taney wanted the South to prevail and Maryland, his home state, to join the Confederacy. Taney would go on to dissent when the Court sustained the legality of Lincoln's blockade of Southern ports, and he wrote draft opinions holding the issuing of paper money and military conscription unconstitutional.

There were four other prominent cases of habeas, all dealing with convictions of civilians by courts martial. The first involved Clement Vallandigham, the most prominent Northern Democrat who supported the Confederacy. After Vallandigham denounced the war and urged resistance to the use of courts martial, the commanding general in southern Ohio arrested and tried him for aiding the enemy. He was sentenced to detention for the remainder of the war. All of this was without Lincoln's knowledge. On learning of the events, Lincoln ordered Vallandigham released behind Confederate lines. An effort at habeas failed because he was not in custody[46] and a subsequent effort to have the Court review the record failed because there was no jurisdictional statute authorizing it.[47]

There was jurisdiction in Lambdin Milliken's case. He had plotted armed rebellion north of the Ohio River and been sentenced to hang. A unanimous Court overturned his conviction by holding that Congress had not authorized courts martial for civilians. Five justices went beyond the facts and held Congress lacked power to do so. As long as civilian courts are open, civilians could not be tried by court martial.[48] This is a core aspect of civil liberties. But it must be noted that the order discharging Milliken came in April 1866, and the opinion was handed down the following December. The war was over.

Two years later the Court had its major court martial case, this one involved William McCardle, the editor of the Vicksburg Times. Properly concerned that the Milliken majority would rule for McCardle and thus facilitate the ending of Reconstruction (before the coerced ratification of the Fourteenth Amendment), Congress hastily passed a statute repealing the one on which the Court's jurisdiction rested. This coincided with the House having impeached Andrew Johnson and Chief Justice Salmon Chase presiding over Johnson's Senate trial. In 1868, the Congress that had been elected in 1866 and that had excluded representatives from the South, was deadly serious about Reconstruction. Thus even though Milliken had been argued before the repealer, the Court wisely held a reargument on jurisdiction and ruled that because of the repeal it lacked jurisdiction and therefore dismissed the case.[49] Nevertheless the Court noted that it "seems to have been supposed, if effect be given to the repealing act . . . that the whole appellate power of the court in cases in habeas corpus is denied. But this is an error."[50] At the Court's next term, in the last habeas case, again involving a Mississippi newspaper editor, albeit one who killed an army officer, the Court followed its McCardle hint and held that it had jurisdiction under a provision of the first Judiciary Act.[51] The editor was then released from custody without the Court ruling on the merits.

WORLD WAR I AND AFTER

The erratic course on habeas was not copied during World War I and its immediate aftermath. Both the Department of Justice and the Post Office were dead set on clamping down on antiwar statements. As Attorney General Thomas Gregory said, "May God have mercy on them, for they may expect none from an outraged people and an avenging government" (quoted in Stone 2004, 153). The Court was fully part of that righteous crusade and even labor leader and Socialist presidential candidate Eugene Debs's conviction was affirmed for a speech praising socialism and pacifism.[52] President Warren Harding subsequently pardoned Debs. Civil liberties were never high in the pantheon of values during the Progressive era and the Court's decisions reflected that. In the aftermath of the excesses of the war, many Americans became far more sensitive to civil liberties violations.

During World War II, President Franklin Roosevelt's attorney general, Francis Biddle, an American Civil Liberties Union supporter, was intent on avoiding a repeat of the World War I repression. To a large extent he was successful, but in all probability primarily because there was little antiwar dissent. But Biddle authorized wiretaps as necessary and there were some symbolic prosecutions of fascist sympathizers, though denaturalization proceedings were the preferred tactic (Steele 1999). Then, of course, there is the most serious blot on civil liberties committed by the federal government in the twentieth century—the forced relocation and confinement of more than 100,000 Japanese Americans from 1942 until after the 1944 elections (even though the president and the War Department knew by then that there was no need for continued confinement).

The Court had visited the Japanese relocation three times. The first dealt with the curfew imposed on only those of Japanese descent. Concluding that they could not second-guess the military commanders on this issue coming in the wake of Pearl Harbor, the Court unanimously upheld the curfew.[53] Justice Wiley Rutledge and perhaps others believed that the vote to sustain the curfew committed him to sustain the relocation as well. In any event that is what six justices did in *Korematsu v. United States*, 323 U.S. 214 (1944), decided right after the presidential election. Black's majority opinion can easily be summarized as concluding that war is hell and that is that. Perhaps no Court could go against the government while the bullets were still flying. Perhaps no justices can vote against the president that so wisely appointed them, though Robert Jackson and Frank Murphy both did.

The same December day the justices salved their consciences by ruling that habeas was available to those in the internment camps and if they could prove they were no danger, they could be released.[54] It was too little, too late. As time passed, with the exception of John C. McCloy, no one involved in the Japanese relocation defended the actions as either constitutional or proper.

World War II witnessed one important judicial extension of civil liberties. At the time of Dunkirk, the Court decided *Minersville School District v. Gobitis*, 310 U.S. 586 (1940), and upheld a requirement that school children commence the day by reciting the Pledge of Allegiance. The children in question were Jehovah's Witnesses who believed that to do so would be to worship a graven image and thus threaten them with eternal damnation. Three years later, in an identical case, *West Virginia v. Barnette*, 319 U.S. 624 (1943), the Court reversed. Barnette is as eloquent a civil liberties opinion as exists and the Court handed it down on Flag Day as a poignant reminder of what the flag stands for.

There are several explanations for the reversal, the easiest of which is that new justices joined the Court, one being Wiley Rutledge, who as a newly minted circuit court judge had criticized *Gobitis*. Three justices, Hugo Black, William Douglas, and Frank Murphy, had concluded that *Gobitis* was wrongly decided. Why? First, on reflection, the school districts (backed, of course, by the state) were putting children who took their religion seriously into an untenable position, and more than 2,000 Jehovah's Witness children were expelled over the next three years. Eleanor Roosevelt chastised Felix Frankfurter for his *Gobitis* conclusions. One hundred seventy-five newspapers, including most of the influential ones, editorialized against the decision. Second, some elements in American society thought *Gobitis* signaled open season on the Witnesses. There were at least 355 violent incidents—including one castration—in forty-four states (Walker 1990, 110). FBI director J. Edgar Hoover issued a public call for their halt. *Gobitis* had placed the Court on the wrong side of public opinion and in camp with vigilantes. That, too, was an untenable position which *Barnette* righted.

THE WARREN COURT

This now brings the story of civil liberties protection back to where this essay started. In context it is no wonder that the Warren Court, blemishes and all, stands out. It was different. Furthermore, by coming after periods where civil liberties received no preferences, the Warren Court actions contribute to the idea of progress that law professors from Harry Kalven (1988) through Geoffrey Stone celebrate.

As the post-Warren Court story unfolds, continuity is the basic theme because after Watergate there were no domestic crises. If one takes away sexually explicit materials and commercial speech, neither of which relates to this theme, from the Court's First Amendment jurisprudence of the past three decades, the Court hasn't done all that much. It was from this civil liberties perspective that the Court faced the war on terror.

After September 11, 2001, administration lawyers studying legal issues that would be forthcoming agreed unanimously on only one issue—those captured would be held outside the United States (and therefore ideally outside the law of the United States). The initial pair of cases to arise asked, first, whether an American citizen, captured in Afghanistan, could be held as an enemy combatant and denied an opportunity to prove that the detention was wrongful and, second, whether noncitizens detained abroad had the right to access American courts with habeas corpus to test the legality of their confinement. The evening of arguments for the former, CBS News broke the story of abuses at Abu Ghraib, and while the opinions were being written, the Justice Department's so-called torture memo (claiming that the president had the inherent authority to override a congressional ban on torture) was released. Neither helped the Bush administration, which received only Clarence Thomas's vote.

Immediately after the decision, the Defense Department created tribunals to review the status of all the detainees at Guantanamo, but before the Court heard another war on terror case, two separate developments occurred. First, there were leaks to the news media of secret programs. First, the executive had created prisons in Eastern Europe to hold some detainees without anyone knowing who they were or what was being done to them. Second, the National Security Agency had engaged in warrantless intercepts of phone calls and emails between residents of the United States and individuals outside the country suspected of terrorist activity, in seeming violation of the Foreign Intelligence Surveillance Act, which states that it authorizes the exclusive method for NSA intercepts. Third, the administration had authorized *enhanced interrogation techniques* (the Bush administration's term for procedures it would not disclose and for what its critics called torture) in violation of the Geneva Conventions' prohibitions on cruel, inhumane, and degrading treatment. Fourth, European banking records had been turned over to the United States so that the transactions could be mined for data. The second development was passage of the Detainee Treatment Act of 2006 (DTA), which required adherence to the Geneva Conventions but also withdrew jurisdiction of federal courts to hear habeas petitions by Guantanamo detainees. In combination, these developments suggested an executive branch that believed it could fight the war on terror without congressional help (or oversight) and a (Republican) Congress that believed the judiciary should keep out of it.

Hamdan v. Rumsfeld was a habeas challenge to the military tribunals created to try detainees.[55] Hamdan, arrested in November 2001, but not charged until 2004, challenged both the definition of the substantive offense he was charged with—joining an enterprise dedicated to attacking civilians—as well as the structures and procedures of the military commissions. The Court—over dissents by Clarence Thomas, Antonin Scalia, and Samuel Alito (John Roberts being disqualified because he had participated in the opinion below anticipating the position of the dissenters)—first concluded that the DTA did not apply to Hamdan's case. The majority then held that Congress had not authorized the tribunals, and, indeed, they were contrary to the Uniform Code of Military Justice and the Geneva Conventions. In an extraordinary declaration, the Court stated "the Executive is bound to comply with the Rule of Law that prevails in this jurisdiction," thereby making clear that the president had not acted in accordance with the rule of law.[56]

Breyer's concurring opinion twice stated that the president could go to Congress to seek whatever authority he deemed necessary. With his hand forced by Hamdan, that is exactly what Bush did, and the Republican Congress responded in barely over three weeks with the Military Commissions Act of 2006 giving him everything he wanted—including the ability to use evidence obtained before December 20, 2005, by cruel, inhumane, and degrading treatment, as well as a specific provision eliminating judicial review except by a single appeal of a verdict by a military commission (limited to issues of law and not fact). Thus, if a detainee is never charged with an offense, he may be held indefinitely without any access to a federal court. Breyer had stated that the Court's "conclusion ultimately rests upon a single ground: Congress had not issued the executive a 'blank check.' "[57] With the MCA, the Republican controlled Congress deposited that check in the executive's account.

At the end of his chapter on World War II, John Yoo highlights the current problem of an imperial judiciary. Thus instead of rubber-stamping the executive as the Court did during World War II, Yoo is concerned that an overconfident judiciary will overstep its bounds and interfere in an area were "courts have little competence in measuring the nature of national security threats, the expected value of potential harms, and balancing them against any costs to civil liberties" (see chapter 3, this volume). Such an intervention could result in errors of judgment that risk both national and individual security by granting rights that endanger the nation. Yoo may be correct, but his further assertion that the Bush administration's policy "has kept courts at the center of the action, sometimes intentionally, sometimes not" is an overstatement. The cornerstone of the policy has been to keep as much as possible off American soil (and therefore supposedly out of the reach of meddling, incompetent American judges).

Yoo is correct that the Bush administration has not received the judicial deference FDR was accorded. One must note, however, that FDR was a popular president with a Court staffed by seven of his appointees, whereas Bush is an unpopular president with only two appointees on the Court. But the reasons for lack of deference go deeper, and are tied together by a rejection of the Bush administration's view of the Constitution, to wit, "it's so pre-9/11."

Yoo's claims of the need for judicial deference hinge on institutional competence. The problem here is that in the aftermath of Hurricane Katrina, the administration was exposed as serially incompetent. It couldn't handle hurricane relief and it totally botched Iraq. Thus Yoo's claim of expertise is best left to a new administration; this one has forfeited any claim that it could get something right. Second, the administration has destroyed America's credibility and standing in the world. It may not be surprising that justices who summer in Salzburg and Tuscany may want to do their part to restore America's standing. Third, and there seems no polite way to say it, the Bush administration is lawless. Given the supine Republican Congresses and the administration's fetish for secrecy, the Court might have seen itself as the only institutional check on an out of control executive. This is further buttressed by the Court's late June 2007 switch to agree to hear the habeas claims of Guantanamo detainees immediately after an army officer who had been a member of the "combat status review tribunals" asserted that the whole review process was "an irremediable sham" (Linda Greenhouse, "Clues to the New Dynamic on the Supreme Court," *New York Times*, July 3, 2007).

Whether the MCA is consistent with the Constitution is a contested question. There are two ways to view Hamdan. One is based on separation of powers, a demand that Congress be brought into the process of deciding how to treat detainees. The other is a rule of law demand that procedures be consistent with the due process clause. The Court successfully cut Congress in. Whether a Court that has seen itself as the only interpreter of the Constitution will cut itself in remains for the future when new elections will hold the keys to judicial outcomes.

CONCLUSION

Learned Hand offered a critique of relying on courts to protect civil liberties when he "wonder[ed] whether we do not rest our hopes too much upon constitutions, upon laws, upon courts. There are false hopes; believe me, these are false hopes. Liberty lies in the hearts of men and women; when it dies there no constitution, no law, no court can save it" (1952, 189–90). Hand was making a couple of points. First, an aroused and caring citizenry is exactly what a democracy wants. Second, that there are limits to law. Both are true, but both proceed at such a high level of generality that neither seems particularly helpful in deciding concrete cases. Furthermore, Hand may have overlooked the very real possibility that Americans have not lost the spirit of liberty; they may occasionally have put it aside because of momentary fear. In these situations, courts might be effective in assisting the people in returning to a spirit of liberty.

There is scant evidence for that reminder and return in the short run. Americans on the West Coast were definitely aroused after December 7, 1941. The result was the Japanese relocation. Perhaps the Court could do nothing about the curfew—indeed it probably should not have. But the Court did not need to sustain the relocation in Korematsu—yet it did. Had it drawn the line between Hirabayashi and Korematsu, the military would have been allowed to take some limited actions in the immediate aftermath of an emergency, but would have been told that there must be real evidence before it starts incarcerating people on less than mere suspicion.

An aroused citizenry—at least an aroused Congress—caused the Court to reverse course on McCarthyism. Maybe it was fear of an aroused citizenry that kept the Court far away from dealing with the constitutionality of the Vietnam War. The point should be obvious. An aroused citizenry is a two-way street and only one of those is to have liberty beating in the heart all the time. Hand is asking too much. We can still love our liberty and believe we are protecting it even as we curtail it for what appears to be good and sufficient reason. That was the point of the *Washington Post* editorial approving Dennis.

I have been surprised at how relatively well civil liberties of those within the United States have been protected after 9/11 with the extraordinary exception of José Padilla (and possibly the National Security Agency [illegal] surveillance ordered by President Bush in 2002 without judicial or legislative authorization). Padilla is an American citizen arrested on American soil being detained in a military installation on American soil and kept from an attorney and the judicial process. Attorney General John Ashcroft initially announced that Padilla hoped to explode a dirty bomb in an American city. The Justice Department, however, retreated from Ashcroft's overheated imagination while remaining convinced Padilla was up to no good—though it was not sure what type of no good Padilla wanted to commit. Thus Padilla was held in a navy brig because some powerful people believed he wanted to commit a crime. This was even worse than Dennis. There is the parallel that Dennis and his codefendants were indicted under the Smith Act because the FBI could find no evidence of an actual act against the United States. But they were indicted; they were able to meet with their lawyers; and they were given a trial. After three years, the Justice Department has finally indicted Padilla for conspiracy to murder, kidnap, and maim in a foreign country. Whether he will or will not be convicted, the point remains that holding an American for three years without charges is telling evidence that the judiciary remains a branch of a government committed to fighting the war on terrorism at seemingly all costs. That there has been no true outcry over this says that for a period, like other crisis times, the public is willing to sacrifice minorities' civil liberties for some supposed higher reason.

Nevertheless, I am aware of no horror stories about overreaching under the PATRIOT Act (though the FBI has overstepped in at least six instances). It turns out that all excesses against liberties and lives take place outside the United States. Every time I go through an airport and see a grandmother being searched, I marvel. First, I marvel at the extraordinary waste of resources. No grandmother anywhere has yet to be a suicide bomber; everyone knows this is a waste. Yet we do it even though a better application of resources would make us marginally safer. Second, I marvel at our reluctance to profile (even to the extent of giving grandmothers a pass). Stone writes of "the aspiration of Americans to be fair, tolerant of others, and respectful a constitutional liberties" and suggests that this may be more "deeply embedded in American culture today" than at any other time (Stone 2004, 157). The unwillingness to profile certainly backs him up; Hand could be proud (if bemused).

Beyond the PATRIOT Act and airport searches, Americans seem to have a strong attachment to the First Amendment (even if the occasional poll suggests the contrary). The Court's decisions seem in accord with that position. Of course, over the past forty years it has been easy to use the rhetorical advantages of being pro speech, but the justices appear to mean it. The *preferred position* was a Hughes era phrase that came into fruition under Earl Warren and has continued to this day. The justices will not lightly turn their backs on free speech and civil liberties though they may give way when confronted with a compelling state interest, which I am quite sure that preventing future 9/11s is.

This is the other cutting edge of what Hand observed. Courts cannot stand up to an aroused populace backed by an aroused government. They may not even want to. After all, justices are drawn from much the same elites that populate the federal government. Justices read the same magazines, watch the same programs, and hear the same policy discussions. They are men and women of their times and, in Benjamin Cardozo's words, "the great tides and currents which engulf the rest of men do not turn aside in their course and pass judges by" (1921, 168). Justice Robert Jackson noted that "measures [ordinarily] violative of constitutional rights are claimed to be necessary to security, in the judgment of officials who are best in a position to know, but the necessity is not provable by ordinary evidence and the court is in no position to determine the necessity for itself" (1951, 115).

The justices knew that Pearl Harbor was a stunning attack by Japan; they knew that the Soviet Union was a threat to America; they knew that (at least) some members of the Communist Party were loyal to the Soviet Union rather than the United States. They might overcome this knowledge—as three did in Korematsu and two did in Dennis. That, though, takes a lot of restraint, and perhaps violates Hand's injunction that the "spirit of liberty is the spirit which is not too sure that it is right" (1952, 190). It is probably asking too much to expect most jurists to be able to do so. After all, what if they were wrong and the government's fears were right? How could justices believe that they have been access to appropriate information than the executive branch?

The unwillingness to act becomes especially paralyzing when the justices believe there will be a different type of adverse consequence to their actions—an attack on the Court as an institution. In 1935 and 1936 the Court struck down ten recently enacted federal statutes—a record that stands to this day. With a landslide reelection of Franklin Roosevelt and a Court packing plan on the table, the justices suddenly found everything the New Deal did was constitutional. Then a series of vacancies filled with New Deal justices created a Court that really believed in the New Deal economic policies. A little over twenty years later, the Court's domestic security decisions triggered a sharp reaction in Congress and, as Warren noted, "legislation [to take away parts of the Court's appellate jurisdiction to protect domestic security programs from judicial invalidation], evoking as it did the atmosphere of the Cold War hysteria, came dangerously close to passing" (Warren 1977, 313). As detailed earlier, a majority of the Court bid hasty retreat and the Court did not return to invalidating the federal domestic security program until 1964—well after the issue lost its political salience.

Echoing Hand, the lessons from the stitch in time that saves nine and the Warren Court retreat on domestic security seem fundamental. The Supreme Court is not free to do just anything in areas where Congress truly cares about the outcomes. Sometimes, like after 1963 with domestic security, Congress no longer cares. Sometimes, like after 1957 with domestic security, Congress does. I suspect that when civil liberties and American lives are truly on the balance Congress will care more about the latter. Whether the Court does or does not, if it is a crisis time, the Court will uphold Congress. The contrary example of Roger Taney stands alone— because he was pulling for the Confederacy.

There are several reasons to believe *Hamdan v. Rumsfeld* may suggest a more aggressive protection of individual rights. First, the decision comes in the wake of a series of leaks about programs that the Bush administration tried to keep secret from the nation and Congress. Second, and related, the administration's Constitutional position was the equivalent of "we can do whatever we wish" and flatly inconsistent with the Court's view of itself as the ultimate expositor of the Constitution. Third, the war on terror has lasted longer than World War II even though there has not been a second attack on American soil. Fourth, President Bush's unpopularity is like that of President Truman when the Court rebuked him in the Steel Seizure case. Only time will tell. If there is another attack or if a new president acts similarly to Bush or if Bush gets to replace one of the majority, then we will see what Hamdan really means.

NOTES

1. *Dennis v. United States,* 341 U.S. 494 (1951).
2. *United States v. Carroll Towing,* 159 F.2d 169 (2nd Cir. 1947).
3. 341 U.S. 494 (1951) at 510 quoting 183 F.2d.201, 212 (CA 2 1950).
4. Ibid. at 581.
5. Ibid. at 589.
6. Ibid. at 588.
7. *Peters v. Hobby,* 349 U.S. 331, 336–37 (1955).
8. *Yates v. United States,* 354 U.S. 298 (1957).
9. *Watkins v. United States,* 354 U.S. 178 (1957).
10. *Jencks v. United States,* 353 U.S. 657 (1957); *Communist Party v. Subversive Activities Control Board,* 351 U.S. 115 (1956); *Mesarosh v. United States,* 352 U.S. 1 (1956).
11. *Service v. Dulles,* 354 U.S. 363 (1957).

12. *Konigsburg v. State Bar*, 353 U.S. 252 (1957); *Schware v. State Bar*, 353 U.S. 232 (1957).

13. *Communist Party v. Subversive Activities Control Board*, 367 U.S. 1 (1961).

14. *DeGregory v. New Hampshire*, 383 U.S. 825 (1966).

15. *Elfbrandt v. Russell*, 384 U.S. 11 (1966).

16. *Keyishian v. Board of Regents*, 385 U.S. 589 (1967).

17. *United States v. Brown*, 381 U.S. 437 (1965).

18. *LaMont v. Postmaster General*, 381 U.S. 301 (1965).

19. *Albertson v. Subversion Activities Control Board*, 382 U.S. 70 (1965).

20. *Aptheker v. Secretary of State*, 378 U.S. 500 (1964).

21. *United States v. Robel*, 389 U.S. 258 (1967).

22. *Bond v. Floyd*, 385 U.S. 116 (1966).

23. Ibid. at 135–36.

24. *Watts v. United States*, 394 U.S. 705, 706 (1969).

25. *Tinker v. Des Moines School District*, 393 U.S. 503, 508 (1969).

26. 395 U.S. 444 (1969).

27. *Masses Publishing Co. v. Patten*, 244 Fed. 535 (S.D.N.Y. 1917) revs'd 246 Fed. 24 (1917).

28. *Whitney v. California*, 274 U.S. 357, 372 (1927).

29. 395 U.S. 444 (1969) at 447.

30. Ibid. at 454.

31. 403 U.S. 713, at 717 (1971).

32. The story of the Eighty-fifth Congress and the Court is best told in Murphy, *Congress and the Court* (1962).

33. "Legislation, evoking as it did the atmosphere of the Cold War hysteria, came dangerously close to passing" (Warren 1977, 203).

34. *Wilkinson v. United States*, 365 U.S. 399 (1961); *Braden v. United States*, 365 U.S. 431 (1961).

35. *Uphaus v. Wyman*, 360 U.S. 72 (1959).

36. In re *Anastaplo*, 366 U.S. 366 U.S. 82 (1961); *Konigsburg v. State Bar*, 366 U.S. 36 (1961).

37. *Scales v. United States*, 367 U.S. 203 (1961).

38. *Communist Party v. Subversive Activities Control Board*, 367 U.S. 1 (1961).

39. *Cafeteria Workers v. McElroy*, 367 U.S. 886 (1961).

40. *Holtzman v. Schlesinger*, 413 U.S. 1304 (Marshall); 1316 (Douglas); 1321 (Marshall for the Court).

41. *Hess v. Indiana*, 414 U.S. 105 (1974); *NAACP v. Claiborne Hardware Co.*, 458 U.S. 886 (1982).

42. *Nebraska Press Ass'n v. Stuart*, 427 U.S. 539, 562 (1976).

43. Francis Wharton, *State Trials* 676 (1849).

44. *United States v. Hoxie*, 26 F. Cas. 397 (C.C.D. Vt. 1808).

45. Ex Parte *Merryman*, 17 F. Cas. 144 (1861).

46. Ex Parte *Vallandigham*, Fed. Case No. 16,816 (1863).

47.   Ex Parte *Vallandigham,* 1 Wall. 243 (1864).
48.   Ex Parte *Milligan,* 4 Wall. 2 (1866).
49.   Ex Parte *McCardle,* 7 Wall. 506 (1869).
50.   Ibid. at 515.
51.   Ex Parte *Yerger,* 8 Wall. 85 (1869).
52.   *Debs v. United States,* 249 U.S. 211 (1919).
53.   *Hirabayashi v. United States,* 320 U.S. 81 (1943).
54.   Ex Parte *Endo,* 323 U.S. 283 (1944).
55.   126 S. Ct. 2749 (2006).
56.   Ibid. at 2798.
57.   Ibid. at 2799.

References

Cardozo, Benjamin N. 1921. *The Nature of the Judicial Process.* New Haven, Conn.: Yale University Press.

Hand, Learned. 1952. "The Spirit of Liberty." In *The Spirit of Liberty,* edited by Irving Dillard. New York: Alfred A. Knopf.

Jackson, Robert. 1951. "Wartime Security and Liberty under Law." *Buffalo Law Review* 1(1): 103–19.

Kalven, Harry, Jr., and Jamie Kalven. 1988. *A Worthy Tradition: Freedom of Speech in America.* New York: Harper and Row.

Murphy, Walter F. 1962. *Congress and the Court: A Case Study of the American Political Process.* Chicago, Ill.: University of Chicago Press.

Powe, L. A., Jr. 1991. *The Fourth Estate and the Constitution.* Berkeley, Calif.: University of California Press.

———. 2000. *The Warren Court and American Politics.* Cambridge, Mass.: Belknap Press of Harvard University Press.

Steele, Richard. W. 1999. *Free Speech in the Good War.* New York: Palgrave Macmillan.

Stone, Geoffrey R. 2004. *Perilous Times: Free Speech in Wartime from the Sedition Acts of 1798 to the War on Terrorism.* New York: W. W. Norton.

Stone, I. F. 1963. *The Haunted Fifties.* New York: Random House.

Swisher, Carl B. 1974. *History of the Supreme Court of the United States. Vol. 5, The Taney Period, 1836–1864.* New York: Macmillan.

United States, and Joseph Gales. 1789. *Annals of the Congress of the United States, 1789–1824,* 42 vols. Washington: Gales and Seaton.

U.S. Congress. House. 1958. *Congressional Record.* 85th Congr. 2nd Sess. Vol. 104, Part 2. Washington: Government Printing Office.

Walker, Samuel. 1990. *In Defense of American Liberties.* New York: Oxford University Press.

Warren, Earl. 1977. *The Memoirs of Earl Warren.* Garden City, N.Y.: Doubleday.

CHAPTER 8

TECHNOLOGY, CIVIL LIBERTIES, AND NATIONAL SECURITY

PAUL M. SCHWARTZ AND RONALD D. LEE

This chapter departs in two respects from the earlier historical discussions of the dynamic between national security and civil liberties. First, the other authors focus largely on interactions among the executive branch, Congress, the judiciary, and to a lesser degree the public. By contrast, in this chapter we consider technological change and its impact on the behavior and choices of these actors. Second, a leitmotif of the preceding chapters has been the collective national response to war, insurrection, or internal threats, perceived or real. We examine the development of technology, which is increasingly driven by a highly globalized private sector rather than by the United States government. Technology itself shapes and influences the national response to war or other national security challenges. The nature of this impact on policy can, however, be difficult to parse.

We propose that, beyond the ongoing debate about the role of the three branches of the federal government in protecting civil liberties and responding to national security threats, fundamental issues exist regarding how our governing institutions should evaluate and respond to technological change. We consider the challenge of incorporating technology into the functions and processes of democratic governance.

Our particular focus is on information privacy, which concerns how public and private entities collect, process, share and store personal data. Information privacy is a key aspect of civil liberties, and one on which technology has an especially strong impact. To set the stage for the following discussion, we initially look at two topics. The first is the path by which information technology became part of the fabric of governance and society in the late 1960s. This era saw the development of bureaucratic systems of data processing. The second topic concerns the dramatic development of computing power (identified in Moore's law) and the rise of the Internet. These two developments had a significant influence on the availability and processing of personal data by both the government and the commercial sector. Indeed, the emergence of greater computer power and the Internet has meant decentralized data banks that can easily share information, and greater information sharing within and between the private and public sectors.

With this background in place, we examine technology's potential both to diminish and to enhance privacy when enlisted in the service of national security goals. We summarize and challenge the standard discourse about the relationships among technology, civil liberties, and national security. In the conventional view, there is a zero-sum game in play—technology either harms civil liberties and helps national security, or vice versa. In a sense, this zero-sum perspective is somewhat similar to the dynamic sketched in earlier chapters of this volume, in which measures taken in the name of national security diminish civil liberties. We propose that the reality regarding technology is more varied and complex than the conventional wisdom accepts, and conclude by offering observations about the challenges that technology poses for governance.

HISTORY LESSONS ABOUT INFORMATION PRIVACY

In the 1960s, the United States government turned to electronic data processing to aid in its expanded social welfare programs, and private companies adopted computerized data processing to streamline and extend business operations. Computerization enormously increased both the volume of stored personal data and the ability of businesses and governments to analyze and extract meaning from this information.

During this period, Alan Westin and Arthur Miller wrote two landmark scholarly works that explored the emerging impact of computerized data processing on civil liberties. Both scholars recognized the emergence of technology that raised new potential threats to civil liberties. They attributed these threats to the computer's creation of novel ways to link, process, store, analyze, and transfer personal information.

In 1967, Alan Westin in his *Privacy and Freedom* surveyed a range of new technologies with special attention to "the computer-born revolution in man's capacity to process data" (158). He saw the computer as creating a new kind of "data surveillance" (366). He then argued that "as 'life-long dossiers' and interchange of information grow steadily, the possibilities increase that agencies employing computers can accomplish heretofore impossible surveillance of individuals, businesses, and groups by putting together all the now-scattered pieces of data" (366).

By 1971, four years later, the public had developed a strong interest in the topic of computers, data banks, and information privacy. One sign of this interest was the appearance that year of Arthur Miller's *The Assault on Privacy* in both a hardcover edition from the University of Michigan Press and a paperback from a popular publishing house. "Institutions of almost every description," Miller noted, "are relying on the computer to increase their data-handling capacity and to improve the efficiency of their operations" (1971, 36). He argued that the accumulation of "dossier-type material on people over a long period of time" represented a threat to "some of our most basic freedoms" (54–55).[1] This fear was based on the coming centrality of new information processing technologies; as Miller wrote, "the emerging information transfer networks can be described as society's electronic equivalent to the biological central nervous system" (273). From this perspective, the domestic intelligence-gathering and surveillance in the late 1960s and early 1970s that L. A. Powe describes in chapter 7 may well have been influenced by the availability of new technologies at the time. The question for Miller and Westin was how to regulate these new systems to preserve civil liberties in light of the new technological capabilities for surveillance. In the conclusion to *Privacy and Freedom*, Westin made two essential points:

1. The strict records surveillance that was for centuries the conscious trademark of European authoritarian systems . . . is now being installed in the United States . . . as an accidental by-product of electronic data processing for social-welfare and public-service ends.
2. There is no way to stop computerization. (1967, 326)

The new information processing systems were in fact not to be stopped. Over the subsequent years, they have made undeniably positive contributions to the effective delivery of government services and to the creation of entirely new categories of businesses. The question, still open to this day, is how best to regulate their impact on information privacy.

From the vantage point of 2008, we can see that Westin and Miller were writing at a critical juncture during which the public and private sectors were increasing their computerized data processing of personal information. In one observer's view, such early periods in the growth of technological, bureaucratic, and physical infrastructures provide critical opportunities to create the legal and social rules that will shape the resulting systems. As Thomas Hughes argued, "a technological system can be both a cause and an effect; it can shape or be shaped by society. As they grow larger and more complex, systems tend to be more shaping of society and less shaped by it" (1994, 112). The suggestion is that a critical window of regulatory opportunity may sometimes be available for each emerging technology.

As a general matter, Hughes's point is surely correct. Yet, the experience in the United States also suggests another lesson, namely, the profound instability of any legal regulation of information privacy due to ceaseless technological developments. Spiros Simitis, a leading international privacy expert, clearly pointed in 1987 to the impermanent nature of regulations in this area. Simitis noted presciently,

> No matter how precise the rules [for privacy], they nevertheless remain provisional because of the incessant advances in technology. Regulations on the collection and retrieval of personal data thus present a classic case of sunset legislation. If the legislator wants to master processing issues, she must commit herself explicitly to a constant reappraisal of the various rules. (1987, 742)

As to Simitis's view regarding the instability of information privacy regulation, technology has indeed had the kind of impact he foresaw.

Over the last three decades, the two most important technological developments in this context have been the increase in computing power as predicted by Moore's law and the rise of the Internet. Moore's law is not a legal rule, but a prediction in 1975 by a cofounder of Intel, a leading semiconductor manufacturer, regarding a continuing, steady increase in computing power per unit.[2] Time has proved Gordon Moore correct, and advances in computing power have also meant steep drops in computing costs and a creation of a wide array of new electronic devices. At the end of the 1970s, the only communication device in wide use was the landline telephone. Today, digital devices—such as computers, mobile phones, pagers, and personal digital assistants (PDAs)—create, receive, and transmit new kinds of detailed personal information, including locational information, at a speed and low cost hardly imaginable to the analog phone user of the late 1970s. The emerging technologies of radio frequency ID and transponders, such as used in the E-Z Pass on the East Coast and Fastrak in the Bay Area, also lead to the collection of personal information.

The second important technological development in recent decades has been the Internet and its widespread use across the population at large. Beginning in the 1960s, the United States Department of Defense's Advanced Research Projects Agency (ARPA) funded research into survivable communication capabilities in the case of a nuclear attack on the United States. The initial ARPANET linked computing research centers at several universities. In the 1990s, a successor network, the Internet, built on the ARPANET model and added use of the TCP/IP protocol. In the course of the 1990s, the Internet became a widespread communications medium with the emergence of the World Wide Web (WWW), based on Tim Berners-Lee's HTML format for hypertext documents.

The Internet is the most widely adopted and interoperable means to date for networking different computers—and for collecting and sharing personal information. Some computer networks have existed at least since the 1970s. In 1977, the Privacy Protection Study Commission noted the phenomenon of a "physical decentralization, but functional centralization, of records" through "computer networking—the interconnection of computers via telecommunications" (United States 1977, 9). The Internet, of course, goes considerably beyond such networks. Its openness and worldwide reach have increased the processing, combination, and transfer of personal data. It has also done so in ways that are difficult for any individual to anticipate or control.

We can develop these points by considering, first, the statute that addresses the privacy of individual videotape rental transactions, and, second, the law regarding telecommunications surveillance. The Video Privacy Protection Act was written in 1988 in such a way that it can be interpreted and applied beyond the simple corner video store to reach even online rental services, such as NetFlix, which did not exist in 1988, and to regulate rentals of DVDs, which also did not exist in 1988. So far, so good. But the statute does not address myriad issues about the application of its principles to video files downloaded, or streaming videoclips watched.

Moreover, the act of renting a video in the 1980s caused the collection of a relatively discrete amount of information. In contrast, complete information about an individual's Web surfing, video file download, and streaming videoclip viewing habits may soon be available. These data include decisions about products ordered or other action taken, and even how often specific scenes were watched and when in the day, week, and year they were viewed. This information may provide detailed insights into an individual's political and artistic preferences as well as her spontaneous self-expressive thoughts and priorities. Constitutional law considers such activities in the pursuit of self-determination as subject to fundamental protections. In these and many other areas, the rapid development and public embrace of the Internet, the digitization of content, and the widespread availability of broadband Internet connections have pushed new privacy issues to the fore at nearly breakneck speed.

As a second example, telecommunications surveillance law initially focused only on the contemporaneous surveillance of communication content. The critical statute for such surveillance is the Wiretap Act, enacted originally as Title III of the Omnibus Safe Streets and Comprehensive Crime Control Act of 1968. This statute establishes a general prohibition on law enforcement's surveillance of the content of a telephone conversation captured in "transmission," that is, in real time, in the absence of a court order (Solove, Rotenberg, and Schwartz 2006, 264–5). Today, in contrast to 1968, the thorniest questions about surveillance concern a range of telecommunications attributes considered to be less than content and to involve asynchronous communication.

Interception of information that falls into these categories is generally subject to the Stored Communications Act of 1986, which tends to offer lesser protections than the Wiretap Act. In addition, although it has been amended on numerous occasions, including by sections of the PATRIOT Act of 2001, the Stored Communications Act still largely reflects technical categories prominent when it was enacted. As Orin Kerr observes, the Act freezes "into the law the understandings of computer network use as of 1986" (2006, 502). At that time, for example, bulletin board systems were the most important kind of networked computer communications. The Stored Communications Act still refers to only two categories of network service providers: those that provide "electronic communication services" and those that provide "remote computing services" used as part of an outsourcing of tasks.

Among the difficulties that flow from these old distinctions is that at present most network service providers fulfill many functions. Hence, numerous questions under the law prove exceedingly complex. One that Kerr points to is central for the information age; it concerns "the surprising difficult case of opened e-mails" (2006, 509). Unresolved questions exist concerning the legal standard under which the government is permitted to obtain access to emails that a person has read and left with an ISP or on a remote server.

In sum, technological developments over the last three decades have both increased the ability of public and private sectors to create, combine, and compare databases of personal information and put pressure on the stability of any legislative attempts to protect civil liberties by regulating information privacy. They illustrate the difficulty of striking an enduring balance between civil liberties and government's ability to derive law enforcement and national security benefits from the use of technology.

BEYOND THE STANDARD DICHOTOMY

Government has also sought to harness the power of technology in the interests of national security. We now discuss the impact of technology on both national security and civil liberties. One view takes a zero-sum approach. First, technology is seen as offering a great, even unique potential for improving national security. Here, we hear the discourse of technological optimism. Drawing on the work of Leo Marx, we can define technological optimism as resting on beliefs in history as a record of progress and technological innovation as the primary agent of that progress (1994, 240). In the context of national security, moreover, technology is specifically regarded as a uniquely powerful means for safeguarding the safety of the nation.

Second, technology is also seen as raising great, even unique, dangers to civil liberties. This discourse is technological pessimism—with elements of a dystopian perspective sometimes mixed in. Technological pessimism represents a "sense of disappointment, anxiety, even menace, that the idea of 'technology' arouses in many people these days" (Marx 1994, 238). More specifically, technology is seen as creating systems of control that inexorably degrade civil liberties. In the context of privacy, the leading intellectual examples of technology gone wild are George Orwell's Telescreen from *1984* and Jeremy Bentham's Pantopicon (as rediscovered by Michel Foucault in *Discipline and Punish*). Popular culture has also sounded this theme in movies such as the *Conversation, Enemy of the State, The Matrix*, and *Minority Report*.

The standard dichotomy portrays a state of constant tension between the two sides. Technology's achievements for national security will lead to a loss for civil liberties. A gain for civil liberties will require limits on technology—and cause an attendant loss for national security. We illustrate this logic in table 8.1.

TABLE 8.1   The Standard Dichotomy

Subject Area	Overall Impact of Technology	Discourse
1. National security	Technology improves national security	Technological optimism
2. Civil liberties	Technology harms civil liberties	Technological pessimism

Source: Authors' compilation.

For a detailed example of the standard dichotomy in action, consider the public discussion and policy debate in 2002 about the Pentagon's Total Information Awareness (TIA) program. TIA was intended to revolutionize the ability of the United States to detect and counter foreign terrorists through its projected development of novel data mining and profiling techniques. This technology is made possible by the ongoing increase in computing power and the emergence of decentralized data banks in the private and public sector. TIA was led and funded by the Defense Advanced Research Projects Agency (DARPA), whose predecessor agency, ARPA, as noted, played a critical role in funding the research that helped to create the Internet. TIA's program managers stated that terrorists engaged in what TIA termed a "low-intensity/low-density form of warfare" that had "an information signature, albeit not one that our intelligence infrastructure and other government agencies are optimized to detect" (DARPA n.d.). The solution? TIA first proposed, "to fight terrorism, we need to create a new intelligence infrastructure to allow these agencies to share information and collaborate effectively." It also called for creation of "new information technology aimed at exposing terrorists and their activities and support systems" (DARPA n.d.).

Thus, TIA sought to use information technology to broaden and even automate the response to the terrorist threat. As Jeffrey Rosen summarized its research agenda, "TIA sought to develop architectures for integrating existing databases into a 'virtual centralized grand database' that would collect data from public- and private sector sources" (2004, 100). The massive TIA database was to contain information about personal finances, education, travel, health, and other areas. As Rosen observed, moreover, the database was to combine information from sources in both the private and public sectors. TIA would then apply advanced techniques and technologies to detect precursors and indicators of terrorism. In brief, TIA sought to use technology to connect the dots and allow counterterrorism officials to search different databases to identity terrorist activities.

The technological optimism behind this project was expressed in graphic form on the initial Web site for the project, quickly scuttled, which featured an eye placed on top of a pyramid and the legend *scienta est potentia* (knowledge is power). This underlying belief in the potential benefits for national security from data mining and other automated data analysis was far from limited to the TIA.

Numerous blue ribbon commissions have demonstrated a similar enthusiasm for data mining of different kinds. These groups include the Commission on the Intelligence Capabilities of the United States Regarding Weapons of Mass Destruction (Robb-Silberman Commission), the Commission on the September 11, 2001 Terrorist Attacks on the United States (the 9/11 Commission), and the Markle Foundation Task Force on National Security in the Information Age. In the academy, Judge Richard Posner has emerged as perhaps the single greatest voice in favor of data mining (2005a, 2008). The devil is in the details, however, and questions remain regarding the safeguards necessary to protect civil liberties within any automated data analysis (Rubinstein, Lee, and Schwartz forthcoming).

The technological optimism of TIA was, however, quickly swamped by technological pessimism. An outpouring of media reports raised concerns about the implications of the program for civil liberties. A central fear regarding TIA was its combination of public and private databases. For example, *New York Times* columnist William Safire objected to the program's dismantling of "the wall between commercial snooping and secret government intrusion" ("You are a Suspect," November 14, 2002, A35).

In response to mounting public concerns, the Pentagon removed the ominous eye from the TIA Web site, changed the name of the program from Total Information Awareness to Terrorism Information Awareness, and pledged that the program would include privacy protections—although the planned privacy safeguards were left largely unspecified. In 2003, Congress voted to deny funding for TIA, though it specifically allowed funding of "processing, analysis and collaboration tools for counterterrorism foreign intelligence." Congress specified in the Defense Appropriations Act of 2004 that the results of this research were exclusively to be used in "(1) lawful military operations of the United States conducted outside the United States; or (2) lawful foreign intelligence activities conducted wholly overseas, or wholly against non-United States citizens."[3] In the discussion of TIA, much of the discourse saw the values of national security and civil liberties as inevitably in opposition.

Beyond these specific provisions in the Defense Appropriations Act of 2004, the government elsewhere has pursued TIA's goal of developing new techniques of database mining and profiling to identify terrorists. Noah Shachtman writing in *Wired* magazine in 2004, for example, identified six governmental programs engaged in activities similar to those sought in TIA. Of these, perhaps the best known is CAPPS II, a program to screen airline passengers by analyzing passenger records, commercial databases, and national security information, including terrorist watch lists. In a June 2005 report about data mining in homeland security, the Congressional Research Service found "mission creep" to be a critical concern and found it present in CAPPS II (Seifert 2005, 10). In a paper for the Center for Strategic and International Studies, Mary DeRosa also raised concerns about mission creep in counterterrorism programs and noted the inadequacy of current government mechanisms for controlling the use of data mining matches (2004, vi).

Delays in the implementation of CAPPS II and concerns about its civil liberties implications led to its replacement by another initiative, Secure Flight. This program is still in development. Thus far, the Transportation Security Administration has published a system of records notice, pursuant to the Privacy Act of 1974 (5 U.S. Code §552a), and a privacy impact assessment. With its privacy and processes now set out in writing, it is conducting tests of Secure Flight.

Overall, the government's technological optimism has been enduring. As the Pentagon's Technology and Privacy Advisory Committee (TAPAC) found in 2004, "TIA was not unique in its potential for data mining. TAPAC is aware of many other programs in use or under development both with [the Department of Defense] and elsewhere in the government that make similar uses of personal information concerning U.S. persons to detect and deter terrorist activities" (United States 2004, viii). At the same time, worries about the implications of technology are persistent. Thus, the standard dichotomy is well entrenched. It is also woefully incomplete.

First, depending on the context and how it is implemented, technology can protect rather than harm civil liberties. Timing is essential—acting the moment technological systems are introduced is critical. There is a great need, for example, for legal regulation of the government's use of data mining systems. The key challenge is to structure procedures and institutions for ongoing analysis of the impact of technology, positive and negative, on national security and civil liberties.

Second, technology may not only be a way to safeguard national security, but also to pose threats to it. We propose replacing the standard

TABLE 8.2   Technology's Multiple Impacts on National Security and Civil Liberties

Subject Area	Overall Impact	Discourse
1. National security	Technology improves national security	Technological optimism
2. National security	Technology harms national security	Technological pessimism
3. Civil liberties	Technology improves civil liberties	Technological optimism
4. Civil liberties	Technology harms civil liberties	Technological pessimism

Source: Authors' compilation.

dichotomy with an expanded analysis of technology's multiple impacts on national security and civil liberties. We present this approach initially in tabular form (see table 8.2).

In terms of this table, the standard dichotomy acknowledges only categories 1 and 4. Full analysis requires more; it calls for a look at other potential implications of technology.

Few policy analyses formally incorporate the four possibilities. More typically, scholars simply note the need for a broader analysis of technology, national security, and civil liberties. For example, in 1967, Alan Westin noted the ability of "scientific activity, especially by such groups as the telephone companies, electronics firms, and data-processing manufacturers" to "develop new systems for the protection of the average citizen's privacy" (379). This observation would fall under row 3 in table 8.2. The Privacy Protection Study Commission made a similar comment in 1977 in noting technology's failure to give "an individual the tools he needs to protect his legitimate interests in the records organizations keep about him" (United States 1977, 18). And, more recently, Jeffrey Rosen aptly called for a more complete analysis of data mining and profiling than was generally present during the TIA debate: "Nearly all [technologies of identification] can be designed in ways that strike better or worse balances between liberty and security. Depending on these design choices, the technologies can protect liberty and security at the same time, or they can threaten liberty without bringing a corresponding interest in security" (2004, 100).

Although widely overlooked in the public debate about TIA, this program at least made some attempts to harness technology to promote pri-

vacy. DARPA funded research at the Palo Alto Research Center that
sought to create different automated methods to expunge from collected
data the information associating that data with a specific person and to
release the data only when overseen by a neutral party (that is, a federal
court). This research was to incorporate civil liberty considerations into
deployment of technology.

To be sure, technical and practical issues will arise and may be difficult
to resolve—indeed, they may sometimes weigh against deployment of a
specific technology, or counsel limits on such deployment. The conceptual
ideal is to develop and deploy technology that advances both national
security and civil liberties (Lee and Schwartz 2005, 1472–81). But this
goal may prove elusive, and the trade-offs complex to calculate. As an
example of the difficulty of the calculus, consider encryption and anonymity
technologies.

On one hand, widespread availability of encryption technology might
make it more difficult for the law enforcement and intelligence communities in the United States to access the plain text of terrorist communications.
Technology, such as so-called onion routing, which allows anonymous communications and communication paths, can also assist terrorists. On the
other hand, strong cryptography prevents terrorists and criminals from
violating the privacy of others and helps to keep our critical digital infrastructure secure. Moreover, onion routing has already been used by a U.S.
Navy unit to disguise its communication patterns. The benefit to the government of a public anonymizing network is that "a widely used anonymity
system provides Department of Defense users the best protection from
prying eyes" (Diffie and Landau 2007, 274). As the developers of Tor, the
most current version of onion routing, have stated, "anonymity loves
company" (Dingledine and Mathewson 2005, 547).

We turn now to row 2 of table 8.2, which concerns the harms that technology can visit on national security. From the perspective of 2008, there
are three distinct developments related to technology that have enormously
increased the potential harm to national security. Just as this chapter has
traced history lessons about the impact of technology upon information
privacy, an element of civil liberties, it is also possible to consider the
impact of technology on national security. These historical lessons are not
cheerful ones.

First, technology has increased the destructiveness of the weapons
at the disposal of America's adversaries; these include a wide range of
weapons of mass destruction, including nuclear, radiological, biological,
chemical weapons, as well as more conventional ones. These weapons

greatly increase the potential for harm to our society—especially in the hands of nonstate actors that hold extreme views and are less susceptible than nation-states to the conventional military, diplomatic, economic, legal and moral pressures that other nation-states can bring to bear.

Second, the United States and many other nations targeted by terrorist groups are highly industrialized and depend heavily on technology, opening the door for asymmetrical warfare to be waged against them. Terrorists have misappropriated the advanced technology of a nation to cause great damage and harm at low cost to them. On September 11, 2001, terrorists armed with box cutters hijacked commercial aircraft fully fueled for transcontinental flights and turned them into large-scale lethal weapons. The 9/11 Commission estimated the planning and execution costs of the attacks at between $400,000 and $500,000 (169). The operation caused inestimable human loss and suffering, as well as billions of dollars in harm to the American economy as well. The New York City comptroller estimated the cost to New York City alone as between $83 billion and $95 billion (Thompson 2002).

Beyond dangers to the United States' air passenger transportation system, the United States faces other risks to the safety of its nuclear plants, its telecommunications and financial systems, and its transportation infrastructure of trains, subways, highways, and ports. The possibility of bioterrorism places new demands on the public health surveillance and response system. The possibility of cyberterrorism poses a threat to the Internet and other communication networks.

Finally, technology empowers terrorists by allowing them to recruit new members and supporters, and to fund their activities more readily, across greater distances, and within shorter time frames. It also allows terrorists to communicate, coordinate, and conceal their operations. The Internet and digital technologies, for example, allow nearly instantaneous, low-cost international communications. In an illustration of this point, as reported in the *New York Times*, in July 2007, Prime Minister Gordon Brown offered the British House of Commons the following tally of the devices and data involved in a terrorist plot against transatlantic airliners that British intelligence had foiled the previous year: 200 cellphones, 400 computers, and 8,000 CDs, DVDs and discs containing 6,000 gigabytes of data (Jane Perlez, "British Leader Seeks New Terrorism Laws," July 26, 2007, A8).

The vast data cloud of world and domestic communications may also increase the difficulties posed for governments in developing accurate and timely intelligence about the intentions and plans of terrorists. In apparent response to these difficulties, President George W. Bush acknowledged in 2005 that he had authorized the National Security Agency "to intercept the international communications of people with known links to al Qaeda and related terrorist organizations" where one end of the communication was outside the United States. The administration asserted that required procedures under the Foreign Intelligence Surveillance Act did not provide for the requisite speed and agility. These administration claims have proved controversial. Nonetheless, sustained attention by legislators, policy makers and an informed citizenry is especially needed for issues at the intersection of technology, civil liberties, and terrorism.

HISTORICAL DISCONTINUITIES, HISTORICAL CONTINUITIES

We close with exploration of a larger question, which is whether (or not) technology has wrought a fundamental change in the historical relationship between civil liberties and national security. In large part, the preceding chapters describe a dynamic in which a public security threat disrupts a balance between civil liberties and national security. The new threat triggers political and public responses. The executive branch plays an especially prominent role, and the judiciary, the Congress, and the public may agree, disagree, or simply acquiesce. Over time, a backlash or reaction to new policies emerges, as the underlying threat is eliminated or perceptions about the magnitude of the threat change. Ultimately, a new balance is achieved.

By contrast, other chapters of this book note that this dynamic may prove different in confronting radical international terrorism because of the potential for this threat to persist without the possibility of a clear and declarable victory by the United States and its allies. There is also another reason for thinking that the dynamic may evolve differently this time; technology may upset the pace and outcome of this traditional ebb and flow. To the extent that it does, this chapter points to a different lesson than the rest of this book.

There are two ways that technology might affect the traditional fashion of reaching a new equilibrium. First, the rapidity by which technology generates new policy issues may mean that any balance between civil liberties and national security is inherently evanescent. A new equilibrium requires agreement among the three branches of government and the governed, stasis among particular technologies or technological capabilities, and consensus about the application of agreed legal principles to the new situation.

Second, the government has traditionally played a central role, sometimes for better and sometimes for worse, in the civil liberties and national security dynamic. The private sector's important role in developing and commercializing technology may lessen the government's ability to preside over the civil liberties and national security dynamic. This impact may be particularly drastic because the private sector driving technological change is inherently global and transnational in its workforce, sources of innovation, economic interdependencies, and market focus.

IMPERMANENCE

In *Perilous Times*, Geoffrey Stone draws a central lesson from the history of major restrictions of civil liberties in the past. Looking at events of 1798, 1861, 1917, 1942, 1950 and 1969, he comments that historical differences in suppression of dissent depend heavily on "the extent to which national political leaders intentionally inflamed public fear" (2004, 533). Moreover, "again and again, Americans have allowed fear to get the better of them" (529). For Stone, "the unimpeachable lesson of history" is that the government has established a pattern of overreaction, leading to excessive wartime repression of civil liberties, and, in particular, freedom of speech (530). In chapter 5 of this volume, Stone ends with an analysis of *Hamdan v. Rumsfeld* and a suggestion that the Supreme Court may be about to engage in more aggressive protection of individual rights.

In *Uncertain Shield*, Richard Posner disagrees with Stone's conclusion. He points to a "continuing ominous evolution in the availability and lethality of the technologies of destruction" and, striking a different note, worries "about the prospects for sound organizational reform" of the American intelligence community (2006, xx–xxi, 211). Like Stone, however, he sketches a process in which civil liberties rebound over time and a new equilibrium is established (2005b, 186–9; 192–7). Similarly, Alan Brinkley in chapter 2 of this volume describes how the reaction to repression of civil liberties in the United States during World War I led Justices Brandeis and Holmes and other members of the Supreme Court to create "the legal and moral basis for our modern concept of civil liberties." For Stone, Posner, and Brinkley, there is a general tendency over time toward equilibrium in the balance between civil liberties and national security interests.

Yet, the history of technology, data processing, and information privacy we have explored here teaches the impermanence of legal regulation and the insistent challenges by technology to existing balances. Nothing has been so constant in this area as change. Sic transit gloria mundi. Another argument about the constancy of change, from a different perspective, is made by Jan Lewis in chapter 6 of this volume. She discusses how the American identity has always been a work in progress, and proposes that in America "citizenship is always contested" and civil liberties "never wholly secure."

THE GOVERNMENT'S ROLE

In the past, the government has been a dominant player in the dynamic involving civil liberties and national security. Consider its role in adopting and enforcing the Alien and Sedition Acts, the suspension of the writ of habeas corpus during the Civil War, the Espionage Act in 1917, the Sedition Act in 1918, the Palmer raids, the internment of Japanese Americans during World War II, McCarthyism, and the domestic surveillance activities of the intelligence community in the 1970s that led to the enactment of the Foreign Intelligence Surveillance Act.

Technology appears to have changed the ability of government to exercise a central role. The greater power of the private sector in developing technology and the greater disruptive effects of technology, as in asymmetrical warfare, are among the factors that have weakened the power of the government. Nonetheless, the government will continue to have an important role, indeed a unique role, in protecting national security and safeguarding civil liberties.

We conclude by pointing to the concept of public liberty that Stephen Holmes develops in the final chapter of this volume. For Holmes, a concept of public liberty is needed in the current debate about the liberty-security tradeoff. Holmes makes an important distinction between "the private liberty of private individuals to behave as they choose so long as they refrain from harming each other" and "the public liberty of citizens to examine and criticize their government, and to strive to out it from power in competitive elections, so long as they obey the law." Public liberty allows citizens to compel government to give reasons for its action. It serves to improve security by preventing policy makers from hiding their errors from the public view and avoiding criticism. As Holmes proposes, "the aim of liberal institutions should be to facilitate the psychologically painful process of recognizing past blunders and initiating requisite mainstream readjustments."

Whether in dealing with new technologies or with new threats to national security, the health of a democratic system depends on an informed citizenry willing to participate in civic affairs. A public discussion about important technological issues, such as data mining or the impact of technological advances on existing statutory frameworks regulating electronic surveillance, would be an important exercise of Holmesian public liberty. Indeed, there is an emerging agreement among at least some policy experts regarding the necessary regulation of data mining (Rubinstein, Lee, and Schwartz forthcoming). As part of this regulation, there must be public debate about the reliability and track record of both government and commercial data mining, and the makeup and operation of data mining systems. Some residue of information may necessarily be kept secret for national security reasons. Nonetheless, public release of information and public debate are needed for the design, performance, and privacy protections in data mining systems.

CONCLUSION

This chapter first considered the history of computerized processing of personal information in the United States. There was no stopping the adoption of electronic data processing by the public and private sectors; the question has been how to regulate the processing of personal data to protect information privacy while realizing the value of computerized data processing for both government and private sector endeavors. The chief lesson of the confrontation of United States law with widespread adoption of electronic data processing has been the instability of legal regulation for information privacy.

We have questioned the conventional wisdom in which technology's benefits for national security are viewed as coming at the cost of civil liberties, and vice versa. In a more complete view, technology can also harm national security, and it can benefit civil liberties. Substantial governmental and public attention is needed to manage the consequences of technology's disruptive effects. Having explored a series of historical discontinuities and historical continuities, we wonder if technology has disrupted the traditional and recurring processes in which civil liberties and national security values have been balanced in the United States. Public liberty, without question, requires increased public discussion and debate about the role of technology and the regulation of technology in shaping and reshaping the dynamic balance between civil liberties and national security.

NOTES

1. Miller also observed, "many people have voiced concern that the computer, with its insatiable appetite for information, its image of infallibility, and its inability to forget anything that has been stored in it, may become the heart of a surveillance system that will turn society into a transparent world in

which our homes, our finances, and our associations will be bared to a wide range of casual observers, including the morbidly curious and the maliciously or commercially intrusive" (1971, 16).

2. In a popular formulation of Moore's law, the prediction is that the number of transistors, and hence the available processing power, that can be placed on a given size of integrated circuits will double every eighteen months.

3. Pub. L. No. 108-87, 117 Stat. 1102 (September 30, 2003).

REFERENCES

The Commission on the Intelligence Capabilities of the United States Regarding Weapons of Mass Destruction [Robb-Silberman Commission]. 2005. *Report to the President of the United States.* Washington: Government Printing Office. Accessed at www.gpoaccess.gov/wmd/pdf/full_wmd_report.pdf.

DARPA. No date. Information Awareness Office home page. Accessed at http://infowar.net/tia/www.darpa.mil/iao.

DeRosa, Mary. 2004. *Data Mining and Data Analysis for Counterterrorism.* Washington: Center for Strategic and International Studies.

Diffie, Whitfield, and Susan Landau. 2007. *Privacy on the Line*, updated and expanded edition. Cambridge, Mass.: The MIT Press.

Dingledine, Roger, and Nick Mathewson. 2005. "Anonymity Loves Company." In *Security and Usability: Designing Secure Systems that People Can Use*, edited by Lorne Faith Cranor and Simson Garfinkel. Sebastopol, Calif.: O'Reilly Media.

Hughes, Thomas P. 1994. "Technological Momentum" In *Does Technology Drive History: The Dilemma of Technological Determinism*, edited by Merritt Roe Smith and Leo Marx. Cambridge, Mass.: The MIT Press.

Kerr, Orin. 2006. *Computer Crime Law.* St. Paul, Minn.: West Publishing.

Lee, Ronald D., and Paul M. Schwartz. 2005. "Heymann: Terrorism, Freedom and Security: Winning Without War." *Michigan Law Review* 103(6): 1446–82.

The Markle Foundation. 2003. *Creating a Trusted Information Network for Homeland Security.* Second Report of the Markle Foundation Taskforce. New York and Washington: Markle Foundation.

Marx, Leo. 1994. "The Idea of 'Technology' and Postmodern Pessimism." In *Does Technology Drive History: The Dilemma of Technological Determinism*, edited by Merritt Roe Smith and Leo Marx. Cambridge, Mass.: The MIT Press.

Miller, Arthur R. 1971. *The Assault on Privacy: Computers, Data Banks, and Dossiers.* Ann Arbor, Mich.: University of Michigan Press.

National Commission on Terrorist Attacks Upon the United States [The 9/11 Commission]. 2004. *The 9/11 Commission Report: Final Report of the National Commission on Terrorist Attacks upon the United States.* New York: W. W. Norton.

Posner, Richard A. 2005a. "Our Domestic Intelligence Crisis." *Washington Post*, December 21, 2005: A31.

———. 2005b. *Preventing Surprise Attacks: Intelligence Reform in the Wake of 9/11.* Lanham, Md.: Rowman and Littlefield.

————. 2006. *Uncertain Shield: The U.S. Intelligence System in the Throes of Reform.* Lanham, Md.: Rowman and Littlefield.

————. 2008. "Privacy, Surveillance, and Law." *University of Chicago Law Review* 74(5). Forthcoming.

Rosen, Jeffrey. 2004. *The Naked Crowd: Reclaiming Security and Freedom in an Anxious Age.* New York: Random House.

Rubinstein, Ira S., Ronald D. Lee, and Paul M. Schwartz. Forthcoming. "Data Mining and Internet Profiling." *University of Chicago Law Review* 75.

Seifert, Jeffrey W. 2005. "Data Mining: An Overview." CRS Report #RL31798. Washington: The Library of Congress, Congressional Research Service.

Shachtman, Noah. 2004. "Start: Homeland Security—The Bastard Children of Total Information Awareness." *Wired* 12(2). Accessed at http://wired.com/wired/archive/12.02/start.html?pg=4.

Simitis, Spiros. 1987. "Reviewing Privacy in an Information Society." *University of Pennsylvania Law Review* 135(3): 707–46.

Solove, Daniel J., Marc Rotenberg, and Paul M. Schwartz. 2006. *Information Privacy Law,* 2nd edition. New York: Aspen Publishers.

Stone, Geoffrey R. 2004. *Perilous Times: Free Speech in Wartime: From the Sedition Act of 1798 to the War on Terrorism.* New York: W. W. Norton.

Thompson, William C. 2002. "Thompson Releases Report on Fiscal Impact of 9/11 on New York City." Press release PR02-09-054, September 4, 2002. New York: NYC Comptroller, Press Office. Accessed at http://www.comptroller.nyc.gov/press/2002_releases/02-09-054.shtm.

United States. 1977. "Technology and Privacy: Appendix 5." In *Final Report of the Privacy Protection Study Commission Joint Hearing Before the Committee on Governmental Affairs, United States Senate, and a Subcommittee of the Committee on Government Operations, House of Representatives.* 95th Cong., 1st Sess. (July 12, 1977). Washington: Government Printing Office.

————. 2004. *Safeguarding Privacy in the Fight Against Terrorism: The Report of the Technology and Privacy Advisory Committee for Secretary of Defense Donald Rumsfeld.* Washington: Technology and Privacy Advisory Commission. Accessed at http://purl.access.gpo.gov/GPO/LPS52114.

Westin, Alan F. 1967. *Privacy and Freedom.* New York: Athenum.

CHAPTER 9

CONCLUSION

STEPHEN HOLMES

What can richly textured studies of wartime curtailments of civil liberties in American history teach us about the ongoing war on terror? Expertly reprised in this volume, the historical record reveals not only that executive power routinely eclipses legislative and judicial powers during wartime. More alarming, it also implies that the United States actually has two Constitutions, the first for peace and the second for war. At least one contributor to this collection suggests, on the basis of such a retrospective, that George W. Bush has not only responded to 9/11 in a perfectly normal fashion but has actually been more respectful of due process, the Constitution, and judicial authority than previous wartime presidents, including liberal idols such as Abraham Lincoln and FDR.

Typically, not to say paradoxically, those who invoke the historical record to normalize the Bush administration's reaction to 9/11 also emphasize the dramatically unprecedented nature of the terrorist threat. In his careful introduction, Dan Farber cites Alberto Gonzales's statement that "the war against terrorism is a new kind of war," as well as Bush's claim that "the war against terrorism ushers in a new paradigm." Utterly new and without historical parallel, so administration spokesmen and defenders assert, is the threat of "transnational terrorist cells that will strike without warning using weapons of mass destruction" (Bolton 2004, 235). Every one of the national security institutions of the United States was conceived and structured to counteract threats to the country posed by organized territorial states with capital cities and military command centers that can be pinpointed on maps. These powerful departments and agencies were certainly not designed to prevent an elusive, transnational, and clandestinely networked murder gang from incinerating a major American urban center. One possible implication of this lack of fit between inherited institutions and newly arisen threats is that President Bush should not be criticized but praised when, responding to 9/11 (and the implicit danger of nuclear terrorism that 9/11 revealed), he tore up the rulebook and began wielding previously forbidden powers expressly to fulfill his constitutional obligation to protect the country.

Those who lavish praise on the Bush administration not only for piously following but also for bravely abandoning constitutional precedents will have to untangle their own clashing narratives. Such eye-catching inconsistencies are of interest to us only as a stimulus to specify with greater accuracy both the continuities and the discontinuities between the Bush administration and its wartime predecessors.

THE POLITICIZATION OF NATIONAL SECURITY

Most of the foregoing chapters suggest that the principal continuity between yesterday and today lies in the insidious influence of partisan politics on the way national security is defined and defended. The politicization of counterterrorism since 9/11 is well within the historical norm. In the past, as in the present, actions contrived to embarrass domestic political rivals have been calculatingly presented as essential to national security. Moreover, the war on terror is not the first conflict during which heated disagreements inside the executive branch concerning the nature, imminence and gravity of a particular threat have been concealed from the public for electoral advantage.

A lethal threat to the nation may or may not alter the motives of an incumbent president, but it will certainly change his opportunities. Fear of a common enemy, real or imagined, often leads otherwise antagonistic groups to rally around the leader of the moment, burying their differences for the duration of the war. Critical impulses are usually put on ice once the enemy is, or seems to be, pounding at the gates. The sudden deference and even cooperativeness of previously obstructionist and rival forces unblocks the political system, opening the way for what Alan Brinkley calls "the existing agendas" of the executive. When deference and passivity are not forthcoming, moreover, wartime politicians are sorely tempted to question the loyalty and patriotism of their obstreperous partisan rivals, demonizing remaining opponents as treacherously disloyal (Michael Abramowitz, "Bush says 'America Loses' Under Democrats," *Washington Post*, October 31, 2006). Even when they are silencing critics to safeguard their own (arguably unjustified) reputation for competence and to bolster electoral support for their party, they may sincerely believe that they are curtailing liberty for the sake of national security. "Victory would be ours," a president and vice president may tell themselves, "if only our irresponsible critics would keep their scornful doubts to themselves."

As we have seen, wartime censorship of political criticism gains whatever plausibility it has from two claims, first, that antiwar agitation raises the hopes of the enemy and thereby needlessly prolongs the conflict and, second, that a tactically shrewd enemy knows how to exploit domestic factionalism and discord. A powerful reason to doubt the vaunted security benefits of such censorship, however, is that many politicians would happily censor their most talented critics in peacetime, too, if such silencing were allowed. If incumbents had a totally free hand, in truth, they would often be sorely tempted to quash dissent. In other words, war legitimates an intolerance of dissent that is constitutionally disfavored in normal times. Formulated differently, the incumbent's perennial dislike of public criticism is weaponized in wartime. That punitive conflations of criticism with disloyalty promote the competent management of national emergencies is by no means obvious, however. Chilling opposition voices may turn the national security state into the pliant tool of a political machine that, in turn, may happen to be seized by a gratuitously skewed and selective vision of the national interest.

The partisan exploitation of the liberty-security polarity is another recurrent pattern in American history. When critics of the party in power speak up for liberty, they are routinely excoriated for opening a breach in the country's defenses through which the fleet-footed enemy will steal. Those who accuse the executive branch of violating constitutional liberties in wartime are also commonly accused of abetting hostile forces and proving that they are not truly committed to defending American lives, whatever the cost. The loud insinuation that, in wartime, the friends of liberty become the pawns of the enemy is another American tradition that remains very much alive.

The central implication of these recurrent historical patterns is not cheering. To expect incumbents to resist the political temptation to exaggerate the threat of an attack or to brand domestic critics as subversives seems fairly unrealistic. If the struggle to defend the nation from its enemies has never been, how can it now become, sealed off aseptically from partisan politics? The unseemly commingling of domestic and foreign rivalries, so we have learned, is a seemingly irrepressible feature of American political life. What most conspicuously unites the counterterrorism presidency of George W. Bush with the war presidencies of his predecessors is therefore the crass politicization, for domestic advantage, of a violent struggle against a dangerous foreign foe.

Having absorbed this discouraging lesson, we are in a position to consider the other side of the coin, namely, the ways in which Bush has parted company with the most noteworthy wartime presidents of the past.

SEARCHING FOR NOVELTY IN THE WAR ON TERROR

Specifying how constitutional liberties have been treated differently in the war on terror than during previous American wars turns out to be rather difficult. The remainder of this conclusion, in any case, will be devoted to exploring this question. I begin with two common but, in my view, misleading ways of differentiating Bush from his predecessors.

The first is the liberal argument that the war on terror is not a war in the sense of earlier existential conflicts in which the very survival of the American system of government was at stake. According to Bruce Ackerman, for instance, "terrorism is a very serious problem, but it doesn't remotely suggest a return to the darkest times of the Civil War or World War II" (2006, 20). Ackerman's distinction implies that Lincoln and Roosevelt were at least partly justified in restricting civil liberties, whereas Bush has been acting with reckless disregard for the Constitution and the rule of law.

Although it has much to commend it, this approach is marred by a tendency to trivialize the extent to which threats to American national security have been radically reconfigured by technological change. The administration's diagnosis of the newly emergent threat environment may be essentially correct even if the remedy it concocted has proved toxic. Neither perimeter defense nor nuclear deterrence will defend the United States from the grave if uncertain danger posed by WMD in the hands of elusive transnational terrorists. Al Qaeda's scattered cadres, it is true, cannot be seriously compared to Hitler's million-man army or Soviet Russia's massive nuclear arsenal. The clandestine marketing of fissile materiel and nuclear expertise, however, combined with the revolutionary transformation of global communications, transportation and banking, function as force multipliers. They deliver global reach to would-be mass murderers of otherwise negligible stature such as Osama bin Laden and Ayman al-Zawahiri. At a nightmarish extreme, committed zealots, super-charged with petrodollars, might manage to exploit nuclear technology to incinerate Washington, D.C., without warning, obliterating America's national government and catapulting the country's political future into the unknown. The danger of losing a densely inhabited American city to crazed jihadists might be, and probably is, remote; but it should not be downplayed as immeasurably less fearful than the dangers encountered in America's earlier major wars.

Conservatives and antiliberals prefer to differentiate Bush's approach to constitutional liberties from that of his wartime predecessors in a different way, namely by emphasizing his administration's admirable "restraint" (see John Yoo's reference to "the relative restraint—from a historical perspective—of the Bush administration" in chapter 3 of this volume). Above all, Bush has refrained from criminalizing dissent in the manner of other wartime presidents. Michael Moore and Jon Stewart have not been jailed for impugning the president's motives or attempting to bring the ruling clique into "contempt, scorn and disrepute." Post-9/11 America has witnessed no political purges, no tarring and feathering of the president's critics, no boarding-up of opposition newspapers or brutal cudgeling of ostensibly unpatriotic editors.

As Dan Farber has explained, however, this failure to criminalize dissent and persecute the opposition is not aptly described as a symptom of executive branch restraint. Bush had no need to enact a new Sedition Act to echo those of 1798 and 1918. Gagging the administration's incoherent, cowed, and powerless critics would have required more effort than it would have been worth; it proved easier simply to ignore what they said. Shouting down opposition media proved less demanding than shutting them down, and planting derogatory stories in the "free and unrestrained press" about the occasional critic whose voice began to be heard above the din has been as easy as lying.

In general, wartime governments fret about inflammatory speech only when the straw is dry, that is, when some part of public opinion is at serious risk of catching fire. Opposition to the Iraq war is increasingly widespread in America; but political opposition to an accurately targeted lethal attack on al Qaeda is virtually nonexistent. The utter absence of a Fifth Column of al Qaeda sympathizers inside the United States, plotting to replace America's elected government with an American field office for an eventual world caliphate, eliminates the practical threat of antigovernment speech. America's teachers cannot reasonably be suspected of teaching Salafism to American children. Nor can the entertainment industry be charged with subliminally beaming Salafi messages to the moviegoing public. When there are no believably witch-like creatures to hunt, in other words, the nonexistence of witch hunts does not need any special explanation. There is certainly no need to credit it, tautologically, to a culture of restraint.

Historically, speech has been criminalized in the United States only when incumbents have been able to mount a plausible case that antiwar activism might obstruct military recruitment. There has never been a seriously disruptive antiwar movement in American history, it turns out, that was not a by-product of an emotionally aroused antidraft movement. Unlike the administrations of Lincoln, Wilson and Nixon, the Bush administration has been successfully shielded from draft card burnings and other rowdy displays of public displeasure by a wholly volunteer army. It has had no need to restrain itself from criminalizing dissent or otherwise persecuting dissenters for this reason in particular. Whatever dissent exists is anemic and of no political consequence because the abolition of conscription has prevented populist hostility to the draft from boiling over into populist fury at the party in power.

To summarize: The war on terror is just as serious as the greatest of America's previous wars; and the Bush administration is not more restrained than its predecessors. So how should we understand the most salient differences between present and past?

THE UNIQUENESS OF THE THREAT

Before zeroing in on the principal discontinuity between Bush and previous wartime presidents, we need to clarify a few additional points about the changed perception of America's national security environment after 9/11. What is truly unprecedented about the post-9/11 terrorist threat? If we can give a clear-cut answer to this question, we will edge closer to understanding what is also unprecedented about the Bush administration's response.

The most commonly mentioned factor is expected longevity. Indeed, that the terrorist threat may never disappear is by now a grim truism. The knowledge of how to create a nuclear weapon cannot be undiscovered. The United States can no more shut down all smuggling routes into the country than it can abolish cheap air travel. As a result, the vulnerability of America's major urban centers, including the nation's capital, to a nuclear surprise attack may have well become a permanent feature of America's national security environment.

That this is a serious turn of events needs no special emphasis. For our purposes, the most important consideration is the following. The historical record suggests that America's most celebrated heroes of civil liberties (such as Justices Holmes and Brandeis) found the moral courage to defend the liberty to disagree publicly with the country's wartime leaders only after serious hostilities had ceased. In the war on terror, where hostilities will perhaps never cease, experience therefore leads us to foresee a bench that is considerably less heroic than American civil libertarians may hope and expect. Many commentators have publicly worried, as a result, that the always belated but hitherto predictable postwar rebounding of civil liberties, without which America's constitutional freedoms would not have endured so long, may in this case never materialize.

Besides its potential lack of an end point, the new terrorist threat has another unique characteristic. It is maddeningly ethereal, obscure and difficult to assess. As former Secretary of Defense Donald Rumsfeld used to say, we lack metrics to discern whether we are winning or losing this war. Not only the courts, but also the Pentagon, the National Security Council, and the Central Intelligence Agency seem to have scant competence in measuring the extent of the terrorist threat to national security. Such radical indeterminacy makes the war on terror different from previous conflicts that shared a similar potential to inflict deep wounds on the country. Hierarchically organized and centrally organized enemies are much easier to keep track of with the naked eye than a fluid, kaleidoscopic, and highly decentralized global terrorist movement, seemingly able to spawn copycat microarmies by sheer force of publicized example. It is very difficult for Congress, the public and the press, as a result, to evaluate the executive's claims about the changing gravity of the threat or about our success or failure in the conflict. If truth be told, it is very difficult for the executive to evaluate its own claims accurately in this respect. This imperviousness to evaluation, both external and in-house, has always characterized threat assessment of the wartime executive to some extent, but it presents a greater problem in the war on terror than in any previous armed struggle of comparable gravity.

RETHINKING THE LIBERTY-SECURITY TRADE-OFF

To deepen our exploration of this issue, we need to revisit the alleged need for a liberty-security trade-off that runs like a *fil conducteur* throughout this volume. The purported necessity of sacrificing liberty for security in wartime (including today) is difficult to assess because both terms are to some extent subjective and open to interpretation. For instance, the American government's tolerance of KKK terrorism after the Civil War, recounted above, compels us to recognize the importance of asking: Whose liberty? Whose security? But the most important distinction for our purposes is the distinction between private liberty and public liberty.

L. A. Powe is speaking for many when he admits to having "been surprised at how relatively well civil liberties of those within the United States have been protected after 9/11," adding "I am aware of no horror stories about overreaching under the Patriot Act" (see chapter 6, this volume). To qualify this observation, it helps to linger for a moment over the distinction between private and public liberty. A constitution is not only a system for protecting individual liberty. It is also a system for organizing decision making to maximize the intelligence and corrigibility of decisions (Starr 2007). Legislative and judicial oversight are not designed primarily to hamstring or paralyze the executive but rather to force the executive to have plausible reasons for its actions and, when necessary, to correct the executive's most egregious blunders.

That those charged with fighting terrorism must balance two competing constitutional values (namely, the president's duty to protect the nation from its enemies and individual rights such as privacy and free expression) is a commonplace; but it arguably misstates what is at stake. Even those liberals who deny that we should sacrifice liberty for the sake of security inadvertently contribute to the erroneous assumption that constitutional liberty has nothing positive to contribute to the protection of national security. The underlying fallacy here only becomes visible, however, when we distinguish the private liberty of individuals to behave as they choose as long as they refrain from harming each other and the public liberty of citizens to examine and criticize their government, and to strive to oust it from power in competitive elections, as long as they obey the law.

According to James Madison, "the right of freely examining public characters and measures, and of free communication among the people thereon . . . has ever been justly deemed the only effective guardian of every other right" (1798). The right of citizens to examine and criticize their government rests on the following empirical generalization: Power wielders, like other humans, usually behave better, both morally and strate-gically, when observed than when unobserved. There is no reason to believe that this rule becomes any less valid during national emergencies (such as Hurricane Katrina) than in normal times. Highly insulated policymakers, who are not kept informed and alert by dissenters and whose errors are carefully shrouded from public view, are extremely unlikely to design intelligent and successful policies.

The confused and confusing debate about the liberty-security trade-off would have unfolded differently if more attention had been paid to public liberty. Indeed, only a one-sided concept of liberty as exclusively private rather than public makes it possible to justify sacrificing liberty for security. That we may increase our security by giving up our privacy makes at least some sense. What make no sense at all is the government's implicit boast that it will do a better job of protecting national security if it is never criticized or forced to give an informed audience plausible reasons for its actions. A government that stops being compelled to gives plausible reasons for its actions will soon cease to have plausible reasons for its actions. The consequences for national security cannot possibly be favorable.

The right to inspect our government includes the right to question the priorities it sets among the multiple evolving threats confronting the nation. In *Whitney v. California* (1927), as we have seen, Brandeis eloquently defended public liberty, namely the right of citizens to challenge the government's claim that the emergency allegedly at hand is so grave that it warrants the infringement of private liberty. That citizens can increase their security by relinquishing their right to question their government's conceivably erroneous picture of the country's threat environment seems highly implausible, if not downright unintelligible. An enemy shrewd enough to take advantage of liberty will have even less trouble taking advantage of foolishly designed policies selected without the benefit of sharp criticism by informed parties.

The constitutional value that public liberty protects is not individual autonomy, in other words, but collective rationality. To reject public liberty is reckless because it frees the government from the need to make a logically coherent and fact-based case for its proposed actions before some sort of tribunal that does not depend on spoon-fed disinformation and is capable of pushing back. An important test for any policy proposal, to paraphrase John Stuart Mill, is a standing invitation to the world to criticize it while offering a superior alternative. A dynamic tradition of public liberty helps remind the president and his party that their own fighting faith, too, may one day be upset. Having embedded a distrust of false certainty in the foundations of American democracy, American liberalism requires that the factual premises for the government's resort to coercion and force must always be tested in some sort of adversarial process, giving interested and knowledgeable parties a fair opportunity to question the accuracy and reliability of the evidence alleged. This includes supposed evidence that the necessity of the current crisis justifies unfettered executive branch discretion.

SECRET GOVERNMENT

After gaining the legal right to obtain the private records of its citizens without showing probable cause, it is true, the Bush administration engaged in covert electronic surveillance of American citizens not only without a judicial warrant but in flat contravention of Congress's express wishes. Nevertheless, the growing transparency of society to the government's prying gaze seems to be a somewhat lesser danger to the American political system than the growing opacity of government to society's inquiring eyes. Secrecy, stonewalling, and overclassification are greater problems than indiscreet spying, however dangerous the latter may be, especially if it involves storing embarrassing information that could eventually be used to blackmail influential politicians. This is true because excessive secrecy in decision making tends inevitably to reduce the intelligence of the decisions made (Moynihan 1998). The stupefying effect of excessive secrecy is strongly suggested by the experience of the last few years when "the process of lying to deceive the enemy imperceptibly turned into lying to hide failures and disappointments" (Friedman 2004, 293). Shielding itself from informed criticisms and outside input, the Bush administration seems to have made one ill-considered choice after another. We can conclude with some confidence that an insular ruling clique poses a more immediate and palpable threat to national security, as well as democracy, than the speculative possibility of a citizenry whose vitality might conceivably be chilled by covert, high-tech surveillance.

The danger that looms most frighteningly today is further irrational decision making based on hunch, impulse, and a craving for action that will plunge the country even deeper into even more hopeless foreign conflicts. We can therefore complete Powe's diagnosis as follows. Bush's presidency has flouted the American constitutional system of government less by violating individual liberties than by violating public liberty, that is, by recklessly dismantling the principal constitutional mechanisms designed and established to facilitate the candid recognition and speedy correction of momentous errors. By emphasizing Bush's unprecedented assault on checks and balances, we can criticize his administration without idealizing or whitewashing its predecessors. Several recent commentators have adopted a similar approach, among them the political scientist Chalmers Johnson. I cite at length:

> Several American presidents have been guilty of using excessive power during wartime. Abraham Lincoln suspended the right of habeas corpus; Woodrow Wilson had his "Red Scare" with the illegal jailing or deportation of people who opposed his intervention in World War I; Franklin Roosevelt conducted a pogrom against Americans of Japanese ancestry, incarcerating almost all of them in the continental United States in detention camps. In addition, there is no question that, from the earliest years of the republic to the 1990s, the United States witnessed a huge accretion of power by the executive branch, largely due to the numerous wars we fought and the concomitant growth of militarism. Nonetheless, the separation of powers, even if no longer a true balance of power, continued to serve as a check on any claims of presidential dominance. (2006, 244)

Abraham Lincoln and FDR can be criticized along many dimensions; but neither of them was so stubbornly oblivious to dissident voices or so unwilling to change course when convincingly criticized as George W. Bush.

A refusal to listen to criticism is dismaying precisely because the threat we face is so new and elusive and the resources we have at our disposal (soldiers, Arabic speakers, satellite coverage, the attention span of high officials, and so on) remain scarce. The extreme difficulty of setting priorities among low-probability catastrophic threats in the war on terror strongly suggests the need to revitalize various mechanisms of political self-correction, including after-action reviews and mandatory second opinions. Consultations with knowledgeable parties outside a narrow circle of like-minded operatives committed to upholding a party line should be not optional but obligatory. Because the country had never before faced a threat anything like that posed by private sector nuclear terrorism, the administration's first responses were destined to be experimental and plagued by mistakes. To respond intelligently, therefore, it should have safeguarded and fortified all existing decision-making protocols containing even residual elements of adversarial process.

Because the war on terror is totally unprecedented, giving unsupervised discretion to a single clique inside one compartment of the executive without requiring obligatory consultations with knowledgeable parties cannot possibly be prudent. The aim of liberal institutions should be to facilitate the psychologically painful process of recognizing past blunders and initiating requisite midstream readjustments. Preserving public liberty means frustrating the impulse of incumbents to silence their critics. The payoff, on balance, is more thoughtful policy. The worst imaginable decision-making system for managing an unprecedented threat that is frustratingly difficult to assess is unchecked presidential discretion, because chief executives are bound to be inhibited by authorial pride from expeditiously correcting their most damaging missteps.

Not only do powerful men dislike admitting their mistakes. Multiparty democracy joins perverse institutional incentives to those stemming from ordinary human vanity. Competitive elections make incumbents view admission of error in questions of national security as a gift to their partisan rivals. Such a problem is so serious, in fact, that it might lead us to invert the conservative mantra that liberal constitutionalism is a suicide pact. Observing the disaster of the Iraq war, we can conclude that granting unfettered discretion to the commander in chief is the real suicide pact. Freeing a poorly equipped individual from all constitutional checks and balances and allowing a president to engage the American military in bloody foreign adventures without giving plausible reasons for his action is a perfect formula for creating the debacle facing us today.

RIGIDITIES OF THE INSULATED EXECUTIVE

Only an executive branch emancipated from legal and constitutional constraints, the administration's defenders argue, will have enough flexibility to defeat a diabolical enemy. This sounds theoretically plausible, but the facts tell a contrary story. Freedom from judicial and legislative oversight has produced not open-eyed flexibility but pathological rigidity. Instead of acknowledging the obvious, namely America's inability to democratize Iraq, the administration has lashed itself (and the country) to a failed policy. Indeed, it continues to act as if its misbegotten project is still on track, only somewhat delayed. Decision making in an echo chamber, refusing to pay any attention to dissident voices, means selecting evidence to corroborate preformed opinions, misunderstanding the challenges ahead, and refusing to ask what if and what then. Dispensing with uninhibited criticism and debate in the face of a threat intrinsically difficult to understand is to doom the country to wild goose chases and a reckless misallocation of scarce national security assets in an increasingly dangerous world. Surrounded by yes-men and sheltered from seriously informed criticism, a pampered and unchecked executive becomes catastrophically disconnected from reality. Concentrating excessive authority in the executive does not increase effectiveness in time of multiple evolving dangers because, for one thing, an all-powerful president becomes unwilling to hear bad news. Thus, the advocates, not the opponents, of an imperial presidency are the ones who have spectacularly failed to understand the true seriousness of today's terrorist threat.

Administration defenders typically imply that checks and balances play into the hands of the terrorists. How can we answer this charge? How can the separation of powers in general and legislative oversight of executive action in particular make a positive contribution to the war on terror? The answer is simple: by forcing the executive to face unpleasant realities sooner than it would do on its own. Checks and balances enforce a psychologically uncomfortable but politically indispensable degree of transparency on the executive. Legislative and judicial oversight forces the executive to give reasons for its actions. Such a system forces the executive to test, in some sort of adversarial process, the factual premises of its proposal to use force. It also encourages learning from mistakes, because we cannot know how to do better next time if we have not made an careful study of what went wrong last time.

To suggest that congressional oversight can improve the performance of the executive branch in the war on terror, incidentally, is not to idealize Congress or assume that its members are nonpartisan, well informed, or even especially intelligent. It is unreasonable to ask legislators and judges, whatever we think of their personal talents, to abandon their critical faculties on the say-so of the demonstrably fallible executive branch. Congress has an important national security role to play for a simple reason. Its members will be less embarrassed than members of the executive branch to admit the perhaps unavoidable errors committed by the president's team in trying to cope with an unprecedented threat.

Congress's relative lack of expertise in national security issues might seem an insurmountable obstacle to its playing a very helpful role in the war on terror. Such a conclusion is too hasty. Congress can compensate for its own lack of expertise by providing official and unofficial forums in which to consider the views of executive branch dissenters, who have an insider's understanding of what is going wrong but whose voices are routinely smothered in the hierarchically organized executive departments. In this way, the separation of powers, far from paralyzing government, gives power to knowledge, a paramount goal of liberal institutions. When they function correctly, the institutions of public liberty are likely to improve the government's performance and especially to enhance its ability to correct its own errors.

Ritual authorizations to use military force (AUMFs), it should be noted, have a paradoxical tendency to increase the rigidity—not the flexibility—of executive action. The Bush administration has insisted that the president can obtain all the powers he needs in the war on terror directly from Article II's commander in chief clause. The post-9/11 AUMFs are therefore redundant, according to the administration's own account. What purpose do they therefore serve? Perversely, they weaken the legislature's ability to correct the executive branch's errors. By feeding disinformation to the electorate in the run-up to a legislative election, the executive can stampede Congress into voting in favor of a military adventure. Afterward, when the faultiness of the intelligence becomes public knowledge, congressmen are reluctant to admit that they were hoodwinked, because such a confession will degrade their future credibility in the electorate's eyes. Having blessed the president's actions, Congress's ability to assess the unexpected and perhaps disastrous consequences with cold-eyed candor is woefully diminished.

The pervasive practice of partisan self-dealing, under cover of national security, is dismaying enough during time-limited wars. In the potentially endless war on terror, the embarrassment becomes even more acute, threatening the very survival of constitutional democracy. One of the principal functions of constitutionalism is to preserve the possibility of *l'alternance*, that is, the rotation of major parties in and out of power. Voting remains a meaningful act only so long as the Ins may be ousted and the Outs periodically invited to replace them. For this to be possible, formal and informal restrictions must be placed on "increasing returns to power." To this end, above all, the United States Constitution grants a high degree of protection to political speech, including speech that is sharply critical of the power wielders of the moment. According to Albert Gallatin, as cited, the Sedition Act of 1798 should "be considered only as a weapon used by a party now in power, in order to perpetuate their authority and preserve their present places." Constitutionalism, in the broadest sense, aims to prevent such abusive power grabs. That is to say, it is contrived to prevent incumbents from using the advantages of incumbency to hide their own mistakes, harass their critics, and weaken their electoral rivals' support base, thereby managing to prolong their hold on power undemocratically.

The regrettable but perhaps inevitable wartime loosening of restraints on incumbent self-dealing has not, in the past, inflicted irreversible damage on American democracy for the simple reason that each of America's wars, thus far, has ultimately come to an end. What this rather trite consideration suggests is that today's potentially endless war on terror might indeed be a political watershed. The danger is unprecedented for a second reason as well. An American president is now claiming immunity from legislative and judicial oversight on the basis of undisclosed information about the nature and imminence of a threat to national security. Is it alarmist to worry about worst-case scenarios in this context? Can we be certain that the inherent potential for executive branch self-dealing, in the face of an inherently indeterminate threat, will not eventually open a pathway to a one-party state? We may hope not. But it would be unwise to dismiss the worry as entirely baseless.

WHY EMERGENCIES REQUIRE RULES

In his introduction, Dan Farber pointedly asked about "the applicability of the rule of law in a period of emergency." A central premise of the national security thinking of the Bush administration, in fact, is that emergencies require a loosening of rules and the allocation of unmonitored discretion in the hands of the executive. Law reduces flexibility, it is claimed, and has to be relaxed to create leeway for mounting an adequate response to the terrorist threat. Due process is said to reduce flexibility, among other ways, by prohibiting the executive from depriving individuals of liberty on mere suspicion and surmise. Dangerous times require uncommon measures. Faced with a grave enough threat, the executive branch must be granted unlimited discretion to use lethal force against anyone it chooses without having to provide an independent tribunal with reliable evidence of any kind.

That this antiliberal approach, rather than being audaciously new, is perennial to the point of staleness is strongly suggested by the statements of Robert Goodloe Harper, cited in chapter 6 of this volume, decrying judicial process and the rule of law as "attempts which are made to bind us hand and foot, until our enemy comes upon us." That we are fighting the war on terror, not litigating it, is one of the mantras of the administration's spokesmen and defenders.

To evaluate this claim we should pause briefly to probe the nature of the rule of law. What is the essence of due process? Is it a system designed to defend individual rights regardless of the burdens it imposes on the government's capacity to protect public safety? Or does the rule of law somehow contribute to security as well as liberty?

Ask emergency room doctors if they prefer discretion to rules? They would probably tell you that the very question makes little sense. Emergencies obviously require creative thinking, but they would be wholly unmanageable without detailed rules worked out in advance. Does the pilot of a two-engine plane who loses one engine throw his emergency protocols and crisis-management checklist out the cockpit window? Do men fighting a forest fire have no procedures for how to behave if the wind suddenly changes? Do doctors and nurses in an emergency room not follow standardized formats to avoid using the wrong type of blood when transfusing an unidentified comatose patient? Does anyone charged with managing an emergency really want to act with unfettered discretion? Don't they all want to take advantage of the experience of past actors, steadying their own panicky judgment by leaning on the accumulated hints and suggestions crystallized in rules of thumb formulated in the past?

Rather than being restrictions on flexibility, rules provide those who have to innovate in an emergency situation with an artificial cool head. Evidentiary rules provide an excellent example. Do counterterrorism officials benefit from lowering the threshold for admissible evidence to the point where unsubstantiated rumors are treated as if they have substantial probative value? This is unlikely for a simple reason. Such a system will encourage dishonest informants and discourage honest ones, the former hoping and the latter fearing that the police will pounce on a secretly denounced suspect without double-checking anonymous allegations. In other words, relatively high evidentiary standards, far from tying the hands of the police, help improve the quality of privately volunteered information on which good police-work palpably depends. Due process prevents the government from myopically and impulsively ignoring this lesson, distilled from centuries of experience, in the heat of the moment.

THE RIGHTS OF FOREIGNERS

An American citizen confined for more than two years without being charged and without access to a lawyer, José Padilla is the exception that proves the rule. He is an exception because, in Bush's war on terror, most of those who have been subjected, say, to unindicted detention have been not citizens but foreigners. Military commissions, admitting hearsay evidence that can be withheld from the accused, are also reserved for aliens abroad. This may make a good deal of sense politically, because American voters do not seem especially interested in the fate of noncitizens at the hands of American officials overseas.

It may even make sense historically, because the Bill of Rights has never been held to apply to foreigners outside the country. For example, the

Fourth Amendment does not require American intelligence agencies to seek a judicial warrant before wiretapping non-Americans living outside United States borders. Moreover, Bush administration lawyers have argued that the Constitution's commander-in-chief clause implicitly grants the executive branch the right to detain and harshly interrogate aliens abroad on the merest suspicion that they might be affiliated with, or simply knowledgeable about, alleged terrorists. They have gone even further, arguing that killing suspects based on undisclosed evidence is not technically unconstitutional, as long as the suspects are noncitizens[1] and the president agrees that each approved extrajudicial execution will in some unspecified way contribute to keeping the country safe.

So, after 9/11, treating non-Americans overseas as if they were guilty until proven innocent may make sense as a matter of electoral politics and narrow legal precedent. But does it make sense?

How do administration spokesmen and defenders respond to liberals who, worrying about disinformation and mistaken identity, wish to extend the presumption of innocence, even during the war on terror, to foreigners abroad? Supporting the president's right to treat foreigners any way he chooses, enthusiasts of executive unilateralism claim that those who object to Bush's policies do not understand that the United States is at war in a constitutional sense. Liberals cling dogmatically to the crime model, it is alleged, especially to the individualization of culpability, because they seriously underestimate the seriousness of the threat. By contrast, those who presumably take the threat seriously recognize, in Farber's words, that "the effort to avoid false negatives inevitably leads to a larger number of false positives." By focusing obsessively on the cost to foreigners of false positives, liberals purportedly expose their countrymen to the devastating consequences of false negatives. It is not America's fault that the guilty hide among the innocent. As a result, those whose humanitarian concern is to defend the innocent, who object to incarcerating and even murdering suspects on the basis of hearsay and circumstantial evidence, are implicitly accused of defending the terrorists. That is the administration's fundamental argument against the crime model, that is, against individualizing culpability in the war on terror.

Is this argument sound? And is the policy based upon it likely to succeed?

The liberal counterargument is easy to state. An overproduction of false positives will harm American national security by alienating potentially cooperative Muslim communities throughout the world. The administration is willing to accept a high incidence of mistaken identity when detaining, interrogating and assassinating suspects, as well as high levels of collateral damage in communities where terrorists hide. It nicely writes off such losses (imposed exclusively on foreign persons) as a cost of doing business. This is not the way in which those gratuitously caught up in undiscriminating sweeps and bombardments, brutal interrogatories and targeted killings, experience America's poorly focused counterterrorism efforts, however. Those on the receiving end naturally interpret American "tolerance" for false positives and collateral damage as a sign that the United States has little interest in discriminating carefully between innocent and guilty Muslims. What the administration conceives as a prudent acceptance of victimized innocents, the victims themselves see as selling Muslim lives at a discount, as a kind of neo-tribal relapse into collective punishment or group-on-group revenge. The consequences are likely to be bloody because the surest way to rouse violent resistance is to communicate to people that there is nothing they can personally do to avoid being attacked.

Even John Yoo, who otherwise dispraises Bush for being overly deferential toward the due-process demands of American liberals, admits that "counterterrorism policy may be more effective by reducing deprivations of civil liberties to maintain" the "support and cooperation" of Muslim communities at home and abroad (see chapter 3, this volume). Practically speaking, the most urgent issue concerns foreign Muslims overseas.

Our authors may not have heard many horror stories about abuses of American citizens under the PATRIOT Act, but they have heard numerous gruesome reports of America's abusive treatment of foreigners overseas, including at least two dozen deaths of detainees at the hands of American interrogators. They also know that tens and perhaps hundreds of thousands of innocent Iraqis who, having never harmed any Americans, have died as a result of an American invasion of an Arab country justified as a response to 9/11.

That such an indiscriminate use of force, promiscuously mixing the innocent with the guilty, may be self-defeating, is strongly suggested by widely accepted tenets of counterinsurgency, especially the maxim that "when force is required it should be used minimally" (Ricks 2006, 266). The principal challenge of any counterinsurgency campaign is to isolate the truly violent actors from their surrounding community. To turn the community against the insurgents, it is essential to minimize collateral damage. Ideally, force should be used only after reliably establishing individual culpability. This ideal can never be reached, admittedly. But its utility as an aspiration suggests that counterinsurgency (and, by extrapolation, counterterrorism) has as much to learn from the model of crime as from the model of war.

By liberating American counterterrorism agencies from the need to individualize culpability, the administration has lent a spurious plausibility to the pernicious narrative of a clash of civilizations. By failing to invest massively in the human intelligence that would make it easier to pinpoint the guilty hiding among the innocent, the administration has not discredited but instead normalized terrorism, that is, the indiscriminate use of violence against civilians and noncombatants on the American side. That this is not a dazzlingly brilliant policy is the least that might be said.

Not only does such a policy seem, on balance, self-defeating. Its positive contribution to counterterrorism remains purely speculative and unproven. Consider the plan to try some 60 Guantanamo detainees by military commission. Could it possibly be true that *none* of these individuals could be tried on the basis of evidence admissible in a regular military trial? Could it possibly be true that, in *every* case, applying ordinary rules of discovery would put the lives of American intelligence operatives and their sources at risk? Ordinary rules of due process, including those incorporated in the Uniform Code of Military Justice, allow the accused to help his or her attorney pick apart the prosecution's evidence. By peremptorily ditching such venerable rules, the military commissions at Guantanamo substantially raise the risk of false positives. Is it worth it?

We may justifiably worry that the mistreatment of foreigners overseas (or in America's stage-set replica of "abroad" at Guantanamo) is embraced not because of its proven utility for fighting terrorism, but for another reason entirely. We may even fear that the underlying rationale might have something to do with the special nature of the war on terror, especially with the lack of reliable metrics for discovering if we are winning or losing. The distorting of counterterrorism by partisan-political motives, which American history suggests may be inevitable, means that the administration deprived of objective metrics of success must somehow communicate to the electorate that it is indeed prevailing in the struggle. What methods can it adopt to convey this perhaps bogus message?

One method would be to violate, in a clamorously conspicuous manner, the human rights of politically voiceless aliens abroad. This is just a speculation, admittedly, and cannot be proved. If the administration is abusing foreigners abroad to send a message that there is nothing it will not do, and is not in fact doing, to defend America, it is making a fatal mistake, however. Not only is it immoral to inflict savage suffering and mass death on foreign peoples for the sake of a speculative strategic advantage. Such a policy is also immensely dangerous for the simple reason that the United States is no longer the sequestered region once celebrated by Noah Webster. Cheap air travel, tourism, and global labor-force migration has irreversibly opened America to the rest of the world, to the handful of individuals raging for revenge as well as to the many hoping to improve their families' lives. In such a changed environment, sticking with the old idea that aliens abroad deserve no protection from an undisciplined American executive and its poorly monitored agents seems like a formula for both alienating potential informants and fanning the flames of anti-American rage, not at all for keeping the country safe as the president is constitutionally obliged to do.

NOTE

1. An American citizen who was killed in 2002 by a CIA-operated pilotless Predator aircraft in Yemen, Ahmed Hijazi seems to have died not as a target but merely as collateral damage.

REFERENCES

Ackerman, Bruce. 2006. *Before the Next Attack: Preserving Civil Liberties in an Age of Terrorism*. New Haven, Conn.: Yale University Press.

Bolton, John R. 2004. "Beyond the Axis of Evil: Additional Threats from Weapons of Mass Destruction." In *The Neocon Reader*, edited by Irwin Stelzer. New York: Grove Press.

Friedman, George. 2004. *America's Secret War: Inside the Hidden Worldwide Struggle Between America and its Enemies*. New York: Doubleday.

Johnson, Chalmers. 2006. *Nemesis: The Last Days of the American Republic*. New York: Metropolitan Books.

Madison, James. 1798. *The Virginia Resolution*. Accessed at http://www.yale.edu/lawweb/avalon/virres.htm.

Moynihan, Daniel Patrick. 1998. *Secrecy: The American Experience*. New Haven, Conn.: Yale University Press.

Ricks, Thomas. 2006. *Fiasco: The American Military Adventure in Iraq*. New York: Penguin.

Starr, Paul. 2007. *Freedom's Power: The True Force of Liberalism*. New York: Basic Books.

INDEX

Boldface numbers refers to figures and tables.

Authorization to Use Military Force
    (AUMF), 111, 221

Baez, Joan, 102–3
Bailey, Dorothy, 81–83, 85
Baldwin, Luther, 130
Baldwin, Roger, 11, 35–36, 160n9
Barenblatt v. United States, 172
Bassett, John Spencer, 156
Benhabib, Seyla, 117
Bentham, Jeremy, 195
Bentley, Elizabeth, 75, 77, 79, 86
Berkman, Alexander, 37
Berners-Lee, Tim, 193
Biddle, Francis, 45, 47, 52, 178
Bingham, John, 151
bin Laden, Osama, 212
Birney, James G., 144
Black, Hugo, 53, 166–8, 170–1, 173,
    178–9
Bond, Julian, 102, 170
Borden, William L., 76
Bourne, Randolph, 29–30
Boy Spies of America, 32
Brandeis, Louis, 11, 18, 38–39, 170,
    203, 216
Brandenburg v. Ohio, 170, 174
Brennan, William J., 168–9, 173
Breslin, Jimmy, 103
Breyer, Stephen, 22n7, 181
Brinkley, Alan, 11, 159n4, 160n9, 203,
    209–10
Brinkley, David, 100
Brooks, David, 125
Brown, Gordon, 201
Brownell, Herbert, 87
Buchanan, James, 142
Budenz, Louis, 80
Burnside, Ambrose, 148–9
Burr, Aaron, 176
Bush, George W.: detention of terror-
    ists, orders regarding, 4–5, 50; as
    insulated executive, 219–22; the

judiciary and, 18, 186; military
commissions, establishment of, 44;
national security focus of, 21;
politicization of national security,
211; praise of, 208–9; violation of
public liberty and constitutional
mechanisms by, 217–8; warrantless surveillance by the NSA
authorized by, 201–2 (*see also*
National Security Agency).
See also Bush administration; war
on terror
Bush administration: civil liberties
and the war against terrorism by,
3, 61–63, 208–9, 211–3; the Constitution, view of, 182; detention of
suspected terrorists, 3–9, 49–51,
180–2; foreigners, treatment of,
223–7; judicial supremacy and, 63;
legalist regime, fight against, 20;
military commissions, proposals
regarding (*see* military commissions); oversight and competence
of, 219–22; politicization of
national security by, 209, 211;
Roosevelt, comparison to, 11–12,
43, 46–49, 54, 58–63; secrecy by, 3,
217–19; surveillance, expansion of,
9–10, 14, 54–55, 109–12 (*see also*
surveillance); terrorism policies,
criticism of, 42–43. *See also* war on
terror
Butler, John Marshall, 172
Bykofsky, Stuart, 159n4
Byrnes, James F., 47

Cabot, George, 123
Cadwalader, George, 176
Callender, James Thomson, 132,
    160n8, 175
CAPPS II, 198
Cardozo, Benjamin, 185
Catholic Church, 72

Women's International League for
  Peace and Freedom, 34
World War I: civil liberties during
  the era of, 27, 29–33, 39–40, 178
  (*see also* Red Scare); dissent, reaction to, 10; progressivism during
  and following, 34–39; Wilson's
  mission during and after,
  27–29
World War II: Court rulings on civil
  liberties during, 178–9; domestic
  policies during, Bush administration policies compared to, 11–12,

43; electronic surveillance during,
  55–58; internments during, 51–54,
  178–9; KGB espionage during, 70,
  76–79; military commissions used
  during, 44–47

Yen, Hope, 43
Yoo, John, 11, 16–18, 109, 159n1,
  181–2, 225

Zawahiri, Ayman al-, 212
Ziesche, Philipp, 123
Zolberg, Aristede, 159n2